Tomorrow's Memories

INTERSECTIONS

Asian and Pacific American
Transcultural Studies

Russell C. Leong
General Editor

Tomorrow's Memories

A DIARY, 1924–1928

Angeles Monrayo

EDITED BY
RIZALINE R. RAYMUNDO

University of Hawai'i Press
Honolulu

in association with UCLA
Asian American Studies Center
Los Angeles

Library of Congress Cataloging-in-Publication Data
Raymundo, Angeles Monrayo.
Tomorrow's memories : a diary, 1924–1928 / Angeles Monrayo;
edited by Rizaline R. Raymundo.
   p. cm. — (Intersections)
   Includes bibliographical references and index.
   ISBN 0-8248-2671-X (acid-free paper).—
   ISBN 0-8248-2688-4 (pbk : acid-free paper).
   1. Raymundo, Angeles Monrayo, 1912— Diaries. 2. Filipino
Americans—Hawaii—Diaries. 3. Filipino Americans—
California—Diaries. 4. Hawaii—Biography. 5. California—
Biography. I. Title. II. Series: Intersections (Honolulu, Hawaii)
CT275.R297 A3 2003
996.9'0049921'0092—dc21   2003040294

Designed by Bookcomp, Inc.
Printed by The Maple-Vail Book Manufacturing Group

*In memory of Mom and Manangs, who left us
with many memories of joys and happiness
amid their struggles and hardships*

Intersections: Asian and Pacific American Transcultural Studies

Contents

Acknowledgments

I want to thank the following people for their support and encouragement, without which this book would have remained just copies of the diary for family and friends instead of published for all those interested in the Pinays (Filipina women) and their roles in the Filipino community.

My family and friends, from the very beginning, gave me encouraging words and support that the diary should be published—Donald and Geri Raymundo, Esther Romero, Betty McCarthy, Wilma Aguinid, and Helen and Ken Dirck.

Kathleen C. Miller and Bettina Aptheker were instrumental in my starting Philippine and Filipino American history research which led to the editing of the diary; Dawn Mabalon and Emily Lawsin encouraged and pressed me on to publication by their countless e-mails and use of the diary in their classes; Irwin Tang submitted the diary to the University of Hawai'i Press. Especially, Masako Ikeda, editor, with patience and support, led me through the process of readying the diary for publication.

Introduction

It is heartbreaking to watch my mother slowly and carefully move around the house. She is eighty-four, blind and physically weakened by a series of major surgeries, but she still insists on feeding and dressing herself, taking care of her personal needs, and getting around the house with her walker. Once in a while I look through our albums of photos, which she began collecting long before she married, and read an entry here and there in her diaries to help sustain my memory of her when she was energetic, enthusiastic, and independent.

I consider myself fortunate that my mother, Angeles Monrayo, began writing a diary when she was a young girl. It is a strange but moving experience to read about her childhood thoughts and life in Hawai'i and then see her as she is today. Her first three diaries cover the years of her childhood in Hawai'i from January 10, 1924, to her arrival in California, November 17, 1928, and her elopement. They end when she was expecting her first child.

Recently she surprised me by giving me five more books—one contains poems she wrote in the 1940s, and four are diaries from April 9, 1981, her third day in the hospital for a major operation (two weeks after my father died), to October 19, 1993, her last entry before she had undergone glaucoma surgery, which left her blind.

This introduction attempts to fill in some of the years before and after my mother's first three diaries. Work on the diaries was a strange experience for me. Whenever I stopped work on the book to tend to that "young girl" now eighty-four, I felt I had stepped out of a time machine from the past back into the present, my mind and emotions caught between two dimensions.

Throughout my childhood until I left home to start my own life (and even then, once in a while she'd reminisce out loud when I visited), my mother told me stories of her childhood in Hawai'i, when she first came to California, the Depression years—stories about the happy and unhappy times of her life. I confess that when I became a teenager, sometimes I would only half listen to her stories. Now I am thankful for her storytelling and will introduce some of her stories here.

One of my favorite stories was told to her by my grandfather of an incident that occurred on the ship to Hawai'i from the Philippines in 1912.

My grandfather and granduncles were Sakadas—Filipinos recruited in the Philippine Islands by the Hawaiian Plantation Association (HPA) to work on the plantations. When they were recruited, my grandmother was pregnant with Mom and did not want to leave home until after her child was born.

Mom was born in Romblon City, Romblon, Philippine Islands, on August 2, 1912. On November 15, 1912, she was on her way to Hawai'i with her parents, Enarciso Morante Monrayo and Valeriana Motia Monrayo, five-year-old brother Julian Monrayo, two aunts (Motia), and two uncles (Monrayo) on the SS *Shinyo Maru*, a three-masted ship of the Maru Line.

Nanay woke up one morning to find her baby gone. In a panic, she woke up Tatay, crying, "Our baby Angeles is gone!" He immediately woke Julian and they searched each and every sleeping person. Julian found his baby sister sleeping between a couple. Tatay angrily woke them. The young wife, frightened and crying, said she was only "borrowing" their baby. She told them she and her husband had been married for years but never had a child. She just wanted to have the baby with her for the night and would have returned her in the morning. The incident did not frighten the woman, as she continued to take baby

Angeles now and then. After that, when Nanay awoke and saw her baby gone, she knew exactly where to go to get her back.

Some of Mom's early memories of Hawai'i were when Nanay sent her to the Chinese store on the other side of the Waipahu Sugar Mill every morning to buy freshly baked buns. Whenever Mom tells the story, she sniffs the air as if she can still smell the baking buns. Her route to and from the store was through the mill grounds, and the workers would smile and say hello or wave to her. Mom smiles when she talks of the days she and Uncle Julian played in the sugarcane fields, but she shudders when she mentions the ditches filled with water. When they had to cross a ditch, he would carry her on his back. She refused to walk in the ditch water because of the "bugs" (leeches) that would cling to her legs. Uncle Julian didn't mind the "bugs"; he just pulled them off.

She sadly remembers when her parents' marriage ended. She was six years old. Nanay, a victim of *coboy-coboy* (kidnapping or abduction of a man's wife by another man), had run away with another man, taking Mom with her. Uncle Julian was left behind because he wasn't around. Mom was ten years old when Tatay finally found them on the island of Kauai and took her back with him to Honolulu. Mom and Uncle Julian were boarded with a family whenever Tatay worked on the plantation. Although she lived with different families, she had to take care of herself and her personal needs. To this day, she is thankful to Nanay for teaching her how to cook, wash, and take care of herself.

Mom had nine full siblings, but seven died in infancy. She had four half siblings; one died in infancy and one Nanay had given away to the baby's godparents. Nanay had a child every year, and Mom remembers clearly the day Nanay gave birth to her half sister. She was about seven years old then. On the day her sister was born, she helped Nanay prepare for the birth by helping Nanay carry a big pot of hot water from the outside kitchen to the bedroom and placing a pile of clean rags by the mattress which Nanay had propped up against a bedroom wall.

3

Suddenly and quickly Nanay settled herself on the mattress and told Mom to run for the midwife. She said she ran as fast as she could. When she and the midwife returned to the house, Nanay was already giving birth and the midwife immediately went to help her. The women forgot about Mom until she started to cry. Mom said she became frightened when she saw blood coming out from her mother and thought she was dying. It took her a long while to get over the experience of seeing her mother give birth to her sister.

When Tatay and Mom moved to California in July 1927, her intention was to continue her education but they lived in an isolated farm in the San Ramon area and there was no one available to help her find a school, so she gave up on continuing her education.

Mom and Dad, Alejandro Salvador Raymundo, met on October 5, 1927. He was a salesman for tailor-made men's suits. Mom said it was love at first sight for her. A month later, when work was finished in the camp, she was ecstatic to learn that they were going to go to Stockton. She had not forgotten Dad, who had told her that he went to Stockton often. In Stockton, she began working as a pool-table girl in Menda's Pool Hall on Market Street. Her arrival raised the Pinay (Filipina women) population in Stockton to seven.

She and Dad met again when he came into the pool hall during her first week on the job. They began to see each other often. One day my father proposed to my mother, but Tatay was vehemently opposed to their marriage. With friends' help, they eventually eloped and got married on January 23, 1928. She was fifteen-and-half years old, he was one month shy of his twenty-fifth birthday.

Mom laughs when she tells the story about getting their marriage license in Modesto. Mom had worn a cloche with the brim turned down close to her eyes. When the clerk asked for her age, she immediately said, "Twenty." She said, "I don't know why I said twenty instead of eighteen. The man looked at me and he said, 'You don't look twenty.' I tried to tell him that we Filipina women are not like white women, we don't look our age. The man behind the window shook his head and said, 'No, you are not twenty, but, oh, well.' Your Dad and Ninong and Ninang Roxas just stood by and didn't say anything."

Mom shudders when she tells of how she and Dad managed to stay just about "a half step ahead" of Tatay. In fact, he arrived at the justice of the peace five minutes after they left. On their way back to the camp, the wedding party stopped at a chicken farm to buy several chickens for their celebration dinner. After they bought the chickens, Dad decided that it would be a good time to find out how to raise chickens. This kept my parents at the farm for an hour or so. Mom believes that it was God's way of saving their lives, as an angry Tatay had been waiting for them at the camp with a gun. Mom believes he would have shot them, remembering how violent he was when he beat up Nanay and went looking for Delphin with a gun.

When Tatay finally, but grudgingly, accepted their marriage, he and Uncle Julian visited now and then, and then lived with my parents off and on—in fact, through most of the Depression years. But Tatay never spoke directly to Dad until his great-granddaughter was about ten years old. Anything he had to communicate about Dad he said to Mom in Dad's presence. Dad tolerated Tatay for Mom's sake, going about his business as if Tatay were not around.

When my parents got married, they lived with their Ninong (Godfather) and Ninang (Godmother). They offered Dad a place with their crew and Mom a job as assistant cook. One day Ninang Roxas, who was the camp cook, became ill and the kitchen responsibilities fell on Mom. She was frightened at first but with encouragement from the others, she said, "I gritted my teeth and took over and it didn't take me long to get into the groove of cooking for a small crew." The experience stood her in a good stead through the years in various camps when a cook was needed.

Their lives as migrant workers began in 1930, as they moved from camp to camp throughout central California. Once, when they moved to a camp, there wasn't a room available in the camp and no housing nearby. The largest things Dad had ever built were vegetable crates or boxes, but he was a man who would try anything once. He solicited the help of the *boys* (a crew or a group of Filipino men) to get lumber and build a house. Whenever Mom tells the story, she laughs because to this day she doesn't know where the *boys* got the lumber; it was good lumber. She never asked, but she had her suspicions. "I know those *boys*," she would say. Dad never talked about it. They went about building the one-room house as if they knew what they were doing. The one thing Dad did know was how to wire a house. "Thank God he was an electrician," Mom would say. When he and the *boys* proudly finished, it was a nice little house, although it tilted to one side. That didn't deter Dad. He moved his family in—it was a roof over our heads! I remember how they always laughed whenever they talked about that little house.

Dad had taken a correspondence course in applied electrical engineering from the Chicago Engineering Works and received his diploma in December 1926. (The certificate is still in our possession.) He was hired almost immediately after his graduation, and his job was to maintain electrical wiring in a business office. One day, he turned off the electricity and put on his rubber gloves. Just as he started work on the wires, the electricity suddenly came on, almost knocking him off his feet. His hands escaped injury, but his rubber gloves had been burned off his hands. He never again attempted to look for a job as an electrician. He returned to fieldwork.

In the summer of 1931, in Ripon, California, Dad and his friends were working in the sugar beets when the price for sugar beets drastically fell. For all their hard work, they received nothing. Broke and with no work available, they lived in a railroad junction building. Times were hard, the Depression had hit, but there was food on the table. Vegetables consisted of mustard greens, mushrooms, and other edible greens from the surround-ing field. Fish were caught and salted. Rice, mushrooms, mustard greens, and salted fish were our diet through the winter months of 1931 and 1932. Bud, my brother, was born on December 30, 1931. The camp cook had been keeping the *totong* (scorched bot-tom of steam rice) in burlap sacks hung on nails outside the kitchen. Mom said it was a godsend that he had the foresight to keep the *totong*, as it kept the *campo* in rice for the winter.

There was a turkey farm nearby, and Mom heard Dad and four men of the crew discussing how to get one of the turkeys. "The farmer has a lot of turkeys. He will not miss one," she over-heard one of the men say. The men wore large rubber boots when they went to the turkey farm and came home with a huge turkey, which they cleaned and split among themselves. Dad preserved our share by packing the meat in lard inside two 4-gallon lard cans he had gotten from the cook. The suspicious turkey farmer showed up at the camp the next day with several policemen. The farmer said he knew how many turkeys he had and one was missing. Mom said the police were all over the place looking for evidence and measured everyone's shoes. They were too small for the big prints the police found around the turkey farm, and there was not a single trace of feathers anywhere. Mom never found out what they did with the boots.

In July 1932, we moved to Delano, California, about 200 miles south of Stockton, where we lived for a few months. Mom laughs when she describes the move. "It was like 'grapes of wrath,' but no one paid attention, as other people were doing it too." Our one big mattress and bedding were strapped onto the car's roof; the huge corrugated tub (used to wash clothes and bathe my brother and me) was strapped to the back of the car. Our large steamer trunk filled with clothes and a few posses-sions was in the rumble seat and next to it a container of rice and fish for our lunch. We were all in the front seat. It was a long trip with necessary stops and lunch along the way; we left early in the morning and arrived in Delano in the evening at the camp.

Dad was told there wasn't any room available in the bunkhouse for a couple. He told the boss the barn would do very well, as the weather was warm. The barn was filled with large grape-drying trays, three of which he stacked, placing the mattress on top for our bed. Mom said it made a comfortable bed.

8   The next morning, when we entered the kitchen for breakfast, the boss was surprised and upset when he saw me and my brother. He had not seen us in the car on our arrival. He scolded Dad for not letting him know he had children. "The barn is not a place for children to sleep in!" The cook lived in a tent next to the kitchen, and the boss told the cook to move into the bunkhouse with the crew. The cook was not happy but he did not complain. For the duration of the grape season, the tent was our home and Mom became the camp cook, to the relief of cook and crew. As the contractor said, "He is a better field worker than a cook." She was paid one dollar a day plus meals for her, my brother, and me. Dad paid for his meals from his wages.

When my brother and I became of school age, Mom's priority wherever we lived was to see to it that we attended school. She didn't want us to spend our lives working in the fields. When our enrollment was settled, she concentrated on making our living quarters a home—whether it was a room located at one end of a bunkhouse, a tent, a two-room shack, or a box car.

Our migrant life stopped when we moved to Salinas, California, in 1939. We lived in a labor camp for about three years until Dad was offered a job as an irrigator and tractor driver for Stolich & Company, one of Salinas Valley's largest farms. He was taking diesel mechanic classes in the evening, and his instructor was the chief mechanic at Stolich & Company and offered Dad a job as a mechanic. When he wasn't driving the tractor, he could work in the shop. We moved into a company house with an outside shower and outhouse. It was not the greatest, but my mother was happy because it had three bedrooms—my brother and I would have our own bedrooms. She was happy we would not be moving from one school to another for a long while. Mom even joined the Filipino Women's Club and became an active member.

Mom said that once in a while she missed the camp life and the get-together after dinner when she, Dad, and several *boys* used to sit outside on the steps of the bunkhouse and sing in the cool of summer evenings. She knew how to play the ukulele and Dad knew how to play the violin and they sang along. I remember those days, sitting with them and listening to their singing.

In the summer, Mom, my brother Bud, and I worked in the field; when we were in school she and a friend worked in the fields. Once, for several weeks during World War II, they and several friends worked in one of the canneries in Monterey's Cannery Row, which was in desperate need of workers on the midnight shift. Soldiers from Fort Ord were also recruited to work in the canneries. One night Mom had fallen asleep but her hands kept moving. She was awakened by the noise of can hitting can and saw she was trying to stuff a can into another can instead of fish. She was embarrassed when some of the soldiers across from her smiled and shook their heads.

During the lettuce season, she and another Pinay friend talked a labor contractor into hiring them as thinners. Thinning lettuce seedlings is a back-breaking job. They were determined to work with the men, who were getting 25 cents an hour, instead of with the other women and children hoeing weeds for 10 cents an hour. The contractor argued that the farmer did not like women doing such work in his fields. They argued that, dressed like the men with bandannas wrapped around their heads topped with large hats and shirts and work pants, they would look like one of them and promised they would not look up whenever the farmer came to the field. He finally gave in. When Mom tells the story she proudly says, "We showed them we were as good as the men. We kept up with them."

It was not all work for my parents. They had their social life. They loved music, loved to sing and, best of all, loved to dance, especially Mom. At every opportunity, they attended dances, picnics, and special Filipino celebrations, such as marriages, births, christenings, July 4, and Christmas; the most important day was Rizal Day on December 30.

I do not remember the Depression years very well. I vaguely remember little incidents here and there, the few friends left behind when we moved, a cabin in Delano with cockroaches, a run-down three-room shack in Visalia whose floor my mother washed and scrubbed with buckets of hot soapy water. I have fond memories of baths in that house in the corrugated tub placed in the middle of the kitchen floor. I can still see the kitchen warmed by the wood-burning stove and rags stuffed under the doors and around the one window to keep the winter cold out and the heat in—those bath times were "nice and cozy" to me.

I don't look back on those years as "the good old days"—not when I now understand the hardships and deprivations. I constantly wonder how my parents and their friends ever made it through those years. Single men and families lived together in camps or in a house, supporting each other. Whoever was fortunate to find a job supported the others. Mom said no one she knew was on welfare. I found out much later that Filipinos were considered aliens and therefore did not qualify for welfare.

World War II was the beginning of the end of the comradery and family of the Filipino community I had known, the *campo* life when the *boys* and families were a "family." Those years of love and care disintegrated when many Filipino men went into the army to form the First and Second Filipino Infantries, others with families moved to the cities to work in shipyards, and children graduating from high school found office jobs in town.

Prior to World War II, many single Filipino men separated from their families in the Philippines tended to adopt families. We children called them *tios* (uncles).

One of Mom's stories is a good example of the deep sense of family and love for children. I was about seventeen months old. The Depression was about a year old. Work was hard to find. At the time Dad and three men were labor contractors of a lettuce-cutting crew. Their hard work was for nothing, as the market for lettuce fell and the lettuce they worked so hard to cultivate was left to rot in the field. They were left penniless. One of the partners, Manong Pedro, in his late sixties, "adopted" our family and stayed with us instead of moving on as the other partners and some of the *boys* did. He always made sure I had milk. Mom never knew how he was able to get milk and he never told her, but every day he had a bottle for me. One day it had been raining heavily and he came home soaked and cold, but he had my milk. That evening he came down with pneumonia. After a couple of weeks, Dad and one of the *boys* took him to the hospital. He died in Dad's arms on the way to the hospital. Dad, with the help of the hospital, contacted relatives of Manong Pedro. Dad did not tell Mom of Manong Pedro's death; he told her he was being cared for in the hospital. It wasn't until a month later through a chance meeting with a friend that she found out Manong Pedro had died. She had never questioned his month-long "hospitalization" as it wasn't uncommon in those days for a patient with pneumonia to be in the hospital a month or longer.

Mom has another side. She loved to read and write. She said that whenever she could, she read. She stopped writing in her diary when she had her first child, saying she was too busy caring for her family and working, but she did manage some writing—lyrics of popular songs of the day and even some lyrics and poetry she wrote herself. She was also an avid pen-pal and has photos of pen-pals from Alaska, India, England, and Hollywood in her photo albums. She began diary writing again in 1981, after my father died, until 1993, when she became blind.

She has a good collection of photo albums—pictures of friends and places were treasured. One of her albums she started in the 1940s contains brief written comments beside each photo. She has a collection of news clipping albums from 1928 to 1949 of Filipino friends, events, and especially of World War II. She is also a collector of mementoes. With all the moving about she managed to keep a couple of large pots and few utensils from her *campo* cooking days. She kept several of her crocheted items, bleached rice sacks, an electric coffee percolator set, a radio, a few treasured dresses, and gifts of ceramics, vases, and figurines. She still has her collections of coins and stamps from the 1940s. How she managed to keep them through the years I don't know. I remember Dad grumbling about her boxes taking up room whenever we moved, wondering out loud why she didn't throw some of the old things away. She would wonder just as loudly about his old fishing poles, reels, and tackle boxes taking up just as much room and why he didn't throw the old things away. She kept his fishing poles, which are still hung up on one of our garage walls, and his tackle boxes, which are still on a high shelf in the garage where he last placed them.

Mom passed away on September 15, 2000. She was eighty-eight years old. This book is a memorial to her and to the Manangs who are gone but have left us a legacy of their fortitude and strength.

Rizaline R. Raymundo
San Jose, California

12

Tomorrow's Memories

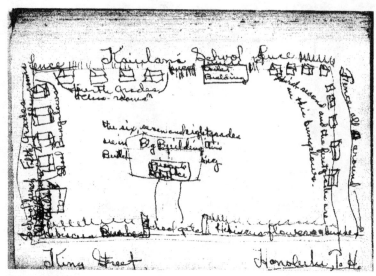

Kauilani School—1925. Hall Street, Honolulu, T.H.

1924

Waipahu, Oahu, Territory of Hawaii
January 10, 1924

Christmas and New Year is now over and this month is beginning of the New Year of 1924, and I think this is the best time
to start a diary my teacher told us about a book that she wrote
about herself. And this is where I got my idea to start one for
myself because, I would like to read about me—what everyday
things happen to me—when I am old woman, right now I am
only 11 years, 5 months. I have been in School just this past
few years but God gave me the mind to catch on how to learn
my alphabets and to put them together so I can read and write
like I do now. I'm thankful. . . .

Waipahu, Oahu, T.H.
March 3, 1924

Dear Diary:

Mary and her folks had moved to Honolulu. I feel so lonely now
without her. The reason why they went to Honolulu, because
it's been heard that all Filipinos must strike for higher pay. Mr.
Pablo Manlapit is the leader of this strike. Mr. Manlapit says
that all Filipinos must strike or else there will be many hurt. So
I think that's why they left and moved to Honolulu to stay. Oh,
why did this strike has to come up for. Now no one to pal with,
now, I have to sleep all by myself from now on, go to school

alone and eat my lunch alone and I'll have to go to shows alone. Gee, I don't think I'll have any more fun, now that Mary is gone. I have other friends but they're not as close to me like Mary is. Speaking of the strike, I wonder if Tatay will go to Honolulu too. Gee, Tatay is making good here tho' he is steadily putting money in the bank. Anyway I'll let you know if we do go to Honolulu. Oh Diary, before I forget, Father bought a new car. An Oakland Touring car. Boy, it's nice to have, I mean, own a car. A friend of our will drive it for us. And my brother will learn from him. Faustino will drive the car—and I'm scared of him somehow. I do not like him.

Strike Camp, Middle St., Honolulu, T.H.
May 10, 1924

Dear Diary:

We just arrive here today, here, at the Strike Camp. There are so many Filipinos here, married couples and unmarried men. They're from all parts of Oahu. There are five other young girls here too. I became friends with two of them already. Their first names are Esperanza and Victoria. They are both very nice girls. They showed me the place around here, as soon as we settled, I mean, found our sleeping quarters. You see, we all live in one big house, and so all we did was put curtains around our bed, and that will have to serve as our room, for how long, we don't know. I guess we have to stay here until this strike is over. And Manlapit is going to feed the whole crowd. We're suppose to go down to his office every other day to get our ration of food. Gosh, I hope this strike won't last long. You see, Diary, Mr. Manlapit wanted the plantation to give the laborers $2.00 a day and eight hours work. I certainly hope Manlapit wins, 'cause then it will be for our own good. Will tell you some more later on as the girls are draggin me. I told them I want to finish this.

Strike Camp, Middle St., Honolulu, Oahu, T.H.
May 11, 1924

Dear Diary:

Another day had gone by. Do you know, as soon as we finished breakfast, I went over to Esperanza's sleeping quarters and she was just finishing breakfast. I asked her if she has anything to do today. She said "No." And I asked her to show me the place again. We looked into everything. The bath room, the toilet, the kitchen and do you know there are so many mango trees close by. Boy! Wait until the mangoe season is in full blossom, by that I mean when they get ripe, and that's not far-off—it is next month, and I'll surely do some climbing again. I haven't climb trees for so long, it seems. Oh well, it won't be long now. I told Esperanza about it, and she says, "That's good, 'cause that means we don't have to ask any boys to get mangoes for us. We can get them ourselves." And Esperanza introduced me to the other 3 girls—Sofia, Marcella, and Trinidad. I don't know which of this girls is the oldest, but I do know I am the youngest of them all. Triny is sort of snobbish—'cause she's better looking—but she has such mannish walk. But just so they are nice to me I'll be nice to them. And Diary, the men here play basketball and volleyball. And there are 3 woman here that "cooks" and "sells" "Maruya," you know, fried bananas and other good things to eat. Oh, I just love "Maruya." I bought four today and gave 2 to Esperanza. Somehow Esperanza kind of fill in Mary's place; but I don't think I'll ever forget Mary. I do hope I'll see her soon. Well, Diary, that's all for now. If something new happens here I'll let you know.

Strike Camp, Middle St., Honolulu, Oahu, T.H.
May 13, 1924

Dear Diary:

Say, there'll be something going on here on every Saturdays and Sundays from now on. You know what? Well, I'll tell you. It's this; there's going to be dances here every Saturdays and Sundays.

Gee, won't that be fun. You see, Diary, I'm so crazy about dancing. And another thing, we are going to charge the men 10 cents
for 3 minutes dance. Gosh, that's not bad is it? You know, Diary,
someone thought of this idea, and it is for our own good, 'cause
you see, we are very far from "show-houses." This dancing busi-
18   ness is for our benefit so that the place here won't be as dull every
Saturday and Sunday. And I know we girls are going to have lots
of fun when that day comes around. Gee, I hope all the girls will
be in it. I'm sure Esperanza and Victoria and Sophia will join in—
including myself.

Strike Camp, Middle St., Honolulu, Oahu, T.H.
May 19, 1924

Dear Diary:

Gee, the dance is tonight and I'm so glad; I can hardly wait for
tonight. I wonder how much I'll earn. Maybe nobody will dance
with me. Esperanza and Victoria are so excited as I am. Gosh,
who wouldn't be, may I ask you? It's now 4 o'clock in the afternoon. Gee, I don't—I cannot eat my supper. Oh well, my dad and
brother will have my share. Father doesn't care if I go dancing
with the girls tonight, 'cause he knows it is all for the fun only,
and adults will enjoy it as well as we children. So until here, Diary
dear, will let you know as soon as I can how I came out. Gee, but
it's grand to have you, 'cause, I can come to you and tell you what's
in my heart, you know, the things I feel and many other things
too. I know you'll keep it a secret just as long as nobody is looking into my things, and get hold of you. This is all for now.

Strike Camp, Middle St., Honolulu, T.H.
May 20, 1924

Dear Diary:

Sorry, I couldn't tell you anything last night when the dance
was over because I was so tired and sleepy, but I was happy,

'cause I made $7.20. I counted it before I went to sleep and I gave it to Father this morning. I kept just a dollar for myself to spend on something that I'd like to eat. Gee, I didn't think I would make that much, but I did. And tonight there's going to be dancing again. Hope I'll make just as much as I did last night. Oh, there were only four girls that danced last night. **19** The other two didn't join in 'cause they say nice girls don't dance at all. Marcela didn't say that but Trinidad did. Gee, I wish one of these days she'd be real jealous about us making some money and she won't, so that she will really join us. That way we'll make her eat her words without us forcing her to. 'Cause she says too, that it's bad for us girls to dance, 'cause dancing will lead us to something else later on. She's just evil-minded, that's all. Gosh, we just dance. I don't see any harm in it, do you? These dancing isn't anything like they have in dancehalls. The dancing we have here is just-clean-good-fun, for all of us here. Oh well, if that's the way she feels about it, well, that's up to her, eh Diary?

Strike Camp, Middle St., Honolulu, T.H.
May 21, 1924

Dear Diary:

Well, I made $6.90 last night. Tho' I made 30 cents less, nevertheless, I was very glad to make that much. I think the other girls made more than I 'cause, they seemed to have danced more. Just Esperanza would tell me how much she makes and I would tell her how much I make too. The other two would just giggle and laugh and they would say, "Not so very much." I never mind them, if they would not tell Esperanza and I, how much they make, it really doesn't make any difference to us. The four of us today had played so many games, we even played baseball with the boys. Oh, it was fun. Oh, Esperanza and I washed our clothes today and we starched them too, just the dresses and my father's shirts and my brother's, but I don't starch the underclothes 'cause they get hard and it scratches our skin. Tomorrow, she and I will iron all the clothes. Yes, Diary, Esperanza and I get along very nicely. You see, she doesn't have any mother, just her father. So I guess that's why we like each other so. But she can never fill in Mary's place.

20 Even now, I wish Mary would come here to visit the Strike Camp, 'cause many people from uptown comes to the camp, to look the place over—and also the people in it, I suppose. Well, Diary, there won't be any dances 'till the May 24–25—this coming Saturday and Sunday. So all we can do now is run around and play, eh Diary. Until here, I'll have to say so long until that time comes when I have something to tell you.

Strike Camp, Middle St., Honolulu, Oahu, T.H.
May 22, 1924

Dear Diary:

I've got to tell you this. Do you know Esperanza and I took in washing today from the men here in the camp, 'cause after all, we just play and play and so it so happened that one of our friends here brought this thing up about us washing his clothes 'cause he doesn't have any wife, he says, and, the laundry shops are so far-away; besides he says he's getting tired of washing his own clothes, and he say he'll pay us like he would pay the laundry-man. And so he says why don't you wash some of the boys clothes here, you'll make some extra money besides dancing on Saturdays and Sundays? And I says, "Gee, that is a very good idea." And he says "sure" and he says too, that I can wash clothes and iron them pretty good for a young girl like I am. Gosh, that made me feel kind of proud of myself. And so I thank him so much for telling me about washing clothes, and to show he was in earnest, he gave me 4 shirts and 4 pair of underclothes. He says as soon as you wash them and iron, bring them to me and I'll pay you. Well, Diary, I put his clothes all bundled-up, and put his name on it and I ran out to find

Esperanza 'cause I want her in it too. You know, her and I wash and iron and whatever we make, we'll divide it equally. I found her, she was talking to Victoria, and so I called to her and says, "Let's go walking," and she came to me as soon as her legs could carry her. Then when we were far from everyone I told her of the good news. Gee, she was so happy as I was. So, we turned and walk towards the camp and asked a few more of our friends, all men, if they have any dirty clothes that they would like to be washed. At first they thought we were just joking but when they saw how earnest we were, they all say, "Sure, we have," but they say, "Be sure and return them nice and clean or else we won't pay you a cent," and I caught them winking at each other. Anyway, they know I can wash them clean, 'cause they always see the clothes I wash every Monday. Boy, they certainly gave us a great bundle. Anyway, we finished them in three hrs. We hung them late this afternoon about 2:30 but I think they'll dry before evening comes, 'cause the sun is shining so hot. Tomorrow we will iron again—'cause yesterday we iron our clothes, you know. Maybe it will take us about half day in iron all the clothes we washed today, but we won't care, 'cause we know we'll be paid well for our hard work. Gosh, I'm glad I could really wash, and Esperanza is too, 'cause she doesn't have much money. You know the money she earned last Saturday and Sunday, her father took nearly all of it. And so this money we earned in washing, well, her father won't have to know about it. And that way she can keep every cent that she'll get. About my father, well, he let me keep the money I earned, only I don't want to. One dollar out every dance-money I earned, is all I want. After all, he saves them and it helps to buy food too. So I don't worry about my father, he is so good to us. Esperanza and I are tired, but we don't care. After we finished washing I took her to the store and we had ice cream and vanilla snaps and we walked home slowly and we told stories all the way home. We laughed so much. It was fun, Diary.

Strike Camp, Middle St., Honolulu, Oahu, T.H.
May 23, 1924, 8 o'clock at night

Dear Diary:

Do you know, we made $3.15 apiece when we delivered the clothes this afternoon at 3:30. Gee that's not bad, is it? I guess **22** starting next week Monday, we'll take in washing twice a week. We collect the clothes on Sunday afternoon and on Wednesday afternoon, and we'll wash them on Monday and Thursday morning, and iron on Tuesday and on Friday. We usually play so we might as well earn some money by washing. And when Esperanza and I finishes our work then we can have our fun. What we made today shows we can really earn some money if we just set our heart into doing something, to earn money. Diary, you'll hear from me on Sunday.

Strike Camp, Honolulu, Oahu, T.H.
Sunday morning, May 25, 1924

Dear Diary:

Here I am again. It's now ten-thirty in the morning and I feel, oh, so happy just being alive and healthy. Well, Diary, I made $7.30 last night—ten cents more than I made last Saturday. Gosh, I'm doing pretty good, and gee, we had so much fun last night. You know, even married couples danced. Of course the men do not pay their wives, they just danced with each other. Sometimes they swap partners and they were really having the time of their lives. Of course when they, I mean the married men, danced with us girls they have to pay like the single boys do. So most of the married men are contented to dance with their wives only, that way they don't have to dig into their pockets and pay. But still we girls make some money 'cause most of the single men here—and married men have work of some kind up town. Esperanza and I made the same I think. The dance started 7 o'clock last night and stop at 12 o'clock. You know, we wanted to pay our musician but they won't take the money 'cause they say they enjoyed the evening as well as we did. There are only two boys that plays for us, a mandolin and a guitar player. They play good music. Well, tonite is another night of fun for me, and also for everyone here in the camp.

Strike Camp, Honolulu, T.H.
Monday morning, May 26, 1924

Dear Diary:

Well, Diary mine, just made $6.90 last night but that wasn't bad, was it? We had as much fun as usual. There's always a big crowd. Oh say, there's 2 sailor boys that came here. I just noticed them last night. They are both Filipino sailors. These sailor boys were either visiting relatives or friends. And do you know, Trinidad just told me this morning that she likes one of these sailor boys, very much. She likes him well enough for a "sweetheart." I wasn't surprised because she's already 15 and come to think about sweetheart she has one already. He is a nice-looking boy that lives above us. What is she going to do with two sweethearts? Gee, that's impossible, don't you think so? Not unless she thinks of giving the other up. Oh, well, that's her business. Boy! she was so excited over this sailor guy. I wonder what he's got to make her so excited and happy every time she see him. You know, Trinidad was watching us last night and I bet she wished or still wishing she could join us. And I know too that the sailor guy knows that Trining likes him a lot, and I can tell he likes her too as Trining isn't bad to look at—and the same with the sailor guy. If Trining falls for him that's her business, eh Diary.

Strike Camp, Honolulu, T.H.
Wednesday noon, May 28, 1924

Dear Diary:

Esperanza and I just finished our washing and we just finished hanging them up to dry. Boy, are we tired. But we don't mind really, Diary. Tomorrow we'll iron and deliver them right away and collect our money. Right after we hang the clothes up, we figured how much we'll collect for washing and we're going to receive $2.50 each when we deliver them tomorrow. We had freshly cook "Maruya," fried banana fritter, after we finished our washing. Gee, but these "Maruya" taste so very good. I like to eat them when they're still hot. Yep, Esperanza and I really enjoy each other. She is kind and nice and we are in the same boat, meaning she has no mother and I have no mother. Tell you some more tomorrow, Diary, so long—

Strike Camp, Honolulu, T.H.
Thursday noon, May 29, 1924

Dear Diary:

It's now 4 o'clock in the afternoon. We had delivered the washing and collected $5.00 all told, so we have $2.50 each. We went down to the store and we bought ice cream and pies. Before we went home we watched the streetcars and automobiles passed back and forth and many people are in the streetcars. They look at Esperanza and I and we'd stare back at them. Funny thing about me, I like to sing. I like to hum or sing a school song or our native songs. I'd always hum some part of the song called "The Japanese Sand-man," and "My Isles of Golden Dream." Well, Diary, day after tomorrow will be dance night again, and that'll be another fun night again, I wonder if that sailor guy will come back for Trining.

Strike Camp, Honolulu, T.H.
Sunday morning at 9:00, June 1, 1924

Dear Diary:

Made $9.20 last night and I think Esperanza made just $6.20. Anyway she didn't mind. She was very glad she made that much. You know, that sailor guy was here again. He just danced with all of us. He says to me I danced pretty good for so young a girl and I told him—"Oh, that's because I loved dancing." He smiled, then he looked at Trining who was watching us. I know, Diary, that she wished she was on the floor dancing with the sailor, and I think he wanted that too. And if I'm not mistaken he'll be over tonight too—just so he can see Trining. I've a feeling these two will be what people called sweethearts yet—even if Trining already has a sweetheart. I think she'll give the other guy the air. You know, Diary, I forgot to mention to you that I've been delivered letters to and from Trining to the boy upstairs, 'cause her mother is so strict. So she makes me give her love letter to him—and I read them even if I was not suppose to. Gosh, but these people in love say the craziest things! I wonder if I'll be as silly too, five years from now, eh Diary?

Strike Camp, Honolulu, T.H.
Wednesday night, 7:30, June 4, 1924

Dear Diary:

It's night now, and the stars are winking and blinking up above. Yes, another day is over. Today we collected some dirty clothes and we washed all morning. And just about an hour and half ago, we got thru sprinkling the clothes with water so they will all be ready to iron tomorrow. Esperanza and I figured we'd have about $1.55 apiece for the clothes we had washed. Right now I'm glad I'm alone. Esperanza had gone to her sleeping quarters upstairs but she'll be back and I never tell her I have a diary. Somehow, I just don't want her or anybody to know that I have you. I like Esperanza very much, but not as much as Mary Ehapon. They are both very nice girls. I wonder what Maria is doing now. Maybe she is now seeing a picture show or she maybe in bed, sleeping, huh. Anyway, I hope she is well and her mother and step-pa too. Well, Diary, this is all for today, I mean tonite. Gosh, there's so many people here in the camp, and they are all so jolly and nice. Right now, I can hear babies cry, little boys and girls squealing with delight over something, and grown people talking—just telling tales and laughing so loud. Seems like we are just one happy family here in the Strike Camp. I still wonder tho', just how long this strike is going to last. I said this is all for tonight and I'm still here. I will close now. I know Esperanza will be back soon, so I better put you away.

Strike Camp, Honolulu, T.H.
Thursday night at 9:00, June 5, 1924

Dear Diary:

Esperanza and I finished the ironing today and we delivered all the clothes, and we collected our money and we exactly have $1.55 each. As usual, we spend a little on "candies & ice cream" and saved the rest. To tell you the truth, I give my share to my father, so he can buy food. I just keep 25 cents for myself. Do you know, my father has never yet to scold me or be mean to me? He just advise me and my brother to behave and be good; not to do anything that he is going to be ashamed of; I can honestly write, Diary mine, my father is very good to me. I could not ask for a better father. I am really having fun, now that I am living with him. When I was with my mother I did not have a chance to play with other children of my own age. I have to take care of my half brother and half sister. My half brother is William Fernandez and my half sister is Incarnation Fernandez. I had another half brother, name Enastacio Fernandez, but Mother gave him away—he was a pretty baby, he had such pretty curls. I felt sad when I found out about it. Mother gave Enastacio to his godmother and his godfather because they couldn't have a baby of their own, but, young as I was, I know the real reason why Mother gave Enastacio to her Comare and Compare. I think at times about him, as well as I think about my mother and about my half brother William and my half sister Incarnation, where are they now and how they are getting along. William must be about 5 years old now, he was born 1919 in Kauai. So did Incarnation who was born the following year 1920, she is four years old now, and Enastacio 3 years, he was born a year later after Incarnation. Another baby was born in Waipahu. The following year, Father took me away from her—but this baby died, I was told, the same year it was born. Perhaps it was God's wish, 'cause I was told by my father that Mother and Delphin was having a hard time. I hear that Mother and Delphin and my half brother and half sister are living here in Honolulu. I hope they are all alright. Yes, Diary mine, I feel sad whenever I think about my mother and father so far apart now—why do things like this happens to a family? When Nanay was pregnant with Enastacio, a young man who lived several houses away loved to tease Nanay. Whenever he saw her, he'd say, "Hello, tambor," which means "drum." She hated the word. No matter where he was, if he saw her, he'd go out of his way to say, "Hello, tambor." Once, I saw her chasing him with a kitchen knife, threatening to cut him up. Her anger turned to hate for the young man, who was dark with black, kinky hair. Enastacio was born a "marked" baby—he was dark with black, kinky hair.

Strike Camp, Middle St., Honolulu, T.H.
June 9, 1924

Dear Diary:
We had our "dancing" 2 night straight—I made $7.00 the other nite and $7.50 last night—gosh, so many Filipino sailors came, last night and the other night, too. I gave Father $13.50. I kept 1.00 for myself. The men tell me for as young as I was, I can follow them easily like fox-trot and waltzes. I'm not even 12 years old yet, but because there are only few girls living here, I guess that's why they let me. There's a saxaphone player, too, only he does not play every time we have a dance. I like the music very much if he plays with the guitar and mandolin player, because the music sound so much better, and it makes you want to dance

so much more. I can keep on dancing and forget about eating. Yes, Diary, that is how much I like dancing. I better put you away before my brother gets back, I do not want him to know I have a diary. Tatay sees me writing on you, but he just smile at me— his knowing smile, I call it—he seems to know things. I feel kind of sad for him because he can't read or write, but he knows his numbers. You can't fool him about money, he knows his cents and dollars, of which I'm glad he does. He knows where I put you. We have a big steamer trunk. I have a hiding place in it. Tatay told Manong Julian not to be disturbing or looking for things in the trunk without his permissions, of which I am glad, so when Tatay says something about do not touch or take any-thing—you had better not.

Strike Camp, Middle St., Honolulu, T.H.
June 12, 1924

Dear Diary:
Esperanza just told me this morning that her and her father are going to move, where to, she do not know. I feel sad again. Gosh, every time I find a friend they have to go away. But she tell me that there is nothing that she can do. When her father makes his mind to do something, he is going to do it. She tells me that they are going to move in a few days—maybe tomor-row or next day. So, she says, "Angeles, I cannot be with you today. I have to help pack our things, our clothes especially. Maybe if I do the things I'm suppose to do and finish them sooner, maybe we still can play and have some fun for today." I do not feel like going out and play with Trinidad or Victoria. I'll just stay here and read or crochet. I think I better read. You know, Diary, since I have learned to read and write, I have a better picture of this world and the people that are living in this beautiful world we are in. I am so thankful and grateful to our Heavenly Father, also to Tatay for letting me go to school—'cause I wanted to go to school so very much, so I can

read and write. Within the past 3 years that I went to school, I learned fast the alphabet.

Strike Camp, Middle St., Honolulu, T.H.
June 14, 1924   **29**

Dear Diary:
Esperanza and her father just left the Strike Camp. We both cried and we said "good-bye." I do not feel as lonely and very sad as when my "Igso" Mary Ehapon left Waipahu, I think because there is Triny and Victoria. Like Esperanza they are about four years older than I am. I know I am going to miss her. We had been close and we had some fun together and we got along alright—no quarrels. Yes, Diary, like I ask before, why do friends leave or separate. Is this the way of life? Like my mother & father. They have been together for so long—then they separate—somebody comes, and take her away from Father? Is that right? Perhaps someday I will understand things about life better. Anyway, Esperanza is gone now, I have to get use to that—again—like when Mary moved away—oh, you get that lonely feeling inside of you. I am glad that there are a lot of people here. I wonder if I'll meet her again?

Strike Camp, Middle St., Honolulu, T.H.
June 20, 1924

Dear Diary:
You know, Trinidad, one of the older young girls here in the camp, she joined us in the "dancing group." When, just a few months ago, she said she won't join us, because dancing is bad. Anyway Triny (as she is called for short, for Trinidad) joined us dancing last night. Victoria and I had a good laugh when we remembered the things she said to us about not wanting to join us on the dance floor. Oh well, I guess that's her own way of thinking about things and such.

Strike Camp, Middle St., Honolulu, T.H.
June 22, 1924

30 Diary, do you know that Trining is a sailor-sweetheart—oh, that's alright to be a "sailor"-Sweetheart, but she is already a "sweetheart" to a young fellow here in the camp? Boy! She is really asking for troubles. Before the "sailor boy" came to the "Saturday night" dance here in the camp Trining was crazy about this guy living here in the camp. She even gave him some strands of her hair (that's crazy) to prove that she loved him. Now that she is in love with this "sailor guy" she wants her hair back, but the Strike Camp young man refused—he's going to keep them her letters too. And do you know I'm Trining's "messenger-girl." I deliver her letters to him and to her from him. Naturely I read them before I deliver. I know I should not read their letters, but I wanted to know how people or what they say to each other. Gosh, they get so romantic, so much "love you" in their letters. Am I going to be like them when I get old enough to fall in love? I wonder?

Strike Camp, Middle St., Honolulu, T.H.
June 29, 1924

Diary Mine, It's now night, about 8 o'clock I think. My curtained room is by a window. I look out there. It's very dark, but I can see lights close by and far away. Oh, I didn't tell you that we made our sleeping quarters on the second floor of the building, with many of the Filipino families that went on strike. I was lucky to get a place by a window, and Tatay fixed my sleeping place. He put curtain around my cot bed, so I can have some, how do you say, so people can't see me when I get into bed. So whenever I write in you, no one can see me writing. Tatay is having a good time, too. He's somewhere downstairs talking to friends. In fact we are all friends here, just one big family it seems. As for Manong Julian, I don't see him too often. When I get up in the morning, he is gone—he is, I mean there are so many boys of his age here, so he had many friends to play with. He is 17 years old, and I think he goes into the city of Honolulu with his friends to see movies. You see, they can ride on streetcar, they get on it down the street called Kalihi Street. I have not tried to ride on one, maybe someday I will. Since we have come here to the Strike Camp I have not gone anywhere, just to the grocery store when Esperanza was still here in the Strike Camp. (I miss her, I feel so sad sometime I come up here, and cry.) But something inside of me tells me not to feel sad all the time, but I cannot help to feel sad, like the time I remember and I see Tatay beat up Nanay. I think I was five years old at that time. I cry so much and wonder why my Tatay was hurting Nanay so much, but now I know why. Then I feel sad all over again, 'cause now they are not living together anymore. She is living here somewhere in Honolulu with Delphin and her children. I do not know if she has born any more children. Tatay told me that Nanay and her family are living here in Honolulu. I wish she is well and happy and her family, too. Maybe I will never see my mother again.

> Strike Camp, Middle St., Honolulu, T.H.
> *June 30, 1924*

Dear Diary:

It's night now, I don't know what time it is, but I think it is still early, because my father is outside talking to friends, and too, we finish eating not too long ago. I can hear so much talking—someone is telling a joke, I think, 'cause now they are laughing. Anyway, what I'm going to tell you next is no joke. Trinidad's mother gave me a good-bawling out, oh how she scolded me. She caught Trinidad reading one of her love letters from the young man upstairs. Her mother won't have known about me, delivering the "love letters" to and from him if she had only kept her mouth shut—no—she had to tell her I was the "messenger." From now on, I'm not going to deliver no more love letters, they can do it themselves. Trinidad did not have to bring me into her "love affairs," I told Trinidad that, no more will I bring her letters to anyone. She can do it by herself. One "scolding" from her mother is enough. Trinidad's mother was the second woman that scolded me, that I can remember. The

32 first one, beat me up. I was ten years old at the time. It was the same year Tatay took me away from my mother. Yes, the woman beat me because I push her daughter down—I was just trying to defend myself, she was coming at me like a wild bull. This happen about 2 years ago. I was only 10 years old. Some women as mothers are very mean—you know what—they should always find out first who is wrong. I hope I won't grow up like her—mean and terrible person. I will never forget her, I mean, play with those girls again, after that beating from their mother.

Strike Camp, Middle St., Honolulu, T.H.
July 5, 1924

Gosh, oh gee, I have to get sick. They say I got the Measles. I got sick yesterday. Tatay, my brother, the driver of the car (our car). There were 2 other people that were in the car with us. I did not watch the parade, I just sat in one corner of the car all hunch up because I felt cold and I thought if I double up I will feel warm. The sun was shining down on me where I sat and the warm sun felt so good. I told Tatay I felt sick. This is the first time I have been sick that I can remember. I did not eat when we came home—I did not feel hungry somehow. I hope I feel better tomorrow. I sure don't like being sick, I do not feel good. You know, I do not really remember being this sick before. I sure do not like the feeling—I just like to lie down and close my eyes. Thought of playing with my friends has not entered my head. "Oh, Dear God in heaven, please help me and let me be well again, Amen!" Afterwards, I feel all hot all over. I heard the people around me say, "I have a fever." I just lay in bed and closed my eyes. The women all wives and mothers all were talking in Visayan—some were feeling sorry for me because I have no mother to take care of me but they were wrong. Tatay took care of me the few days I was feverish. And Tatay had been taking care of me and my brother. Yet, down deep in my heart, I wish, oh so very much, that Tatay and Nanay were together again. I miss her, right now, I wish she was here— but, that was not to be.

Strike Camp, Middle St., Honolulu, Oahu, T.H.
July 10, 1924

Dear Diary:

I feel better today, the fever is gone. I do not feel cold anymore, so I took a cold bath today. I missed taking a bath every day. I did not have a bath since July 4th. So today I feel better, without telling my father I took my bath. Gee, the water feel so good. I soap myself good—I feel so dirty after so many days, that I did not take a bath. I feel clean and good after I bathe. Do you know that the dance is tonight. I'm happy I can join in the fun tonight; I missed last week's dance, because I got sick. Gee, I hope I would not get sick again.

Strike Camp, Middle St., Honolulu, T.H.
July 11, 1924

Dear Diary:

Gee, I was feeling so good last night, dancing I made $8.50. I gave Tatay all the money. I feel that he should have it all. Since we have moved here, Tatay has not work at all. I know he is spending his savings on food. So I figured he should have the money I earned. I do not know how long we are going to stay here in the Strike Camp. I like it here very much, so many people and they are all so friendly. They all are very nice to me, accept Trinidad's mother, she is a terrible person. I wonder if she was glad I became sick? Oh well, I would not think about it whether she is glad or not. I feel bad as it is, when I got sick.

Strike Camp, Middle St., Honolulu, T.H.
July 13, 1924

Dear Diary:

Gosh, I feel sick again. I woke up with a terrible head-ache, but only on my left side of my head. Funny, just half of my head hurt so much, down to my neck and back. Our mandolin player knows how to massage, so he massage my head and neck for a long time, it seemed, but he finally stop—the aches and pain was still there so Tatay told him that may be the aches go away later, but it did not. Anyway Tatay thank him very much. He smiled and said, "Oh, that's alright, may be someday I will have a head ached and somebody will massage my head, too." Anyway he went on to say, "I hope she feels better tomorrow." Oh, I hope so too, because, I really do not like being sick. Yesterday, I washed clothes—I started to, but I didn't finish washing, Tatay did, 'cause as I soaped and rubbed the dirty clothes, the skin on the palm of my hand start to peel off and I see the red flesh but no blood coming out and my hand start to burn and hurt; I had to rinse my hands fast so the soap suds won't go into the flesh. I dried my hands and showed my hands to Tatay and he said, I'll finish the washing, and he did. And this morning, I woke up this morning just half of my head hurting. I hope the hurt will go away.

Strike Camp, Middle St., Honolulu
July 14, 1924

Dear Diary:

I wonder what is happening to me now. I got up this morning with a terrible pain in (my) left leg and thigh and every time I take a step the pain would go up my back and I had to sit down—it hurt so very much. I told Tatay how I feel, but he could not tell me or help me to stop the pain I was feeling. All day I try to walk but I hurt every time I try, so I feel better when I just lie down in my cot bed. I just get up to go to the toilet. The people here are also wondering what is happening to me. They seem to be very worried about me now, because my sickness had got worse. I know Tatay is worried. I can see his face when he looks at me and tells me to just lie in bed and not try to walk around. It seems I would not be able to play with my friends for awhile, if I'm going to be like this.

Middle St., Honolulu, T.H.
July 25, 1924

Dear Diary:

I am really sick now. I can't walk now, I get up I hurt, I try to walk. I cannot help but cry as I lie down in bed. I tried to walk this morning, but every step I take, I hurt all over now. My legs hurts going up my leg and to my back and up to my neck I hurt. I hear people talking around me—"What is happening to that little girl?" Some say, someone made a "Kahuna" on me, Voodoo or black magic. I hear stories about "Kahuna." This is a Hawaiian word for "Voodoo." Anyway Tatay took me to one lady who is a "Witch" or "Voodoo Woman." She told Tatay that someone made a "Kahuna" on me and she sold a bottle of medicine $7.50 told my father how much to give me, I should take the medicine every 3 hrs. I took every or rather I finished the contents of the bottle but I did not get well—instead I was sicker it seems. I did not feel better at all.

Middle St., Honolulu T.H.
July 27, 1924

Dear Diary of mine:

I am getting, I think, worse every day. I am not getting better. I don't know if I am going to get well. I have been asking for my mother. It seems when I wake up I call for her—they tell me. I am writing this to let you know, until I get well, this is my last writing anything down in this book of mine. If I should die, then there will be no more to write in this book of mine. I'm not able to walk anymore. I've been vomiting so much I don't remember going to the toilet and I have been calling for Nanay, every time. I can hear myself—calling for Nanay, before I go to sleep. The days go by now. I don't know what day today is—I just hear people talking and their voices fade away when I fall asleep. And so, my book of memories, I have to stop writing in your pages. I have to put you down in the bottom of Tatay's trunk So, my diary, this is the last time, (for now), until I get well—that is, if our Father in Heaven will help me get really well again.

1925

River St., Honolulu, T.H.
January 27, 1925

Dear Diary:

Oh, I have so much to tell you. First I must tell you, I am so very thankful and forever grateful to our Father in Heaven that He made me well again, in truth, like He gave me a second life to live again. You know, I thought I will never get well, that I would just die and thinking I was only 12 years old. All those days in bed—never knowing what day it is, and seems like I was asleep most of the time and those last days we live in the Strike Camp at Middle Street. I remember I was really sick at that time. I could not walk and I remember eating and I vomit right after I have eaten. I was asking for Nanay most of time I was sick. So Tatay found my mother & her other family living here in River Street. I'll tell you what I remembered. After I had put you away in the bottom of the trunk, all I did was lie down in bed and sleep all the time, it seems. When Tatay found a friend to help him, we moved away from the Strike Camp. I remember someone I know is helping Tatay when I was sick. When we moved away from the Strike Camp I was put on a cot bed and blanketed, and Tatay was saying good-bye and thank you to friends he had know for just such a short while. The first time we moved away from the Strike Camp, we moved to a friend's house. I remember, when I woke up, we were in this house. I do not know how long we stayed in this house. I know we stayed here until Tatay found out where Nanay lives here in Honolulu. In this house where we lived for a while, I just remembered waking up a few times, then I go to sleep again. The first time I woke up, it was the sound of running bath tub water. The sound of water sound so good I wanted to go in and take a bath. I know I have not been in bath before. Tatay found me trying to sit. I told him that I wanted to take a bath. He told me in a quiet voice that I cannot take a bath yet. Oh, but I wanted a bath so bad. I know if I was only able to crawl, I would have been in that tub—and who knows, maybe it would have been my last bath too. It was after they gave me a quick sponge bath and change my clothes and put me in a sitting position so I can eat my soup. Seems like that's all I can eat is soup. Other times when I woke up I see people come into my room and they watch me and say, "Poor me why does a Mother-less child" get sick for. Next thing I know, I feel being lifted up and I was put on a cot bed again and covered with white sheet and put on to something. Anyway I could hear Tatay saying "thank you" for taking care of me and for him to stay in their house for a while until he found where Nanay is. I know Tatay paid the people for letting us stay at their house. When they put me in the car, I fell asleep. And I woke up. I had a feeling we were going up-stairs, and I hear voices, so many voices—just like being in the Strike Camp again—only I cannot see because I was covered with a sheet. You know, even when I was getting better, I hardly see Willie and Incarnation. Delphin I have never remember ever seeing him around. Nanay was the one I always see near by. As for Tatay he works. I was so glad when I woke up, one morning, to see Nanay's face smiling down at me. She held my hand and gave it a squeeze. Another thing I can remember like in a dream, I had large sores on my face my arms and elbows, oh, on my ears, too. These sores left scars. Another thing happened. While just lying down, I felt so hot I could hear Nanay saying I was having a high fever. At the same time my throat got big and I can't swallow, it hurts. Tatay was gone for a while. Nanay tried to feed me some soup, but I could not swallow the soup even the way she put up my head so the soup can go down my throat. The soup just runs out at the side of my mouth. I do not know how long I was that way—3 or 4 days. I fell into sleep again. I was asleep but I felt something cool wrap around my throat, I feel it get crisp, someone takes it away and put on a fresh one. I don't know how long Tatay and Nanay kept this up until one day, something woke me up. I felt soaking wet all under my pillow my back and I smell terrible, something rotten, and some kind of yellow water mixed with blood running out of the side of my mouth. I cried out for Nanay. Nanay came running and she said in Visayan, "Ay dios ko, salamat," "Oh, I thank you, my God." Nanay was crying and I was crying too, because I think I was feeling better than the last time I was awake and Nanay cried because she felt I was going to be better—my fever was gone, the swelling in my throat has come down—I found out later the watery thing that came out of my mouth was puz. Nanay made me gargle something and told me to spit the water out, so I did. Nanay told me to do this many times. After that she clean me up and change me. Imagine, I really could not do anything to help myself, and Nanay change my blankets and pillow. Oh, I really smell terrible. I felt better after Nanay cleaned me up and then I felt hungry, so she gave me some soft rice soup. I swallow, I do not have to chew. I could swallow the soup, but my throat still hurts. I think my throat is going to hurt for a while. Anyway, Nanay told me to finish the soup, because I did not eat for a few days. So when the swelling in my throat broke, I feel so much better. After that Nanay and Tatay took turns morning and night rubbing ginger root juice which has been boiled and put in a sack all mashed with a certain amount of olive oil and they rub me all over with the ginger juice. It is Nanay that usually do this.

Oh, before I forget, the thing that this "Old Man" that Tatay met, during my long illness, told Tatay what to do to make me well again. You know what, I believe down deep in my heart, that it was God, our Father in Heaven, who guided Tatay to look for this "Old Man" and told Tatay just what to do. Oh, I must tell you, that the cool-soothing-thing that Tatay and Nanay put on my swollen throat was a shoot of a unopened banana leaf. The leaves really felt so cool and soothing. I still remember the feeling I feel, when they take off the dry-crisp leaf off my throat and put a new fresh leaf on my throat. Nanay and Tatay kept this up until the swelling on my throat broke and until I did not spit blood anymore. I do not know how long, but with God's help, I got well again. I must write here, that while I was lieing down on a cot bed, right under a window—I must have been sleeping, 'cause I heard the birds singing. They sound so beautiful, as if they were singing to me to wake up that the day is beautiful and I opened my eyes. I saw the sunlight and the beautiful blue sky up above and the birds still singing on the trees close by, and do you know, I felt some feeling going thru my body as if to tell me, I am going to be alright again. I think I was not ready to go, or die, as the people that live around me say. Anyway I felt happy inside, oh so happy, so from that day on I tried to sit up especially when I'm by myself. I feel too, that the ginger juice that Nanay putting all over my body, over my legs, feet and my shoulders arms and hands is really making me well again. I feel stronger. Another thing I notice the sores on my face, my ears, I have 2 big sores on my elbows, smaller ones on my arms and legs. I really look bad. I think people were afraid to come near me. I do not blame them. I remember in one of my dream seems Mary come to visit. She heard I was sick, but she did not come to visit me, again I think she was afraid to come near me. Something in my mind kept telling me to get up. Oh, I tried and tried. I was able to put my legs over the cot bed, then I feel tired so I lie down again. I must have went to sleep because when I woke up I was on a mattress on the floor. So, I think Nanay and Tatay think it would be better for me to sleep on the floor. I'm glad they did, because it was easier for me to sit up and do you know, I started **40** to learn how to use my legs. It was hard. I could not stand on my feet, so I tried kneeling, that I could not do for a time, I don't know how long I kneel. When I felt sore and tired I sat down. I do this every time I feel good and I want to walk again, and I would do this when Nanay is busy outside, washing clothes or cooking. Seems like I was doing this for a long time. I tried to use my legs, every day, just to stand up. I found out as the days go by, I feel stronger and I can stand up longer, and I don't hurt as much as when I first tried to stand up. The time I tried to take a few steps. I fell forward. Seems like my legs did not have bones. You know, I felt my legs and my feet, they feel soft. Oh, I was thinking, will I walk again? Anyway, I put that out of my head. I am going to try again and again and again until I do walk again, and I did—with our Father in Heaven telling me to keep on trying and trying harder each time. I sit up, I kneel, I grab the window sill, and I stand up. I would stand for a long time, just looking outside, every thing look so beautiful—below—I see banana trees, a big pear tree, a mangoe tree and see papaya trees too. I say below, because I just found out we are living upstairs, and I'm feeling well again and I am awake most of the time now. I hear so much voices, so many people downstairs seems to be talking so much, and laughing and they must be playing some games. Anyway, like I say, I stand. Oh, I can see houses thru the trees and there are houses over the fence. Truly it is good to be feeling well again and to feel I am going to get well again. After I have stood up for a long time, I turn around. I walk or tried to take a step or two forward. I thought I was going to fall, so I stood still, until I feel alright again and walk 2 more steps and 2 more. I am feeling hurt on my feet, my legs and knees, so I got down on my knees and crawl back to my bed and lay down. I do

this every day and as much as I can. I'm more awake now, and I
do not sleep so much like I use to. I like to hear the people talking below. I can understand what they are talking about, so I
think there are more Filipinos living here. I hear Portuguese language but not so much, and hear Chinese talking too. And so I
stay awake and keep on trying my best to walk and one day I sur- **41**
prised my Nanay by walking to the door. I stood there and looked
at her cooking—a few steps down. She look up and saw me, she
drop the big spoon and run to me and said in our dialect, "Oh,
thank God you can walk again." She was crying and I was crying. I was standing shaking, so I sat down right on the door way
and Nanay sat down by me. Our friends living in the same tenement came to us and say too, "Thank God you can walk, you
will get better now," and I did. Diary, that's why I am writing you
all this. I do not go outside or down stairs yet. Nanay says it's too
soon. I have to be really strong again to go downstairs or anywhere. Oh, yesterday Nanay gave me my first bath in hot water,
which she boiled some Eucalyptus leaves. The water smell like
it had medicine in it. She made me sit in the tub, while she wash
me up and really soap and scrubbed me good—me, I could not
have given myself a good bath. After the bath and she gave me
some of my clothes to put on. It was still hard to dress, but I did
dress by myself without Nanay's help and I feel good, oh so good
to be well again, no more pains going thru my body. After I finish putting on my clothes, she made me sit down in front of her,
where there was a big piece of white cloth in front between her
and I and she told me to bow my head forward so she can comb
my hair—and when she did oh, my, so many little bugs fall onto
the white cloth. She kept combing and combing until no more
bugs falling into the white cloth. Then she said we are going to
do this every day. Then she roll up the cloth and put in the tub
and pour boiling water into the tub to kill those "bugs." She has
to do this right after she finish combing my hair. I feel good and
clean after the bath and the combing of my hair. I still feel weak.
I tried combing my hair, every chance I can, but I know in my

heart that I am getting well and that I am really going to walk again, run around like I use to. Nanay let me or told me that I can walk out onto the front porch sit out there and watch the people below. Oh yes, now that I feel good and well, I do not want to lie down and sleep, but Nanay told me to go in the room and lie down when I start to feel tired. So I listen to her and do what she says. She knows what is good for me. And do you know, it is so good to get up in the morning now to wash my face and clean up and put on my clothes and sit on the porch and look around and watch the people. On the front porch, Nanay would curtain off one end so I can take my tub bath. It is really good to be walking around even if it's in the house only. Pretty soon, Nanay and Tatay will say I can go downstairs and walk out on the sidewalk again and go to shows and go into stores to buy candies, and I'll be going to school again. I miss school, there are so many things I have to learn, now that I can read and write, I want to keep on learning. So when I feel good and strong again, I have to go out and look for the nearest school and say, "I want to come to school," like I always say, when I first started first grade. Yes, no one was with me, when I first went to school. I always go by myself, because I want to learn. Now, I have to do that again. Do you know that if I did not go to school and learn how to read and write, I would not have been able to start this diary. So, the first time I think I am alright and can walk far without getting sick and tired, I will look for the school that is close by. I will put you a way for awhile now. I am getting tired.

River St., Honolulu, T.H.
February 20, 1925

Dear Diary:

I feel so sad today, I cried like a baby. When I woke up I did not see Nanay or Willie and Incarnation. The rooms seem empty, so I ask Tatay where's Nanay and then he told me that Nanay and her other family have moved away because I am alright again, that I no longer need her, and that Tatay can take care of me from now on. For a while there, I could not understand why she have to move away. Oh why, I ask God, things like this happen. I remember now what Nanay told me and that I must remember. She told me to keep myself clean and do not let any man touch me, to keep away from them. She told me that some men **43** are good and some are bad. Anyway she said, "Do not trust them." No wonder she was telling me all this, because she knows she must leave me and Tatay soon. She did not tell Tatay where they are moving to. Tatay also told me today that we are moving away from here as soon as he can find a family where Manong Julian and I can stay and live with, while he goes to work in the plantation. Of course he pays for our eats and room. Now that I am stronger and feeling so good, I stay out here on the porch and watch what is going below. Watching people below, I kind of forget the sadness I feel. I made little friends here, there are many children but few would come up and talk to me, but that is alright, because I do not talk too much myself. Like I say, I watch people below. It is fun to watch them—they are gambling group here below plays the cards and on the ground some are playing 3 large coins which one person throw upwards and let them fall to the ground. I do not know how they win in this kind of game. On another corner—roosters fighting. I do not like to watch this, you see blood and that makes my stomach hurt. Oh, they have a watchman outside. One day I was watching like I always do. The watchman come running into the backyard saying, "Police, police!" Oh, you should see the men and women scatter. Some jump over the fence, which I know they could not do if there was no one chasing them or afraid of. I see silver coins rolling down the cement walk and some are left on the dirt. Of course some get caught. When the police have left, some come back and look for their money. I see some boys help looking for the money but they keep the money for themselves. The people here are nice, they are all family people. I like them. I am, I mean, I stay close to our rooms and just stay on the front porch and just watch people all around me and have been seeing many sailor men come around and soldier men. I know the reason why the soldiers and the sailors come around here, I won't write down the reason, I will just say, "business women," okay. You see, there are about 2 or 3 living below us.

44 All family people are living upstairs, and you can bet your last nickel that there are pin-holes on the bedroom floors—ours have. I use to wonder when I was unable to walk yet, why people come to the room and start looking through the floor? So when no one was around—I look for a hole, and I found one. I was seeing a woman on the bed picking out something like lice from your head and she was killing them with her thumbnails. I got sick. I put the strawmat over the floor again. So when the sailors and the soldiers come to this place I just stay out on the porch 'cause our bedroom is full of people, watching a show below, makes me want to throw up. I sit out on the porch and I think will I grow up and be like them?

River St., Honolulu, T.H.
March 1, 1925

Dear Diary:

I can go down and go outside, and I found out that this houses are called tenement houses. Where we are on the inside tenement houses, the outside row of houses, faces the street called River Street because past the street is a sidewalk and brick wall, where people sit on. The other side a small river as far as I can see goes out far out towards King Street and I think goes into the ocean afterwards, but enough of that. I'm just glad that I can walk out and see all around me now and the beautiful sky above. Oh Dear Father in Heaven, I am so happy and so thankful that You made me well again to make me walk again, and see all this beautiful things around me. Oh, I feel so good inside, for all this things. It is good to be running and jumping around and playing with the girls around here. We play hop-scotch and jump-ropes and we laugh and giggle at most things. Yes I am so glad and happy inside. Only sometimes, I can not help feeling sad, because I do not see Nanay anymore. Will I ever see her again? Oh I just tell you, I am going to write better, I cannot help but turn back the pages in this book and see my writing looks terrible. I am going back to school as soon as I found out where I can go to. So I must try and write better.

River St., Honolulu, T.H.
March 6, 1925

Dear Diary:

You know, what happen, Mary and I are going to live together again, oh, it is good. Tatay found them, I mean Mary and her father and mother. Remember, I told you Tatay was looking for married people or family that Manong Julian and I can live with while he works in the plantation—well, Tatay went to Hall Street yesterday and found Mary and her father and mother are living in Hall Street, and so they talked and they said it was alright for Manong Julian and I to stay with them. Oh, I jump for joy. Oh, I am so glad that Mary and I are going to be together again. Oh, what fun we are going to have again. Oh, I am really happy. So today we start packing and start our move to Hall Street. I wonder how far that is from here. Anyway, that does not matter. Tatay says that it is not too far away. So I better finish and put you away in the bottom of the trunk again and you will hear from me again when we have moved to Hall Street.

River St., Honolulu, T.H.
March, 7, 1925

Dear Diary:

You know what? A young man around here. Oh, he talk to me and I try to talk or be friendly with him, too, but I did not think he have some love thoughts about me. He said, "I love you,

Angeles" when I was coming out of a friend's house. I was telling
Elisa I was moving away tomorrow. I was sad. I know how it is,
when a friend leaves. Anyway we hug each other and say, "Maybe
we will see each other again" and was walking on the veranda.
Felipe walk to me and told me that he love me. I was surprise,
nobody have said that to me before. I hear stories about "love"
from the older people and I understood the full meaning of the
word, the good and bad of it. And so, I answered Felipe, that I do
not love him, I'm too young for thoughts like that, I am only 12
years old. He ask me if he can kiss me. I said, "No." I told him to
go find somebody else to kiss. He just laugh and he let me pass
by. I really ran down the stairway. Man like that scares me. It's a
good thing he did not grab me. Maybe I would have scream. I
cannot believe that a man is telling me about love? Gosh, and I
am only 12 years old—and already someone is telling me about
love. I do not think about those things yet, to me right now everything looks so bright and beautiful. I feel good and happy inside
and truthfully, I feel as if I just woke up from a long, long sleep—
which I really did because, when I was sick and just being down,
I do not remember the days going by. I was just sleeping all the
time. Our friends around here have told Tatay and understand
what they are talking about, that our Father in Heaven has given
me another chance in life. They say it was a miracle that I live
through that illness, without a doctor. Tatay repeat himself, that
the Old Man was sent to him and told him what to do, to make
me walk again, yes my getting well and strong again, it was "God,"
our Father in Heaven who really made me well. I feel and think
that our Father in Heaven had guided Tatay to this "Old Man."

Hall St., Honolulu, T.H.
March 12, 1925

Dear Diary:
I must tell you, now that I can walk and run and jump-rope (I
like to jump-rope very much, double-eye), that is, I feel as if I

Diary

did not get sick at all, what happen to me was like a dream. But down deep in my heart I know I have been really sick, and to prove that, the sore scars on my face, my ears, on my elbows. I have them, the big sores are healed but I have the scars. I have 2 big scar patch on my elbows, one on each elbow, and Manong Julian teases me, by calling them baboon-ass. Oh, he is right, the scars look red and big and I have seen the baboon's behind, my elbows scars look like that. I do not get angry. I do try to wear longer sleeves dresses especially, when I go back to school, so the other boys and girls would not see the scars.

47

Hall St., Honolulu, T.H.
March 15, 1925

Dear Diary:

We are now living here in Hall Street. Yes, Mary and I are together again and I am so glad we are together again. I am going to school with her and I will meet her teacher. Mary is in the 3 grade and I hope we will be in the same room. I will tell you more about that when it happen. Mary and I share the bed in one corner of the room and her mother put a curtain between our bed and her father and mother's bed. And Tatay and Manong Julian share the smaller bedroom. Anyway, Tatay will go to the pineapple plantation in Kahuku to work, so Manong Julian will have the room to himself. You know, Tatay bought me when we were still living in Waipahu, a sewing machine, called Singer. You see, I can sew dresses for myself. I learned how to sew when I was still living with Nanay. I have a Victrola, a phonograph-machine, and I play all the phonograph records over and over. I just like music and I used to danced to it. I know Mary and I will be dancing like crazy when we have the time for it. Right now it's in Manong Julian's room. Now, that we are living with Mary and her mother and father, I am or must help with the house cleaning, washing of the dishes, and do whatever Mary's mother tells me to do in the house. I do not cook, Mary's mother do that. I can cook, but I am not going to say so. Now that Mary and I are together again we are doing things like we use to do when we were living in Waipahu. It is really good to be together again. I do not feel lonely anymore, and I try not to think about Nanay. Even now, when I am by myself I wish, oh **48** so very much, that she had said, "We are going away now" and tell me that her and family must move away from Tatay, Manong Julian, and me but she did not tell me anything. I would have understand. Maybe as the days go by I will kind of forget her and not feel too sad whenever I think of her.

Hall St., Honolulu, Oahu, T.H.
March 30, 1925

Dear Diary:

Mary and I are going to school together again. It is good to go back to school. I was kind of afraid I will not be put in the grade III, because I did not have any papers to give to the teacher from the other school. I told the teacher that I did not have time to pick up my school-paper that she wanted, we have to move right away, which was the truth. Anyway, the teacher was nice and she said, "Alright, you can start in today." So I started today. Oh, I was so glad. Our school is called "Fern School" and it is far from our house. Mary and I have to take the streetcar. It was a good thing Tatay left me some money, because we have to pay for our fares to and from school. We cannot walk to school, too far. Mary and I wake up early about 6 o'clock. This give us time to take a bath, comb our hair, and change clothes. I have short hair right now I just put on clip to one side. We eat our breakfast. We wash the dishes, afterwards I sweep the floors but I am going to change my way of doing things—tomorrow I sweep first, then I take a bath. You see Diary, now that I am well again, I take a bath—a cold bath—every morning. I feel clean all over after I take a bath. Mary do not like to take a bath every morning like I do. Our teacher's name is Mrs. McCabe. She is really nice. I like her. The other boys and girls in our class just look at me. Some girls smile so I smile back.

Hall St., Honolulu, Oahu, T.H.
April 5, 1925   **49**

Dear Diary:

I am so glad to go to school again. I have so much fun now, talking and playing with other girls and learning more in school. I like spelling and arithmetic and reading. Oh you know what, we have to move to a new school way down Kalihi Street. The teacher will be with us when we are all going to move together. It is going to have the same name "Fern School." I hope Mary and I would not forget the way. Anyway we are all excited to move to the new school and see what the new school look like.

Hall St., Honolulu
April 5, 1925

Dear Diary:

Mary and I are not only very good friends, we are "god-sisters" too. Mary's mother stood for me when I took my Confermation last Sunday. So Mary's mother is my "Ninang" and Mary is my "Igsoo"—it means "god-sister," so we call each other Igsoo from now on. I am very happy that Mary's mother brought up the talk about my taking Confirmation more so now because I just got well over a terrible sickness and I am about the right age to take or be Confirmated because my religion is Catholic.

Hall St., Honolulu, Oahu, T.H.
April 10, 1925

Dear Diary:

Our new school is nice. It is a new school. Mary and I wander all over the place and the grades are from the first grade to the eight grade. Mary and I are both in the 3rd grade. At first, I thought, we were going to be separated. Oh, I was so glad when we were put in the same room. Oh, we have a new teacher must be Korean, her name is Miss Dang. She is pretty. I think we all like her. I know I like her. Many of the girls here do not like to talk to us, so we do not talk to them. We just look at each other. These are the new ones, the ones that has move with us to this school, they are still friendly with us. And do you know that this school is close to where the Strike Camp was (it's no longer there). Mary and I went to the place where the buildings are. I remember the road, Middle Street. No wonder it look like I have seen this place before. So today, Mary and I, on our lunch hour (half hour only), we ate our sandwich as we walk to the "place" and I show her the building and the place where I got sick. We just stood outside the place and look at the place. To me, it brought back thoughts that I would not like to think about. I gave a sigh of thank-fullness that I am well and alive looking at the buildings in front of me. Mary was quiet but she just gave my hand a tight squeze and we turn around and ran back to school. We drank water from the school-water-fountain and we were trying to breathe easy when some of our classmates came forward and ask us where have we gone to and Mary and I look at each other and said together, "Oh, we just went to look at some old buildings," pointing to the direction where we came from. I do not think I would go back and look at the place again. Anyway, Diary, school and homework are not hard, like some of my classmates think. I like it. I am so glad and happy that I know and able to read a book not just to look at the pictures, and I now, I can read and understand what I am reading about. Yes, I like school very much. Even when I first started I like school, I really wanted to learn, learn how to read and write. Now I can, I feel happy inside and good feeling too.

Hall St., Honolulu, T.H.
May 25, 1925

Dear Diary:

Oh, Mary and I go to the matinee every Saturday afternoon at
1 o'clock at the Palama Theatre. It is very close here to the
house. But before I can go anyplace, I wash school clothes and
petticoats and bloomers. I do not let my bloomers pile up, 'cause
I wash it as soon as I change every morning, after my bath but
when I ran out of washing soap, the dirty clothes really pile up
for Saturday morning-wash-day. Anyway, I do my washing
every Saturday morning, starch my dresses and hang them to
dry. Sunday morning I iron them all. Oh, when I finish washing, I do the housework as soon as I can, so the afternoon will
be all mine. After Mary and I finish our work, Mary tells her
mother that we are going to the Palama Theatre and see a movie
and when we have left over money, we go into the chop suey
house next to the Palama Theatre and have a bowl of noodles—
oh, they are so good. I get full up when I finish my bowl of noodles, Mary too. And the picture was good. We talk and laugh
about it all the way home, we take our time going home. After
we eat supper we wash the dishes and do whatever that we have
to do. Me, I sprinkle my clothes, so I can iron them tomorrow
morning, after Mary and I come home from church. Yes, we
just started to go to church. We walk to the 4th Street Catholic
Church every Sunday and we can only give five cents when the
donation box is passed around. Anyway, that is better than not
giving anything at all. We see so many people in church. Some
girls are really so pretty, they wear such pretty clothes, they look
so much better than Mary and I. We wear such plain cotton
dresses, but we look clean and I think we look alright. But we
do not feel jealous, which is alright, do you not think so? When
we come out the church we always stop at an ice cream parlor
and I ask for strawberry or pineapple ice cream cone. I like them
very much. Mary ask for the same kind of ice cream. We pay
the man 5 cents and we go on our way, talking and laughing and

lapping at our ice cream cone. Oh, truly we have fun. By the time we come to the little river, we have finish our ice cream cones, and we feel full. When we have the time, we look into store windows and look at the pretty clothes and shoes. They must cost so much money. Mary and I look at the clothes, but they were for older girls and I told Mary they would not look nice on us anyway. Oh well, we sigh, when we grow older, maybe then clothes like that would look nice on us, huh?

52

Hall St., Honolulu, T.H.
May 30, 1925

Dear Diary:

Oh say, an old friend of Manong Julian just moved in below us with his aunt. Manong Julian told me that they know each other in Waipahu. I was with Nanay at that time. That is why I do not know him. His name is Joe Flores. I kind of like him. He is as old as Manong Julian, 19 years old. Oh, but Manong Julian and Joe talk so much about the days they were little boys in Waipahu, the good fun that they had, and all that kind of doings. And from what I can understand, Joe is working at a place where they wash and clean the outside of cars and it is called "car wash" and the name of the person's or owner's name. Anyway, Joe is going to try and see if the owner of the place will need another car washer. Manong Julian is hoping that he will get the work. I heard Manong Julian ask Joe if he remembers me, and Joe said "oh, yes" he said and motion his arm under his nose and said I used to do that. I think he was lying 'cause I do not remember him at all. And when he said what he said, I do not like him. Diary, he makes a girl feel ashamed and I do not like that kind of feeling. He and Manong Julian talk English all the time. I have not heard him speak Visayan or Tagalog. Joe calls me and Mary "greens," because we are only 12 years old. You see, I won't be 13 years old until August 2 of this year and Mary just became 12 years old. So Joe call us "greens." The name do not make me feel bad, to me, it is just funny.

Hall St., Honolulu, T.H.
June 4, 1925

Dear Diary:

We had our exmanition test at school today. I pass and another the other day, I passed that one too. Mary also pass her exmanitions and we are going to the fourth grade in September, when school opens. You see, next week will be our last week of school for this month, then we are going to have our school vacation for 3 months. Gosh, that is really nice. Mary and I are both happy that we have pass our tests. We were worried for a while, we did not know how the test will come out—but now we know and we are glad and we are happy and that soon school will close for vacation time, too. Oh, I know we are going to have a wonderful vacation.

Hall St., Honolulu, T.H.
June 15, 1925

Dear Diary:

School is closed for the next 3 months, and you know, Mary and I have been transferred. I didn't know this word so I asked Miss Dang. Oh, she said, "Oh, that means you are going to another school that is closer to where you live. That way, you just walk to school, instead of taking the streetcar to come to school." Miss Dang told us what to do. We bring our report cards to the Principal of Kaiuilani School and she will direct us to the fourth grades rooms. So I put my report card in Tatay's trunk and it's going to stay there until school will open again. As soon as we finish our work around the house we ask Mary's mother that we would like to look for Kaiuilani School and we told her why. She said yes. We found the school further up or going towards the same way we take the streetcar to Fern School, only not that far. We walk, we pass the Palama Theatre and walk some more. We finally come to the school. There is a big building right in the middle and from the left, there are small houses then it turns right, there are small houses and it keeps going and turns right again. I'll draw the Kaiulani School, it is a big school. I am glad that Mary and I went to the schoolyard to look around.

Hall St., Honolulu, T.H.
June 26, 1925

Dear Diary:

You know what, Joe—since he move in with his aunt—after we finish eating and we have washed and dry the dishes we sit on the front porch, Manong Julian and Joe would play the ukulele. I can play the ukelele too but not as good as they are so Mary and I sing. We know a few songs and Joe taught us new songs and I learn them fast. I think it is because I like to sing. So, if Manong Julian and Joe do not go to the show, we sit on the porch and sing until 9 or 10 o'clock at night. Around here, it is like one big family. Everyone knows each other and they talk to each other from one top-front porch to the one across top-front porch. It is a nice feeling. Usually the older people play cards in the parlor while we sing out on the front porch. Nobody try to stop us from singing, anyway we do not sing too loud. I learn a few new song from Joe. Manong Julian learn them too, same thing with Mary. The songs are "Five-foot-two," "Drifting and Dreaming," "Sweet-Violet," this is a long one 5-verse. We are practising to sing duets and if I say so myself, we sound good. Oh, I nearly forgot to tell you. Manong Julian is working at where Joe is working. Manong Julian is really happy about his work and he hope he'll always be working for a long time. Oh, the name of the place where Manong Julian and Joe work is call "The Royal Hawaiian Sales

Company." Another thing we found out about Joe is that he can speak the Japanese language very well. There is "Japanese-business woman" that lives here and he talks with her. I was surprise, we all were, the "Japanese woman" too. We did not believe what we heard at first, but the "Japanese woman" told us that he speaks the language very well. Joe just smile when we praise him for what he knows. Joe told us afterward that he went to school, Japanese school, because he wanted to learn the language, but he could not write Japanese. He says that was too hard to do. He says talking was much easy to do.

Hall St., Honolulu
June 30, 1925

Dear Diary:
I have noticed Joe looking at me most of the time now. I look at him as if to say why are you always looking at me that way. Before I can say anything, he said, in his favorite words, "Hello, Green," so I answer, "Hello, Joe." I like him, first boy that I can say "I like." And do you know what Manong Julian and Joe called each other? Bananas, yes, bananas. They have crazy ideas, those two. They would say, "Hey, Banana "or "Let's go to the show, Banana," or some other words, or whatever goes in their mind.

Hall St,, Honolulu, T.H.
July 20, 1925

Dear Diary:
I have not write down in your pages because I did not have anything to write down about. Every day is almost the same. Mary and I go to church every Sunday and 2 times a week Mary and I go to the fish market at Aala Park to buy fish for Mary's mother, which we eat for supper. Sometimes she boil it and sometimes she frys it. But tonite, Mary is taking a bath so I can

take you out and write what happen today. I feel excited and sort of thrilled. Here's how, I mean, what happened this evening about 6:30 after I finished washing our supper dishes. (Mary did not go with me.) I went to the store close to the house, it was still light, to buy some red coconut candies. I was walking to the store. I noticed someone following me. I did not turn around until I reached the store. Who do you think it was, but Mr. Joe Flores himself. He came to me smiling and said, "Good-evening, Angeles." I was surprised because this is the first time he called me by my first name. And I answered, I smiled, too, and said "good-evening." I bought the candy I wanted, he bought a package of Chesterfield cigarettes and he asked me if he can walk home with me. I said, why not. We walk in silence. I have nothing to say. He then asked me (we were walking slowly) if I believe in "love at first sight"? I said "No," and he said that he did, with me. Really, Diary, I was surprised to hear him say that to me, because all this time that he has moved here to Hall Street, he always teases me and calls me "green" or "fatty," though I am not fat. I just have more flesh on me than Mary, but I weigh only 105 lbs. and I am 4 feet and 11 inches tall. Anyway, I do not get angry when he calls me "fatty." And now he tells me he loves me. I don't know how love is or how it really feels but I like him and I feel shivers going up and down inside me especially when he hold my hand. It was getting a little dark when we were walking home, and there were not anybody walking around. When we reach the houses, we have to go thru 2 tenements of houses before we reach our tenement. Anyway, Joe stop walking, I did too. He put his arm around my waist, I look up at him and he kissed me, and oh, what a wonderful feeling that went thru me, and I like it. I just stood there and I just let him kiss me once more and I had to tell him he better stop kissing me before some of our friends sees us, we were near the house. We start walking apart. Oh, before, we start walking away from each other, I told Joe to be careful—he must not try to kiss me even there is no one around. I really do not want the people to think I am a "bad girl." They will think so, because I do not have a mother. And he said, "Okay, Angel" and he kiss me one more time and, "I'll try to remember," and I went ahead of him and he called after me and said will see you later. I turned to him and nod for my yes answer. Mary was still in the bathroom when I came into the house. Tonight is a wonderful night for me and I feel just happy inside to know that Joe feel that way about me.

Hall St., Honolulu
July 30, 1925

Dear Diary:

I was washing dishes tonite when Joe got behind, turned me around, and kiss me long. Mary was surprised, she did not know. Now she knows, so Joe gave her a peck of a kiss and said, "Do not tell." He tried to kiss me again but I turn my face away from him and say, "Mary's mother might come back in here," and he said, "I don't think so, they are sitting down on the front porch telling jokes to each other, but anyway we can hear them if they are going to come in." And so that is the way it is around here, and do you know, Joe kisses Mary too, not the way he kisses me, though, I do not get angry or jealous. I get sort of tickle funny whenever I see Joe kiss Mary 'cause it is more of peck. I have to tell Joe to go outside and talk to Manong Julian, who is strumming his ukelele banjo. Mary and I join them as soon as we finish cleaning up the kitchen and putting the dishes away. Oh, before Joe left us he told Mary and I that he will treat us to show at "Palama" this coming Saturday matinee.

Hall St., Honolulu, T.H.
August 6, 1925

Dear Diary:

I just become 13 years old last week and Joe kept his words. Joe treated us to the show last Saturday. We went to a matinee. The movie started at 1 P.M. We went to the theatre half an hour before the show start. When Mary and I reach the Palama Theatre Joe was already there. He bought the tickets as soon as he saw us coming. We sat on the balcony—the left side—and we sat on the third row down from the top, because people was there in the rows below us. And so Joe had the chance to kiss me all he wants. He was kissing me so much, he did not see much of the movie. I did not see much of the movie myself, because he was covering my face most of the time, but I did not care, because I like his kisses too. And when the movie ended, Mary and I went home alone, because Joe stayed behind to see the movie again. With me gone he can watch the movie. It was a good movie, from what I have watch. Mary like the show too. You know the men that were running the movie reel, I know that they saw Joe kissing me. Those men can see everything from where they are. Anyway I do not know them, so they do not matter and too we were just kissing. I think all people that are in love kiss. Do you not think so? Anyway Mary and I had fun.

Hall St., Honolulu, T.H.
August 26, 1925

Dear Diary:

You know, the vacation time is nearly over and next month Mary and I will be going back to school again. I can hardly wait for that time to come. Mary and I have been going to the public library. Miss Dang at Fern School told us about the library, that we can borrow a book or two. First we fill out a card she says and they will give us a card that we keep so they date the card for the books we take out and return—this is truly a good idea, 'cause I like to read now so Mary and I went to the library. We went to a lady standing behind a desk. I thought she was the person to talk to about borrowing books. Like Miss Dang said the lady gave us a piece of paper to fill out, writing down our name, our father and mother's name and street where we live, and how old

I am and other things. I answer all I know. Mary copied the way I'm writing down the answers, her own father and mother's name and her age and where she was born. Anyway, we got our library cards and we were so happy about it. Mary and I took out the same kind of books, "fairy-tales." When the lady was stamping our cards she told us not to keep the books too long, be sure and bring back the books before the due date comes around or we pay the past dues. And too, Diary, I have nothing much to write about, it's the same thing we do around here. At nights we sing, Manong Julian, Joe, Mary, and I, out on the porch, and Joe can not kiss me as much as he wants to, but always kiss me good-night and it's always a stolen moment of happiness for us. To me it leaves me quivery and my heart seems to pound faster, I think because of the thought of being caught. I hope no one will see us kissing each other. And so, that's how the days have passed. We have not been to the show this past weeks. Do you know I forgot to tell you, since Tatay, Manong Julian, and I move here I notice that there are no big children like Mary and I, but there are few little boys and girls about 3 or 4 or 5 years old, Joe's aunt have about 4 children. The families upstairs have children I don't know how many, but I can hear many feet running on the veranda upstairs. But though there are no other big girls around here to play games with, I really don't mind, because when Mary and I finish our work in the house and we don't have to go to the fish market, we sit down on the front porch and read. We like that, and like I told you, after we eat supper and all the dishes washed we sit on the front porch and sing all the songs we know.

Hall St., Honolulu, T.H.
September, 2, 1925

Dear Diary:

Do you know, Joe really got so jealous today, over nothing. A friend, that lives around here, was telling me something funny and we both laugh, and Joe happen to come near us. He was looking at us. When I look at him, and he did not smile, I know he was angry or something was wrong. My friend left. He said, "Good-bye." And Joe ask me, "Who's that fellow?" I answered, "Oh, just a friend who lives around here." And Joe said he felt jealous over the fellow, when he saw us laughing and talking. I say, "Of all things to get jealous of. Joe, we're just friends, he has not said I love you." Anyway, I guess we all get jealous sometimes, ha—especially when you are in love.

60

Hall St., Honolulu, T.H.
October 2, 1925

Dear Diary:

I could not write to you right after school. I have been so busy with classes in school and busy at home when I come home from school. Yes, school is open and I am truly glad it's open. We have so much fun in school. And fourth grade is different. We have 5 rooms to go to. So that means there are only 5 fourth graders. 1 fourth grade room teacher (my room) hygiene and civics, and my teacher's name is Miss Hayashi, the 2 fourth grader teaches language and spelling and the teacher's name is Mrs. Boyd, 3, fourth grader teaches history and storytelling and the teacher's name is Miss Duncan. The fourth, fourth grader is Miss Wong and she teaches arithmetic only. Miss Simeona teaches geography. These five grades rotates every day; it is really something different but it's so much more fun. We'd march out in file and the next room will march in file into our room and so on all day. The teachers have their time all planned out, just how long 1 class stays in the room and out we go to the next one. Before school is let out we're all back in our own room. We're all given homework, oh, the other fourth grade teachers gave us homework too. And I must tell you, I like all this going to school, this learning about writing and reading. I learned something new today about other countries and people and this is geography. I did not know that we live in such a big world, so many different nationalities and countries, they live in far away places. I read in my geography book that there are four season in a year, Spring, Summer, Fall, and Winter. It is truly wonderful to know these things, and I also thought there are only Japanese, Chinese, Porto Ricans, Portuguese, and Filipinos. Oh, there are so many other things in the geography book that I must learn and from the history book and about hygiene, oh really, so much to learn and remember.

61

Hall St., Honolulu, T.H.
October 10, 1925

Dear Diary:

Tatay came home to visit us and to see how we are getting along and to pay Mary's mother for our food and shelter for the month. Tatay comes home whenever he has the chance. He is working at Kahuku right now. And Tatay brought home sad news, for me it is. I do not know if Manong Julian feels like I do. We never share or tell or talk how we feel. He goes his way, I go mine, only I stay home. I do not go out at night like he does. Tatay told us that Nanay and her family had been given free passage to the Philippine Islands, and so that means they are not coming back to Hawaiian Islands, and I know now, I will never see Nanay again. I will always remember how she look at me when I stood at the doorway, at the time she did not think I can really walk and stand on my feet again. I surprise her and she look happy and ran up to me and hug me. I can remember still, she was saying a prayer of thanks in "Hilanggo," my mother's dialect as she ran up the few steps to where I was. And those last days that she was taking care of me. She did not leave until she knows that I am really alright and well again. Right now, I am thinking that God, our Heavenly Father, made Tatay find where Nanay was living so we can be together again for the short but the last time. Back to Tatay, he is going back to Kahuku tomorrow. He is still working there. He says when they are finish with their work there he will be home. You know what, Diary, remember the "Pablo

Manlapit strike" last year? Well, we have not heard anything more about it. And Tatay lost a good job at the mill. Tatay never talks about it and we do not ask him about it. Tatay told us that he will be home for Christmas. He thinks the work will be finish then.

Hall St., Honolulu, T.H.
October 30, 1925

Dear Diary:

You see, last night was the opening night for "Somu" Japanese wrestling. It is fence in, 'cause there is an empty ground space here on Hall Street, and it is fence in. You cannot watch the wrestling or go in with out a ticket, you have to pay. But us, because we live on the second-story tenement we were able to watch the "Somu" for free, so we all gather toward to the front balcony or front porch. Joe, Mary, and I stayed at the back of the people. Manong Julian went out front where he can see really, he does not have to stretch his neck to see the wrestling. He called out to Joe to join him but Joe answered, "I like it here," of course he does because he can kiss me without being seen. You know this wrestling is so rough, it is a wonder they do not break their bones when they slam each other down and they are noisy. They grunt and groan and make such swooshy-noises with throat or mouth. Anyway I really do not like it. Tonight is the first time I saw wrestling. I would not pay to see a wrestling match. I rather see a good moving picture.

Hall St., Honolulu, T.H.
November 4, 1925

Dear Diary:

Igsoo and I really go to places together. We go to the open market close to Aula Park. Ninang always tell us to go buy fish for supper. She gives me 50 cents to buy fish, all of the money she says. So Mary and I go to one fish seller and another to ask just how much a so big-piece-of-a-fish would cost us. Ninang wanted tuna. We finally found 1 fish seller and pretty good size tuna fish and I ask the man how much the fish. It's the only fish he had left. I have been buying fish before and he said fifty cents. I will buy it if you let me have it for 30 cents, and he said, **63** "No!" I said, "Okay, we are going somewhere." We were about to leave when he call us back and said, "Okay, you can have it for 30 cents." He wrapped the fish and I gave him the fifty cent piece Ninang gave me. He took the money and mumbling under his breath he said we cheated him, we had the money all the time. Anyway he gave me 20 cents change, and said to me, "You smart girl" and I answered, "This is the last fish you have and I know you have to sell it, you will have some fresh fish for tomorrow." I gave Mary 10 cents, for me 10 cents and we bought ice cream for 5 cents, we still have 5 cents a piece for tomorrow's lunch. I told Igsoo I am going to buy apricot pie for 5 cents because there is a bakery in front of the school and the bakery have fresh bake pies every day, and I like apricot pies. They are so good when they are freshly bake. My mouth is already watering, just thinking about it and Igsoo said, "Me too." After we eaten our ice cream we hurried home, 'cause Ninang have to cook the fish for supper. She just look at us, when I handed the fish. We always do this, when we have the chance.

Hall St., Honolulu, T.H.
November 10, 1925

Dear Diary:
Everything are going along fine, at home and at school. Oh, there are some new families moving here. 2 families have 2 boy each, 1 family has a son they call him Pedring so his real name must be Pedro, the other boy, his friends call him "Shorty," he is as old as Pedring, 15 years old, but he's so short and Pedro is

tall. I look up to him while I look down at Shorty. I guess that's the way it is. The other family that moved here has a daughter, and she's 15 years old, too, and she is pretty and her name is Nancy. Mary and I like them, they seem very nice and friendly. Mary and I found out that they go to different school, and they are in Eighth grade, just 4 grades higher than we are. Anyway we do not care. Besides Mary and I started late in school, and best of all, we are learning.

64

Hall St., Honolulu, T.H.
November 22, 1925

Dear Diary:

You know what? Our teacher Miss Hayashi ask the class this morning who wants to go on a around the Island-trip. Right away Igsoo and I raise our hands up and a few more went up. Each person must pay $3.00 and we bring our own lunch. All the fourth graders are asked. Miss Hayashi told us we are going to ride in big trucks. She adviced us to bring enough food for the whole day. She said we must be in the schoolyard by 8 o'clock in the morning which is this coming Saturday morning. Oh boy! this is going to be really fun. We are told to bring the money tomorrow.

Hall St., Honolulu, T.H.
Saturday night

Dear Diary:

Oh, we enjoyed our round-the trip today. There were 2 trucks. I did not count how many there were of us that went on the trip. Anyway we really like the trip. Igsoo and I were at the school grounds before 8 o'clock and we were all excited. It was about 8:30 before we really left the school grounds. Miss Hayashi sat with the driver with one of our classmate, Itsutae and she advice

us to be good and behave. We all chimed in, "We will, Miss Hayashi." As the truck turn we wave good-bye to the school and say, "We will see you later," and we all laughed and giggled. Our teacher told us we are going towards the Pali first then down, stop for 15 minutes just to see the view—the ocean and the Island around. It was windy up the Pali, the wind there is for-
ever blowing, but the view from the Pali was beautiful, the white sand on the beach and the ocean waves going over ever so lightly it seems. The ocean water look so blue out there in the deep but on the shallow part of the beach you can see the white sand. As we look to the left we saw Pineapple field growing, really every-thing looked beautiful. We started down, zig-zaging down the road and the road looked narrow. Oh, King Kamehameha's monument is on the Pali. The legend says that he overthrow his enemies over the Pali and so it's truly fitting that his plaque and monument should be placed on the Pali. I did not get the name of the place we stopped to eat our lunch. It was a park kind of. Anyway we stayed there for about an hour. We took our time eating and then we looked over their stores. We bought some candies and crack-seed. We shared our candies with our class-mates and they shared theirs with us. And we laugh most of the time. Oh, we told riddles when the truck was going. We went into Kahuku, another Hawaiian name of a town. We drove into Waipahu. Igsoo and I told our classmates that this town is where Mary and I first met when we went to the first and second grade together not too long ago, and they said together, "Really?" and I said, "Yes, really." I could not show them the school we went to because we did not go that far. We just went through the main part of the town and turn around. We could not go to Ewa because we did not have the time. We made one more stop at the Waialae Beach. We took off our shoes and waded in. It was fun. Then Miss Hayashi call out, "Let's go!" Miss Duncan did the same. Miss Duncan took care of the other group of the other truck. We all grab our shoes and sat on the dry sand to clean our

feet off—sand, so much sand. As soon as we put on our shoes we piled into the truck home-ward-bound. It was 4:30 when we reached the schoolyard. Then we thank Miss Hayashi for a wonderful day, we told her we really had fun. She answered, she is very glad that we enjoyed the trip. And before we each went our way, she said, see you in class Monday morning. And we said "sure." We arrived home in time to take a bath and have supper. We told Mary's mother all the happening of the day. She just listen and when we finish, she said, "That's good." Afterward I told Joe about our trip and he was glad that we enjoyed our around-the-Island trip.

1375 Hall St., Honolulu, T.H.

November 28, 1925

Since I was able to understand and see what was going around me, I have the strongest feeling about going to school, so I can read and write. When I was with Nanay, I told Nanay (this was in 1919, I was seven years old) when school starts again, I would like to go to school. She told me that I could go. I went to Kaliea School Kauai with some of my friends when the school open that year. Oh, I was so glad to go. I walk with my friends, they were nice to me. I did not know where to go and who I should see and talk to about my wanting to learn how to read and write. Anyway I waited in the schoolyard and something in me told me or guided me to where a group of small children playing who were as tall as I am. With this group, I saw an older person, who was the teacher of the children I was watching. I do not know how long I stood there watching them, but I found out later that the teacher was watching me, too. So she came to me and ask me if I would like to join the rest of the children. I nod my head and say, "Yes." She ask my name and I told her but I guess I did not make myself clear, so she gave me a piece of paper to take home so my mother or father can fill it out and bring it back next day. I was really happy that I can go to school, even if I don't have many friends here. I'm to myself most of the time I went to school, but that did not mean nothing to me. I just go over to the swing and slide and play by myself. My going to school did not last long, because I had to take care of my half brother, Willie, who was 1½ years old and my half sister, Incarnation, who was 3 months old 'cause Nanay gets sick quite often. So I could not go to school every day in the week. I do not know how long this went on, but one day I went back to school as soon as we were in the classroom my teacher told me to go to the Principal's office, because he wants to talk to me, I feel scared because something is wrong. You do not go to the Principal's office for nothing. I ask myself, "What did I do wrong?" Anyway I went and as soon I got in the office, he ask me, "Why do you not come to school every day in the week?" So I look up at him (feeling so scared inside) he looked so tall and big, I told him that I had to help my mother to take care of my brother and sister, that's why I can not come to school every day. Then he says, "If that is the reason, then, you might as well stay home—do not come to school anymore." I know he was angry. I just nodded my head for my yes answer, then he said, "You go home now." I feel so sad, that I could not come to school anymore, I cried all the way home. I stopped for a while by the side of the road and look down (because the school was on a hill). I see our house straight across way out in front of me and to think I cannot come to school any more. And all I had learn was to say my A B C letters. I feel good that I had learned the alphabet but I did not learn how to read and I learn also how to count 1 to 100. I learn to write the alphabet and numbers but that is all. I went home feeling so sad and I told Nanay what happen, and she says in our dialect, "There's nothing we can do about that." And so in July 1922 Tatay found out where we were and took me away from Nanay. Later in this book I will write more about my parents. I want to write here, I must have been 4 years old when I know I was in this world. I was walking on a dirt road going home. I was holding on Nanay's skirt, I just know she was my mother.

67

We just left the slaughter-house and Nanay's arms were full of bundles of meat. That's why she told me to hold her skirt. As we were walking along the road I saw trees and scattered white houses along the side of the road, and when I look up and I saw the big-beautiful-blue sky above and birds seems to be singing all around me. Ever since, I know I was in this world, I noticed a lot of people around. Mother always take me with her wherever she goes—and we always walk.

The day I realize I was in this world, Mother and I just came from the slaughter-house, where they kill pigs and cows and they sell the meat there, so Mother make sure she is there right after they kill the cows and pigs and clean them of course, to buy the freshly killed animal. So we walk to this place one or twice a week and then other days Mother and I walk to the big plantation-store. At that time, we were living at Ewa Plantation. When I realize I was in this world, I realize too, that I have a father and a brother. My brother is 6 years older than I am. He is always outside the house, he comes in the house when Mother calls him in to eat, and when it gets dark outside then I see him in the house. I really do not remember too much of those years. I remember mostly I was always with my mother; Tatay, I do not see too much of him. My parents were immigrated to the Ewa Plantation in 1912. From what Tatay told me, I was only 2 months old and my brother was 6 years going on 7 years, when we left Romblon, Philippines. There were a lot of families that immigrated to the Hawaiian Islands at the same time because the plantations offered good-pay-bonuses and nice houses to live in. Somehow I know the plantation kept their word and their promises. I know too that Tatay worked hard. I just see him at night, 'cause he goes to work early in the morning, because when I wake up, I do not see him around. Another thing Tatay tells my brother and me, is that when we came to the Hawaiian Island, we rode in a big ship—"Bapoor" he calls it, a schooner, a big ship with large sails. And Tatay told us that it took a month for the ship to reach Honolulu. And from there we were taken

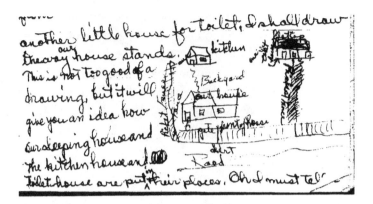

to Ewa Plantation where Tatay worked hard and where five years later family troubles started. Even now that I am 12 years I remembered those troubled days so very much, I cry. It is so sad to see my parents seperated. At that time, as young as I was, I sensed something bad is going to happen. I must have been 6 years old when I see this man come to the house when Tatay is working. So Nanay put me out of the house. I play outside until she calls me to come in and eat and my brother too. I remember, I play so much outside I started to climb our toilet house which is not far away, it's really in our back yard. You see, each family that is working for the plantation is given a 2-room house—1 kitchen house separated from the main house where we sleep and another little house for toilet. I shall draw the way our house stands. This is not too good of a drawing, but it will give you an idea how our sleeping house and the kitchen house and toilet house are put in their place.

Oh I must tell you about our toilet house then, now that I'm living here in the city the toilet is cleaner, it is flushed down and away, I do not know where our waste go to. Anyway back to Ewa, we do it into a box, which is emptied early in the morning into a big box. 2 horses pulls this box. 1 man empties the waste into the big box. The man does this work every morning, and puts some kind of oil into our toilet-box after he empties and puts it back into the toilet house. And you know he is a Japanese man. No Filipino man would do this kind of work. They say they would like to cut sugar cane, better than to do this kind of work. The Filipino children, especially the boys, when they have a fight with Japanese children, the Filipino boys

70 would sing out to the Japanese boys a rhyme that goes like this

> You know what your father use to do
> some years ago—
> Filipinos "Kookay," Japanese "hapay"

and the Filipino boys laughed at them So they just turn and run away, they know it is the truth. So back to where I used to climb the toilet house and stay on the flat-top just a little-bit slanted until my Nanay calls me in. I feel scared for her somehow. Every time Delphin, the man's name, comes to visit Nanay. I feel that what was going on was not right. To me this man is not to come to the house when Tatay is not home. I really do not know how long this was going on, but one day I was on top the toilet house. I heard a roaring noise coming in the back-road. I look. It was a motorcycle, only police man use this motorcycle, that's what the older people talk about. The motorcycle came straight into our backyard. He stop the motor, got out and knocked on the back door so hard, the noise or sound was loud—our neighbors just women on both sides of us came out and look and look. When the policeman knock on our back-door, I was really scared. I don't know how long before Nanay opened the door. The sheriff went into the house and drag Delphin out in his underclothes and shoved him into the seat that was together with the motorcycle and he started his motorcycle and he went away—to Pearl City Jail, I'd heard my mother telling our neighbor. From what I can understand—'cause I listen—some "busy-body" reported to the plantation manager that there was a man, not working at all he just visits a woman, every chance he gets. You see in the plantation every man of age must work, so when "Somebody" reported Delphin is not working and that "Someone" gave the address where Delphin can be found—so a sheriff was sent out to pick up Delphin and put him in jail. And when this happened, the neighbors start talking about Nanay. It is terrible when people start talking about my mother. Of course the neighbors feel sorry for Tatay 'cause Tatay was a hard-working-man and my Nanay was bad, no good, they say. For quite some time when Tatay goes to work and Manong Julian goes to school, my mother and I go walking again—this time we go to the train depot. She buys a ticket for herself, I get on the train free—and we go to Pearl city. I stay outside and wait for her, while she visits Delphin in jail. She stays as long as they will permit her to stay. Then, we come home by train. She cooks dinner before Tatay come home. This happen many times, before Delphin was set free and he was told to leave Ewa. I could not remember everything what happen later. Next thing I remember, Tatay moved us to Waipio. He said he didn't want to stay or live in Ewa anymore. After what happened you can't blame him, how people talk and talk; it was bad. But I had a funny feeling that Tatay was thinking of something else, he had something planned. From what my young mind can understand, he was thinking of catching Nanay and Delphin together, and from what he told Nanay that since Delphin is not working steady he can watch over us—Nanay, Manong Julian, and me—in Waipio, while he goes to Schofield and work there and comes home when there is no work, or whenever they give him, his day of rest. Delphin agreed to this. I was young, but I know that something bad will happen, I sensed it. Waipio is a small place, but there seems to be a lot of people here, mostly family all working for the plantation. I noticed too, we are close to the beach, and there is railroad tracks close by. I go out and play as I always do. So every morning after I wash my face Nanay combs my hair and braids it and ties a small ribbon to it. So my play days in Waipio was the same in Ewa, only I did not have the toilet house to climb onto now. The toilet house here is far away from the houses. I'm afraid to go down to it and do something. If Nanay go with me, I feel not afraid. I am always afraid of deep black holes. That's the way they make the toilet house here in Waipio. Then one night it happened—the bad feeling I feel since Tatay moved us here in Waipio. Before I close my eyes to sleep, I remember telling Nanay in our language to lock the door downstairs—Tatay might come home. Nanay answered me in Hinilonggu. We cannot lock the door because we are not the only ones living up here, and she added, besides "Your Tatay won't come home now, it is too late now." But I found out later that Tatay had come home earlier that day and stayed with the couple who was staying below us and didn't go upstairs until he was sure we were all laying down to sleep. As I was lieing down, I was on my back, my eyes wide open, sensing something, I could not close my eyes to sleep—then, I saw a bundle flying over me. I think Nanay scream. I sat up crying. Tatay reached over and grabbed someone. At first, I thought he grab Delphin, but it was Nanay. I heard broken glass. I found out next day Delphin had jump thru the window. He did not break his leg he just sprained his ankle. This time I was standing up and crying. I saw Tatay grab hold of Nanay's long hair and drag her downstairs. My mother just hang onto Tatay's belt. Someone grab hold of my hand and Manong Julian and led us downstairs, 'cause by this time seems like everyone is awake and when this someone took us downstairs, I saw Tatay really beating up Nanay. This is the first I saw Tatay angry and hitting Nanay. And this "someone" didn't let go of my hand nor Manong Julian. We stood some distance from Tatay crying. By this I felt afraid of him, standing there watching Tatay hurting Nanay and there was so many people watching. Soon, the "someone" took us Manong Julian and me to another house and he told us to be quiet and just stay there and not come out until he come back for us. Pretty soon, we heard someone running toward the house, so we crawl under the bed to as far back to the corner of the bed and lay as quiet as we can. We saw the door open and I know it was Tatay. He just look and saw no one, so he closed the door and ran off again. I found out later that Nanay was able to get away from Tatay and during that night Nanay and Delphin got together and hide, someplace, somewhere in Waipio. Manong Julian and I were taken to the couple who was staying below us. The person who took us there was the same one who had taken care of us when the trouble with Nanay & Tatay started. Soon after that, I notice that things are going on like nothing had happened but I didn't know then and understand was that Tatay had something planned. I do not know how long this "getting-together" with Tatay and Nanay lasted. Delphin was staying with the working-men at the plantation sleeping quarters and he was walking about like nothing had happened. Then one morning, I could not find Nanay, she was gone. I started to cry. I don't know how Manong Julian feel, but I wanted my mother. I was really afraid. The people or couple who was taken care of us told me not to cry, that they will (my Tatay and Nanay) come back for us. As the older people talk, I could understand what they were talking about. I just listen to what they were talking—they were saying that Nanay and Delphin were arrested and are in Honolulu Jail. Tatay had them arrested. That's why I do not see Nanay around anymore. I feel sad that this things are happening to Mother. A few days later Tatay took us to Watertown, my brother and I. This time, we lived with Uncle and Auntie Natad. Auntie is Nanay's younger sister, and they have two children also, Alfredo and Rose. I don't know how old Cousin Alfred is, but Cousin Rose, she's 3 years younger than I am. From what I understand, Tatay is working at the Hawaiian Pineapple Cannery, and as soon as he finds a place for us he'll pick us up. In the meantime, we are with Uncle and Auntie Natad. When Tatay brought Manong Julian and me to Uncle and Auntie Natad's house, it must have been at night and I must have been really tired and sleepy because I do not remember walking in water. Tatay carried me into the house. When I woke up next morning, I got dressed, and Auntie told me to be careful because I would fall into water. I walk to the back door. I saw and I understand why she told me to be careful. The house where we or Auntie & Uncle Natad live is standing in ocean water and not too far away from where I stood, the water looks very dark, so that mean it's deep out there. Oh my, and I'm so afraid of deep water, I shivered, I felt cold. I went to the steps that lead to outside and I saw water but not dark. I could see sand and I found out later I could not get out by myself. I have to be carried in and out of the house. Manong Julian can, he swims out whenever Auntie or Uncle Natad lets him—him and Cousin Fred. And so this means I could not go out and play. Anyway, I am not by myself, there's Auntie and Cousin Rose, I think she was about 3 or 4 years old then. Anyway I just play with my rag dolls, which Auntie made for me. When I get tired playing with the dolls and looking at the blue-sea, I just lay down and sleep. I really don't remember the days going by. At times, I go in the room by myself and cry. I feel scared this happen to us. I do not remember how long we live with Uncle and Auntie Natad; but anyway Tatay finally was able to find a place for us to live in Honolulu at Ewelae. And Tatay found himself a job at the Hawaiian Pineapple Cannery. At this new place we moved into, we have a 3 room place on the 2nd floor, 1 bedroom, living room, and kitchen and everybody in the building uses the same bathroom. On the second floor there's a long front porch and it so happen that we occupy the left 3-room place. Since we moved here, I was afraid to go down by myself or wander around, afraid I would get lost, so I stayed upstairs all the time on the front porch and play. The porch gives a good view all around. And across from where we are staying I noticed houses surrounded with trees and by tall fences around. One morning, I was running back and forth on the front porch and my long hair flying in every direction, I think. All of a sudden, I saw this big woman come

to me and ask me if my name is "Angeles," I say "yes." Then
she took my hand and said, "You come with me. Do not be
afraid, I will bring you back here." I went with her without a
word. She guided me down the stairway, out through the
downstairs front door and we cross the street up to the big
wood gate open it and led me inside, plenty of big trees and
houses then I saw Nanay. She came to me and hug me and kiss
me on the forehead. She was crying and I cried too, and I heard
her say "thank you" to the "big lady" who brought me to her.
From where we were standing I can see where we live, across
the street—upstairs, that's how Nanay saw me and recognize
me running back and forth. She says my hair flying all over my
head. I must have look awful to her. So she asked the police
woman if it was alright to bring me to her, so she can clean me
up and comb and braid my hair. The police woman said it was
alright. And so here I am I was in jail with my mother who got
busy and clean me up and comb and braid my hair. As soon as
she finish cleaning me up she kissed and she hug me and told
me to be "good" and told the police woman to take me back
where she took me from. So now, I know where Nanay is and
the houses among the trees are jail house. And Nanay told me
that it won't be long now that we'll all be together again, and
I feel good inside because Nanay is going to be with us again.
So now I play up on the porch but I cannot see Nanay because
of the trees but I am sure that she can see me. Nanay taught
me how to comb my hair, when I was with her. I could not do
a good braiding of my hair but I tried and I tie the end as best
as I know how. It was 2 more times, that I remember the police
woman came for me so Nanay can clean me up and wash and
comb my hair and she hug me and told me to be "good" when
she tells the police woman to take me back. As the day went
by, I wonder and I waited for the police woman to come and
take me to see Nanay, but the police woman did not come anymore, and so many times I stand on my toes to look down at
the house across the street and tried to look for Nanay. I see

people walking inside the fence but I can't see their faces too good. One day, Nanay come home I was in the living room and I saw Nanay walk in the room. I ran to her and hug her around the hips and she stroke my head. She said something, but I did not understand what she said. I saw tears in her eyes and she said, more clearly this time, "I am home now. I am not going back to the jail." To me, it seem she was gone a long time. Every day that she was not home, I wish she was home, and now she was really home. I feel so good and happy inside that I cried, too. She told me she was not leaving me anymore. She ask for Manong Julian. I told her I don't know where he is. I told her I don't see him to much. When I wake up in the morning, he is gone. I don't know where he goes. Now, I can have my father and mother together again, it is so good to see them together again. I was happy for a while because I see my father and mother together again but that did not last long. I think that Nanay do not want to stay with Tatay anymore, because one day, I saw Nanay spread out a big white cloth on the floor and she start folding her clothes and mine too on top the white cloth. I just look at her doing all this. When she had folded enough clothes on it she tied up the four corners together and made a big bundle. I had a funny feeling coming over me again, so I ask Nanay, are we going someplace? She put her finger to her mouth and she said quietly, yes, we are, just you and I. She put the bundle of clothes to one side of the room, then she changed my clothes, then she combed and braid my hair, she gave me a bath early. When Nanay said, yes we are, I kept quiet after that. I just let her lead me about. I just watch and waited. As for Manong Julian, he was gone. Nanay could not find him. Tatay was still working. He leaves early in the morning to go to work at the Hawaiian Pineapple Cannery and I remember he comes home in the afternoon for lunch and goes back to work as soon as he finish eating. Nanay already fix or cook his food, but I know she was nervous. She was busy doing this and that until Tatay came home to eat and go back to work and from what I can understand I hear Tatay tell Nanay that they all stop work 4 o'clock in the afternoon. I remember the day so well. As soon as Tatay left to go back to work, Nanay finish what she was doing. She cook some more for Tatay and Manong Julian to eat when they come home. I just watched her. I sat on one corner of the room and watch and waited. I watch her fix the bed, sweep the rooms, wash the dishes and pots, she put away things in their place. Then she stood on the middle of the room and look around and see if she has missed doing or putting away something. Then she took the bundle of clothes out of the hiding place, came to where I was and took my hand as if to say, "We are going now." When she lock the door, I know I'll never come back to this place again, and in my young mind, I was wondering if I'll see Tatay and Manong Julian again, and I start feeling sad again. Nanay seems to know I was about to cry, because she told me I must not cry, people will hear me and that must not happen, because she says, I do not want anybody to know we are leaving this place, so I did not cry. I just followed her out of the building. She was holding my hand with her left hand and bundle of clothes with her right hand. We did not wait long outside, when here comes Delphin with horse and wagon (someone was driving the horse). He pick me up and put me in the wagon together with the bundle of clothes. As the wagon drove away, I feel sad, sad again. I cannot understand then why this is happening—but I really know now, Mother did not love Tatay anymore, and that she has met another man that she like better than Tatay. Anyway, the horse and wagon did not go far it seem, when we reach some buildings. Nanay took hold of my hand. Delphin was carrying a lot of things. Nanay and I followed into the building then we walk on a big flat board to go into a big boat. I had a chance to look around. Then in my mind I know we are going someplace far away from Tatay. I do not remember too much after that, I know this much, I remember Nanay's face look so worried before the boat started to move away, then her face look so much better after the boat really moved away from the building. I saw she give a sigh of relief. Then, I did not understand the worried look, now I do. We sailed all night. I think someone carried me out of the ship 'cause I do not remember walking, and next thing I remember I was in a house and Delphin and Nanay was talking to people. I do not remember too much about that time so I will just write down here, we are far away from Tatay now. I was wondering and thinking at that time if he will ever find Nanay and me, yes, Tatay did, 4 years afterwards. All the time, I was with Nanay, Delphin taught me how to do some acrobatic tricks, tumbling forward and backward landing on my hands and my feet. I was small, he had an act where he would throw me to another man's shoulder, of course I was taught to bend my knee and keep my balance when I land and the man grab my ankle, and I stand up, keeping my balance. Many time I think I would miss him, but he always catch me. Delphin tried to teach me how to walk the wire (like he does, 'cause wire-walking was his special act) but I could not walk the wire, I fall. Nanay put a stop to that. She told him that I could not learn to walk the wire. I am just going to get hurt if he keeps on trying to make me walk the wire, of that, I am so very glad, because I feel so afraid to climb up the wire. I feel better when I do a act on the floor or ground. I will not write too much of the time I was with Nanay. Many time, I wonder and think if my Tatay will find us again. When I go out to the beach, 'cause it is close to the house, if Nanay calls me I can hear her. I always tell her I go to play on the beach. I play on the sand by myself and many times I just sit and look far out—all I see is the blue sea and the blue sky and I think about my father and mother and all the bad and sad things that happen, then I cry to myself. I do not go to school no more, all we do now, if Delphin is not working in the mill, he goes and talk to his friends who help him put a show of "sirco," acrobatic tricks and we go from 1 town to the next one, to put a show on. I have a feeling that this is how Tatay found us, thru friends. It was the last year that I lived with Nanay, which was 1922. I was ten years old. I remember that day so clearly. We were in Lihue, Kauai. I was on the veranda of the building (we were going to play "sirco" that night) sitting down looking at people. We just finish practicing our acts. I was told to go where I would not be in the way, because they were going to be busy putting up the "wire" the bars, the rings, and other things they have to do. I missed Nanay. She is going to have another baby, this will be her number 4. That is why she did not come with us. She stayed home in Kaliea. I was thinking about her when I saw this man running to me. He ask me where Delphin is. I said, inside. I have this funny feeling coming to me again—something is going to happen, from the way the man acted. He was all excited and he was talking fast to Delphin. I can hear him telling Delphin that Tatay told him to bring me back to Kaiea right away. Delphin, I know, was afraid of Tatay. Instead of bringing me back himself, he told the same man that brought him the message to bring me back. Tatay was glad to see me but Nanay was not, she was sad. She hug me tight and told me I was going back to Waipahu with Tatay, so "today I washed and iron all your clothes, they are all folded and bundled up," 'cause we are leaving early tomorrow. She told me to be "good." I was sad, yet I was glad to go with Tatay. So this is why I was feeling funny. All this happening, I feel in my body. I feel good yet I feel sad because Nanay is not coming with us. Nanay told me that her place now is with Delphin and Willie, Incarnation, and Enastacio. Nanay was crying and hugging me, and I was crying with her. Tatay and me left Kaliea, Kauai. Early the next morning we docked in Honolulu early. Oh, we rode on a big boat or ship like the one we (Nanay, Delphin, and me) took over four years ago. I sleep with my clothes on. I had no shoes, I walk around with no shoes. Nanay could not buy me shoes, she need the money for food so we can eat. My clothes she makes them, I'm glad about that I learn to sew from her. I just watch what she is doing. She taught me how to cook rice. So when Tatay and me finish eating, oh, yes, Tatay and me went to a restaurant and we eat, the food was good, and then we went to a store where they sell shoes. First Tatay ask for something, a piece of rag so I can clean my feet with and tried 2 pairs of shoes. They fit good. So Tatay bought me 2 pairs of shoes and he bought me 3 dresses, they are so pretty, I like them all, Tatay told me he will buy me some more later. With the dresses and the shoes I was so happy. And then he bought some tickets so we can ride the train back to Waipahu. I carried the bundle I had my 3 new dresses in and Tatay carried my bundles of clothes that Nanay had washed and ironed and the shoes. When we got out of the train, Tatay called a man with the horse and wagon, so we ride on a horse and wagon from the station to the house that the plantation gives to its workers. We stop at a Chinese store where they sell food, vegatables, fruits, clothes. He bought food, a lot, and the Chinese lady just wrote everything Tatay bought. Oh, Tatay told the lady, that if I come to the store, if I want something just write it and he is going to pay for them. The Chinese lady said "alright" and "okay" and she smile. We reach the house. The building was shape like a step there was rooms about eight rooms in the building, we have 2 rooms—1 for kitchen and 1 for bedroom. I sleep on a cot bed—we all we sleep in cot beds. It was not long, I found out where the school is—I just followed the small children like myself and they lead me to the school. I just stood in line. The teacher, she was nice, she came to me and ask me if I wanted to come to school. I nodded my head for a yes answer. So she let me come into the classroom with the rest of the children. Before we sat down, we recited the "Pledge of Alligiance" to the American flag. Oh, before that, our teacher said, "Good-morning, children" and the children answer, "Good-morning, Teacher," then they all sat down but I stood up because I do not know where to sit. The teacher called me to her, calling me "little girl." I went to her and she ask what my name is, so I told her and she ask how old I am. I said, I am ten years old. Then she ask me if I went to school before and I said "yes" only they made me stop coming to school because I cannot come to school every day in the week. That was over 3 years ago. I was with my mother that time, now, I am with my father I can come to school every day in the week. Then the teacher said to me, "I am Miss Duncan. I am your teacher. I will be your teacher until I pass you to the second grade. Now, you are in the first grade. You must study and listen in the classroom. If you are a good and obedient pupil, you will not be punish, you understand me?" I nod my head and I said, "Yes, Miss Duncan." Really, I was very happy that I can go to school every day now. I learn to read and write, and I learn to add and take away in arithmetic. The teacher told me I am a very good pupil, what she tells me makes me feel good inside and all over.

I must tell you that I have found a friend. I was not in the school long when she came in one day in the same classroom I was in and she stayed—the teacher accepted her, I do not know where she came from. I found out later she came from another Island, and she tells me she does not have a brother or sister, there is just her mother and father and that her father is going to work in Waipahu cutting sugar cane. I told her I do not have a mother here. She is at Kauai, another Island far away from here. I told her that I am living with my father and I have a brother. My friend's name is Maria Ehapon and she is one year younger than I am. And do you know she is living close to me. She took me to her house and I met her mother and father, they are nice people, I like them. And they are Filipino just like me— Visayan—only they speak Cebuhano. I'm Visayan, too, but my mother and father are from Romblon, Philippine Islands. They let me sleep with Maria. And this is how Maria and I became very good friends. We are always together. Oh the teacher calls Maria, Mary. Our teacher say it's easier to call her Mary than Maria. Anyway, when her and her parents moved to Honolulu,

I felt so sad and lonely. I never had a friend like her before and now she is gone, I cried when they left. Anyway, this is why I am writing this, so you will know, that if it was not for Tatay, I do not think I would have been able to go to school. I love my Nanay, but I am glad that Tatay took me away from her, because I like very much to go to school. In my first Book, my Diary, I wrote also how Mary and I became very good friends, how and when we moved to Honolulu because of the strike Manlapit had started, and when I become so sick. I thought then, I was going to die, because I could not walk anymore. Yes—I believe it was God's will that I live. In the other book, I wrote what happen so I am not going to write about those days again. Oh, I must write here, Mary and I were together for 2 years before her parents moved here in Honolulu.

1375 Hall St., Honolulu, Oahu, T.H.
December 12, 1925

I think I have written all I can remember about my father and my mother. It is sad that my father and mother are no longer together. In my heart, I wish so very much, that God, our Father in Heaven, would bring them together again—to live together again like before. I would be very happy if that would happen— but I wonder if they will get together again? Tatay never talk about Nanay. When he comes home from the plantation, he stay home for a few days or a week. He and friends around in Hall Street would gather around especially in the evening. They tell stories and they laugh a lot. I understand the Visayan dialect very well. I just listen and I laugh to myself. Mary understands the dialect too and we both speak Cebuhano. When they finish telling stories, they play cards—Filipino card playing like "Entre-quatro" or "Hoong-kiyang." Mary and I would watch them play and we finally learned how to play the card games. Sometimes they ask one of us to play with them especially when they can't find one to fill in as a partner.

1375 Hall St., Honolulu, T.H.

December 14, 1925

Gee, there's going to be a carnival at the back of the Palama
Theatre. Mary and I are anxiously waiting for the day it will
open. I hear people talk that it will stay open until January 2nd
of 1926. I have some money saved from the lunch money that
Tatay gives me everytime he comes home from the plantation.
He gives me 15 to 20¢ a day for lunch, and I spend only 5¢. I
saved the rest. I hide my money from Manong Julian. Sometimes he goes broke—he spend his money fast—he ask me if I
have some money—I answered him, "I do not have money to
give you. I just have enough for my lunch, until Tatay comes
home." He is 6 years older than I am. I tell him, why do you
not find work, you are old enough? You do not want to go to
school anymore, so why do you not look for work? My brother
tells me, "Oh, you better not get sassy with me." So I shut up
before I get a slap on the face. Anyway, I hide my money high
up on the rafter or sill, I do not know what the right word is. I
put my money up there when no one is at home—even Mary
does not know that I hide money up there. I know if Manong
Julian finds my "hiding place" I would not have a nickel left.
So I am very careful when I put some money "up there." I make
sure Manong Julian is not home, and also I make sure no one
is around. I know Mary and I will have a lot of fun when the
carnival opens. I must tell you, I learn how to dance the new
dance. They call it "the Charleston." When I first saw it, I
called it the "Crazy-dance" 'cause you see legs flying forward
and backward and at first I could not catch on. But then I watch
closely how they move the feet in tune with the music—then I
caught on, and boy, once I caught on, I dance the dance when
I come in thru the door. I Charleston to the kitchen, to the bedroom, even to the bathroom, but when an outsider, I mean one
who is not living in the house, is watching me, I stopped dancing. Joe said to me, "You really like to do that dance, huh?"—I
just nodded my head.

1375 Hall St., Honolulu, T.H.
December 16, 1925

You know what, the carnival will open tomorrow or maybe, the day after tomorrow. Gee, Mary and I found out that the carnival will stay open until after New Year's. Gee, that much fun we are going to have. Manong Julian and Joe are anxiously waiting for it to open, too. When we went to school this morning we noticed tents are up and the merry-go-round and there's 1 large round-green circle—like a very large ring—but it is covered with a green material. Anyway we will found out what it is, when the carnival opens. Oh, we were told this afternoon that we would not have any school next week. We are going to have 2 weeks vacation. We won't go back to school until after New Year. My classmates and schoolmates were glad to hear about our school vacation starts next week.

1375 Hall St., Honolulu, T.H.
December 18, 1925

The carnival opened last night and oh did we have fun. There were so many people there and Igsoo and I rode everything that was there to ride in. We rode the merry-go-round and caterpillar—this covers you up as it goes around and around and before it stops the covers folds back to let the people out—it is really fun and exciting. Oh, I fell in love. His name is Felix. He must be 17 or 18 years old or maybe older, but anyway here's how it happen. My Igsoo and I already bought tickets to ride the caterpillar, and we were standing on the flatform close to the railing, hanging onto the railing because there were a lot of people. And pretty soon the middle of the flatform cracked in and some fell in, especially the ones that were standing in the center of the flatform. Igsoo and I hang on fast onto the railing while they were fixing the flatform. While we were in this position, a bunch (about 5 or 6) of Filipino young boys come by and stopped in front of us. They looked at us, Igsoo and I. Two of them I know by sight, my brother's friends, Willie and Joe Sarmiento, the other boys I don't know them. Oh, one or two of them were Porto-Ricans, the rest was all Filipinos youths. I looked at each one, and my heart stopped at one face and he was looking at me, too—I don't know how long he has been looking at me, when my eyes fell on him. He smiled so I smiled back, and my heart seems to beat faster and I could feel myself blush. I never felt this way with Joe. Anyway, the young man that smiled at me turned to Willie Sarmiento and asked him if he know me. Willie must have given him a "yes" answer, 'cause he turned to me and smiled again—so, I smiled back. Pretty soon, the flatform was fixed and we were told to take our seats. Felix come close to where we were standing and he asked me if he can ride with us—I answered "No." He looked at me steady. "Maybe" next time. I did not answer because at that time his friends called out to him—"Hey, Felix, come on now, maybe those girls belongs to someone." I had a good look at him when he come close. He was good-looking and has very light complexion. The caterpillar started to move and soon we were covered. When the caterpillar's covering folded-back and it came to a stop I looked all around into the crowd of people. I did not see Felix or his friends so I thought they have left the carnival. Anyway, Igsoo and I, holding hands, so we won't lose each other, went around the carnival grounds. We just saw a couple of side shows. Mostly we rode the caterpillar and the merry-go-round. We limit ourselves to the rides. We did not want to spend our money all at once. It was about 10 o'clock, when we were about to leave the carnival—we were walking towards the gate. Who do you suppose came after us. It was Felix, I really did not expect to see him again. I guess he was watching us or he just saw us leaving so he ran after us. He talked to us while we were walking and when we reached the gate we stopped. He asked me where I live. Oh, he introduced himself and I told him I was Angeles and Igsoo, her name is Maria and that we live at Hall Street. He ask me if I go to the Palama Theatre. I answered, "Yes. We go there every Saturday matinee at 12 o'clock." Then he said, "I'll see you there next Saturday." I feel all shivery and thrilled at having talked to him and to think he like me and he said, "I'll see you there next Saturday," and he said, "Good-night, Angeles." I answered, "Good-night." He turned and went back to his friends, who were waiting for him. I could hear his friends teasing him about me. I turned around to look at him one more time and he turned also—I waved at him a good-bye wave and he did the same and I turned to Mary. I told her I like the guy and I know he likes me too, maybe for one thing only, I do not know, but we shall see. Do you know, when I saw and met Felix, I forgot all about Joe. I really felt sorry for him, but anyway, I'm not sure about Felix, so like I say—we shall see. Igsoo and I talked all the way home. Since the carnival was close to home, we got home in no time at all. Our parents (Tatay came and says he'll be home till Christmas) asked how we like the carnival, we told them that we like the carnival very much. We enjoyed the rides very much. We told them we went in to see some shows—just 2 of them. We like the rides better. We describe the caterpillar ride to them. I took a bath before I went to bed. We walk on dirt, so you can imagine the dust and dirt, that's why I took a bath—Igsoo did, too. We talked some more before we went to sleep, We had to be quiet—Ninang, Igsoo's mother, told us to be quiet, she told us to go to sleep, we can do some more talking tomorrow. So go to sleep we did—giggling as we dozed off. And I felt warm all over remembering Felix—and hoping I would dream about him but I didn't. When I woke up this morning, I felt good and happy. Mary is still sleeping, which is good. I do not want her to know about my book, things I write when I am by myself. I am in the bathroom—most of the time I write in the bathroom, so nobody will see what I am writing about.

1375 Hall St., Honolulu, T.H.
December 20, 1925

Oh, went to the carnival again last night—Igsoo's parents went too—they went to see a few shows but they did not ride anything. They watch us ride the caterpilar tho'. We did not stay long, because Igsoo's parents wanted to go home early. Anyway Igsoo and I had fun just walking around. Oh, Tatay went to the carnival also. He went with us. Manong Julian and Joe went by themselves. I guess they had fun too. I forgot to ask Joe if they did. I did not see Felix at the carnival last night. I was hoping I would see him. Manong Julian and Joe and Igsoo and I rode the merry-go-round. It was fun, the horse goes up and down while we go around and around. Oh, there was a dance floor at the carnival. There were people dancing on the floor and they were dancing the crazy dance but the real name for the dance is "Charleston." Igsoo and I watch the people dance. The ones that could not do the dance, they were dancing Fox-Trot, a fast 2-step. Igsoo and I would have stayed longer just to watch the people danced, but Igsoo's parents says, "Let us go home now," and so we had to go home with them. Anyway, we had fun.

Hall St., Honolulu, T.H.
December 25, 1925

Today is Christmas. I bought Mary some pretty handkerchiefs, I bought Tatay, Manong Julian, Joe, and Mary's parents handkerchief too. That's all I can buy. I didn't have too much money. Anyway they were really nice handkerchiefs. And Joe gave me a Parker fountain-pen and pencil. It's really a nice set, he had my name on the pen and the pencil set "Angeles Monrayo." I told Joe I was only able to buy handkerchiefs for everyone I like. Joe said, "That's alright, don't worry." After we ate tonight, and Mary and I finished washing the dishes, we four, Igsoo, Manong Julian, Joe, and me, we sat on the front porch and we sang all the songs we can think of. Joe plays the ukulele, he plays that instrument very well and Manong Julian played the ukulele banjo. Manong Julian plays the banjo good, too. Sometimes Igsoo goes off key, so Joe taps her on the shoulder, she looks at him and he shakes his head—but we all keep on singing. When we finish singing, we all laugh. Igsoo finally said, "I can't help it—it just came out that way"—and we all laugh again. While we were singing on the front porch, we didn't know that other tenement dwellors were listening to our singing. We just found out, when they start clapping their hands. So we all said to them "Merry Christmas." And they answer back, "Maayong Pasco," meaning "Good Christmas" and we kept on singing. We did not think of going to the carnival tonight—we were having fun here at home. We sang songs and tell stories until 10 o'clock, because all the men around here go to work tomorrow.

Hall St., Honolulu, T.H.
December 28, 1925

I just found out today Igsoo and her father and mother are going to America sometime next March. Oh, but I feel sad—I ask Igsoo why they are going to America. She told me a friend had told her father that they pay good wages in California. Igsoo is excited about going to America. Igsoo told me she is going to write to me. Oh, we talk so much, she promised that she is going to write to me, that she would not forget me. I told Igsoo I am going to miss her and we are going to be separated again, like in Waipahu. This time she is going very far from me. Maybe, I said to her, maybe we will never see each other again, once they leave Honolulu. "Anyway, from today on, until the day you leave let us try to be together most of the time," and I start to say something funny, but I could not. Then Igsoo's mother called us—she wants us to go to the open market by Aala Park, and buy her about 50¢ worth fresh fish. Igsoo's mother gave me the money. I took the money and off Mary and I went. We were only to happy to go to the open market, it is nice to go there, there are so many people buying this and buying that. There are people selling fruits and vegetables. There are people selling meats only and some selling only fish and other good things to eat. We always try and buy the fish for 10 cents less or more. Sometimes we are successful and sometimes we are not, but if we do get 15 cents or even 10 cents we buy ice cream or some candies for ourselves. I know Igsoo and I did not cheat Ninang because we always buy the amount of fish she wants us to buy for her. Anyway Ninang does not question us, because she is getting the fish she wants, so everything goes alright.

Hall St., Honolulu, Oahu, T.H.
December 30, 1925

Today is Rizal Day. The Filipinos here are celebrating "Rizal Day." I do not know him. I hear many stories about him, from what they tell me, he is dead. I do not know why they are making so much of this doing, called Rizal celebration—and 1 girl will be chosen queen and 4 girls will be chosen as princesses. Anyway, I am not too interested in their doings. Seems all the older people around here are interested about this Rizal celebration—maybe someday I will understand what this Rizal celebration is all about.

1926

Hall St., Honolulu, Oahu, T.H.
January 3, 1926

This is now the New Year of 1926 and we go back to school tomorrow. I miss school and my school friends, you know. I forgot to tell or write here that they all like me and I like them too, though I am a few years older than they are. One good thing that is going for me is that I am small and short. I am as tall or shorter than the tallest girl in the classroom and the boys are taller than the girls anyway, and we all get along swell. I already wash and iron my school clothes. Every Saturday, after I finish sweeping the floors, I do my washing, my clothes and Manong

Julian's, than on tomorrow I iron them, after I come back from church. Fel did not show up or come to the matinee last Saturday. I have not seen him since last year December. I think he is playing around, do you not think so? I do not care if he does not come.

Honolulu, Oahu, T.H.

January 20, 1926

I went to the matinee today at the Palama Theatre. The movie was good. It was the second picture when Fel sat beside me and put something silky and smooth and soft in my left hand. We just look at each other—my heart was beating fast. I thought he was going to kiss me but he just said, "I love you, and read what I had put in your hand—later." He gave my hand a tight squeez and he left. For the short moment I saw him made me feel glad all over. I was happy I had come to the show this afternoon, and during the intermission, I went to the toilet and read what he had given me—it is a silk-Pongee handkerchief. Fel had embroidered "I love you." on the handkerchief. That was romantic of Fel. And so I wrote a letter and gave Joe the letter that I am no longer his sweetheart. Poor Joe, I sure felt bad, but I know that I must tell him, I do not want 2 men for sweethearts. After Joe read my letter he said to me, "Are you sure you do not want to be my sweetheart anymore?" I answered him, "I'm sure." He said, "Then I'm going to leave Hall Street and go back home."

Honolulu, Oahu, T.H.

January 30, 1926

Joe kept his words—he left Hall Street today. He said "good-bye" to me and to Maria. Joe did not say good-bye to my brother because they work at the same "car wash." There will be no more singing around here, now that Joe moved back to his mother's house. It's going to be very quiet around here during the nights. My brother does not know the real reason why Joe moved away. Anyway, I feel a little sad now that Joe left. And Igsoo and her parents are leaving this coming month of March, and I will be alone again—going to school all by myself and I'll be going to church by myself and I'll be going to the library by myself. And Tatay will have to look for another couple that I can stay with, also Manong Julian.

Hall St., Honolulu, Oahu, T.H.
March 7, 1926

Gee, I'm alone again. Igsoo and her parents sailed for America this evening. I feel really sad today. I went to school today feeling so alone again. Why is it one feel so sad, when your friend leaves you? I came home from school. Mary and her parents were gone. They have left the house early. It's a good thing the people, a married people, man and wife have 1 baby a few months old, and a little boy about 2½ years have moved into the house. I have to share the bedroom with them, since I have my own little corner with a curtain around it. The rest of the bedroom the man and wife will have and for the boy and the little baby. I was so glad to find them moving into the house. I was afraid I would be by myself. The people themselves told me that this was all planned quite some time ago, that they would moved in as soon as Mary and her parents leaves the house to go to America. The night came, we ate together like always. I washed the dishes, and I do the same work as I did for Igsoo's parents, clean and sweep up the house before I leave for school in the morning. I'm thinking about Igsoo as I am writing this and I feel lonely and sad. I think I am going to cry. I am thinking that they are so far away from Honolulu now. Although I am a few years older now, I still feel that feeling so alone, like I did when Igsoo and her parents moved from here to Honolulu 3 years ago and now, I am going thru that again. I hope the lonely feeling will go away like it did 3 years ago, only that time I got sick so I was able to forget to be lonely.

Hall St., Honolulu, Oahu, T.H.
March 16, 1926

More than a week has passed since Igsoo left for America. I think by now, they have arrived in America. I hope she will not forget to write to me. It is a good thing I have homework to do and, after dinner, I'm busy with the pots and dishes and I do not see much of Manong Julian these days. The only time I see him is when we eat at night. So, this way, I do not feel so lonely. I'm busy most of the time. I do not think about being lonely. I pray every night before I go to sleep and I think so very much of Igsoo, wishing that she and her parents are still here in Honolulu with me.

Hall St., Honolulu, Oahu, T.H.
March 30, 1926

My Igsoo did not forget me. I went to the mailbox and there was a letter for me and she and her parents are living in Salinas, California. They are working and staying in a Filipino labor camp. She writes me that there are a lot of Filipino men in the labor camp, under a Filipino contractor. She will tell me more in the next letter. She wrote me that she likes it over there. She says, too, that I would like it there, if we go there someday. Gosh, she's making me all excited—I wish I was there with her now; but that's impossible of course. Oh, another thing she wrote me, she says the men there are making love to her. She think they think that she is around 18 or 19 years old but they are wrong 'cause she's only 12 going 13 and I'm 13 years going 14—oh, I take it back, I guess with high heels and the way she dresses one can think she is older. I am so glad to receive her letter, so glad to know that they reached America alright. I hope we can go there someday.

1375 Hall St., Honolulu, Oahu, T.H.

April 20, 1926   **93**

You know, since Igsoo and her parents went to California, I found a new friend, her name is Rose Caballero and she is older than I am, about 3 years older. After I finish with my housework and my school homework, I tell the lady that I stay with that I am going to play with a friend of mine that I will be home before it gets dark. She says "okay," so I go to Rosie's. All we do is talk, and Rosie is like me. We do the things we are suppose to do, so when I get to her place, she has finish what her mother wants her to do and she has finish her school homework too, that we can do what we want to do. Oh, she lives close to the school that she goes to, Kalluwala School. Gosh, it is really a long sounding name, and the school I go to is called Kaulani School. Anyway, since she live close to the school she took me and showed me her school. She showed me the room she is in and she is in the eighth grade. I think she started school late like I did. We both like school very much and you know what, we have been going to places, we both like to read so we go to the public library. We just walked, and we talked and laughed most of the way. We catch ourselves laughing kind of loud and we'd put our hands to our mouth and just say, "Oh my, people are looking at us, I bet they think we're crazy?" so we walk on in silence for a while then we are ourselves again. We stop at store windows and look. My, but they have such pretty things on display—clothes, shoes, and many other things. I feel so good and happy when I found a friend in Rosie. I'm not as blue and lonely like when Igsoo left. Oh, I still miss her, I think I will always miss her. She is my first real friend. Rosie sure fill in the empty and lonely spot that Igsoo has left behind. Another thing I must tell you about Rosie. She's an-indoor-baseball-player of Kalluwala School and she's a slugger. I have watch her play baseball, and boy! can she bat that ball, that is why her school friends call her "Slugger."

1375 Hall St., Honolulu, Oahu, T.H.

May 20, 1926

We just have 3 more weeks of school and I am wondering if I am going to pass to the fifth grade? I will have to wait and see. We have arithmetic test today. We won't know how we make out until she tell us how we all made out in the test and that's tomorrow. I think we are going to have tests all week. I hope I pass all the tests. I don't like to be flunked back, but I suppose, I don't pass the test, than there is nothing I can do, if the teachers don't let me pass. You see we have four teachers, and there are four bungalows of fourth graders. Our teacher Miss Duncan teaches reading and spelling. Mrs. McCabe teaches arithmetic & hygiene & Miss Yap (Chinese very pretty) teaches history and civics and Mrs. Peters teaches geography and language.

Hall St., Honolulu, Oahu, T.H.

May 30, 1926

I received a letter from my Igsoo today. I am sure glad to receive her letter. I receive 2 letters from her this month and I answer her letter right away. As soon as I finish writing in this book I am going to answer her letter. Gosh, she writes such a long letter she has so many thing to write me. She tells there are so many boys or men that are making love to her. Oh, she told me she is not going to school. I could not believe it that she is not going to school. She says she might go to work instead. She is not sure of the work yet—and she will tell me about it when she is sure. About Felix, I saw him once. You would not think we are sweethearts, we hardly see each other and talk to each other, and he has not kiss me yet, he just held my hand, that's all. We sure make a pair of "love-birds." Ha? Anyway, I do not think about him too much. I have my school, my friends in school, my home-work, and taking care of myself. I have plenty to do but to be honest, I do feel a thrill when I think of Felix. When will I see him again?

Honolulu, Oahu, T.H.
June 8, 1926

Wheoeeeee—I passed to the fifth grade. In fact the whole class passed. I'm so glad that we all did. And you can be sure we are happy about it. We all had very good report on our examination tests. Mine were—in reading B+, language A–, history B+, hygiene B, civics B, spelling A, arithmetic A–. Oh, what a report and I'm sure happy to know that I pass. I was worried there for a while. Friday is the last day of school until it opens again some-times in September. We are going to have 2 months vacation—no school for 2 months.

Hall St., Honolulu, Oahu, T.H.
June 16, 1926

Do you know there is an American woman Mrs. Bessinger, she comes around here in Hall Street and she talks to the Filipino women & girls to join a club she has, on 109 Nunuano Street for Filipino young wives or young girls and she teaches cooking and sewing. You know she is a very nice women so friendly. I like her. I told her that I would come to her club. She told us to come at 2:30 in the afternoon and we stay until 4:30 in the after-noon. So next week Tuesday, I am going, because I would like to learn how to cook and about sewing and meeting other young girls that I can meet and make friends like Mrs. Bessinger said. I am anxious to meet other young girls like myself. I live here in Hall Street since last year and there are not too many young girls like my age that lives around here, so my friends, really, are at school.

Hall St., Honolulu, Oahu, T.H.
June 17, 1926

I went with my 4 girlfriends today—we went out to look for work. We went to the Hawaiian Pineapple Cannery. The man that does the hiring took our names and addresses and told us to come back tomorrow. Somehow I had a feeling I was not going to be hired—I am too young—I would not be fourteen years old until the second of August. But, anyway, I am going to try. Oh yes, we got tired walking but we had fun. As we walk we talk and we were all thinking aloud, saying if we'll be hired or not? Before the morning was over—we found out—we did not get hired. So we come home tired but we had fun. First we dropped off Self-iscia at her house and Mercy too and we said to her that we are going to go and try it again—tomorrow, until we get hired or until they stop hiring.

Hall St., Honolulu, T.H.
June 18, 1926

You know we went four days straight to the canneries, but, I was not hired because I was too young. My friends were hired, but not me. I told them I'm willing to learn and do what they tell me. I lied about my age. I told the foreman that I was seventeen. I dislike to lie but I had to so I can get a job. The foreman still insisted that I am too young and that I am not even fifteen (how can he tell?). Anyway, I stuck to my story that I am seventeen going on eighteen. The foreman still didn't hire me. He told me that's all the girls he will hire today. He told me to come back next year. I come home feeling down-hearted because I was not hired and I wanted to work so badly so I can buy my own clothes and shoes and I have my own money to spend on other things I like. Oh, before I left the cannery, I saw Felix working at C.P.C., that was the last cannery we went. I am not going to go and look for work tomorrow. I give up looking for work. He just waved to me and I waved back and smiled and he waved and smile back.

Diary

Hall St., Honolulu, Oahu, T.H.
June 22, 1926

I went to Mrs. Bessinger club. She taught us how to bake "cup-cakes." I like that very much. We spent two happy hours with her. I like her, she is very patient with us—there were only four of us. She taught us step by step in preparing the cup-cakes, and we copied the recipe. I don't know when I'll have a stove with an oven to bake in but if someday I should have one I will bake cup-cakes. You know, after we bake the cup-cakes, we six sat down and we ate some cup-cakes with milk which Mrs. Bessinger had brought with her, of course Mrs. Bessinger joined us. It was fun and wonderful to have someone like her to be interested in us Filipino girls. Next week she says she is going to teach us how to make handkerchiefs.

Hall St., Honolulu, Oahu, T.H.
June 29, 1926

Do you know that there were only four of us girls that come to club. Mrs. Bessinger was hoping that more girls would come because she says that she had talk to the girls and to their parents and they had all promised that they would come. And today only four of us were there—the same ones that came last week. Anyway, we are going to learn how to make handkerchief today. We brought our own scissors, thread, needle, and thimble. Mrs. Bessinger told us some wonderful true stories while we were doing our needlework. I hope to finish my handkerchief before we meet again next week.

Hall St., Honolulu, Oahu, T.H.
July 4, 1926

Today is Fourth of July and so many people are excited and happy and many are lighting fire crackers, there are so much noise around. My friends around here and myself are playing hide-and-go-seek. I was hoping that Rosie will come around so we can talk. I miss Igsoo but I try not to get lonely. I received a nice long letter from her. She writes that they, her father and mother, goes to town whenever her father feels like going into town, when he is not tired. They see a movie or go see a Vaudville show. She tells that I would like Vaudville, these are group of

98   people—they act, sing, or dance.

Hall St., Honolulu, Oahu, T.H.

July 6, 1926

There were six of us girls that came to the club today. Mrs. Bessinger brought another lady with her today and she is Mrs. Patterson. She is very nice too, and she is tall and slender. I think she is younger than Mrs. Bessinger. Anyway we had cooking lesson today. Mrs. Bessinger and Mrs. Patterson taught us how to make carrot salad. It was good, first time I've eaten something like this and Mrs. Patterson taught us how to make a meat-loaf made out of hamburger meat. And do you know that what we made, the salad and the meat-loaf was just right for us? It was 5 o'clock before we all said good-bye. Mrs. Bessinger and Mrs. Patterson told us that we'll see each other two weeks from today, same time.

Hall St., Honolulu, Oahu, T.H.

July 20, 1926

Sometimes in the evening when I have finish my homework and washing the dishes and drying them, I have nothing more to do and it is too early for me to go to bed, I take my brother's ukulele and play some songs and start singing all the songs I know by myself until I get tired and sleepy. Sometimes I play the ukulele and I sing out on the front porch as late as 9 o'clock. A few times these past weeks, I thought no one was around, especially the house in front of our tenement house. It was kind of dark so I did not see anyone sitting on the front porch, there was no light

at their house. I know I sang quite a few songs and when I finished singing "Linger Awhile" I heard hands clapping. A voice
rang out in the dark and said, "Angeles, you sing alright by yourself, you know that?" I said "thank you" but I felt embarrassed.
It is a good thing that it was dark. I felt my face grow hot, must
have been red, like I said, it was kind of dark so they could not
see how I felt. This is the first time Mr. Mariano and his Japanese woman ever paid me a compliment. We've lived here almost
a year now and we only say "Hello and how-are-you" and to me
they are very friendly people, but let me write here, though, that
the woman is a prostitute and Mr. Mariano is a "pimp." But they
mind their business, they do not make trouble, so far, and the
people around here make no trouble for them. So, after the nice
compliment they want me to sing "Moonlight and Roses" and
also "I'm All Alone." They told me they heard me sing these two
songs with Manong Julian and Joe. I said, "Alright, I'll sing the
songs you want me to sing." So, I sang the songs—and a few
more. I said "good-night" to the nice people across from me—
and they answered, "Good-night, Angeles and we thank you for
singing for us." Anyway, I felt good inside when I went to bed,
some people like my singing. Since I was 6 years old, I was
singing—I like to sing. I start singing when "Someone" in
Kaliea, Kauai, started a Filipino Folk-Song-and Dance, and I
was picked to be a little boy—of all things to be a dance partner
to a little girl as old as I am. We were taught to dance to a Filipino folk dance called "Cariniosa." There were 3 other dance
group that we were taught to dance, 2 other group dancing were
all girls dancing to a Filipino folk song and dance called "Ang
Alibangbang" translated in English "The Butterfly." I still
remember the words to it but the others songs I forgot them.
Yes, I like to sing very much. I try to learn all the songs I hear—
even the school songs. I must go to bed now, it is getting late for
me. I have to wake up early as usual. The people I'm staying with
are still playing cards in the parlor. They are having their fun
because they are laughing and talking, telling Filipino jokes.

Hall St., Honolulu, Oahu
July 23, 1926

As I was walking to the club today, I met Amparo, Selfishia, and Victoria on the way going to the club. We were all laughing and talking as we walk along. Amparo said, "I wish the other two would come today, you know we should have more girls here." I know Mrs. Bessinger and Mrs. Patterson would like that very much and too we would have more fun. Mrs. Patterson ask me if I can do hem roll stitches. I answered Mrs. Patterson if she can show me how it is done, perhaps I can do it. So, before we left the club, Mrs. Patterson showed me how to do the stitch and it was easy. Then Mrs. Patterson went on to tell that she has a linen table cloth and 1 dozen matching napkins for me to hand-roll and that she is going to pay me. I told her that she does not have to pay me, but she insisted because, she says, "You are going 'Camping' next year and the money I am going to pay you will go towards paying the Camping Venture, that Mrs. Bessinger and I are planning for you and the other girls, the money is for you alone, the other girls will pay, too."

Hall St., Honolulu, Oahu, T.H.
August 1, 1926

You know what, Joe paid us a visit last night. It was really a surprised to see him. He is looking good. We have not seen him since he moved away last January, 1926. I was in the bedroom when I heard a very familiar voice talking to my brother. Then I heard him ask where are the "greens." My brother answered there is only "me" left. He then went to explain to Joe that the other green left for America to California last March, 1926. All I can hear Joe said, "Oh really." And then Manang Julian and Joe were talking for a while. I could not hear what they were talking about. So I come to the living room and joined them and the three of us went out to the front porch and sat down on the steps and they start talking about old times. And Joe told my brother and me that he had bought a secondhand car and that he would like to take us out for a drive anywhere in the Island. So my brother said, "Okay, Joe, let us go to Waipahu to visit my Aunt and Uncle Mindoro and my cousins on the fourteenth of August." And Joe agreed. We were all excited about the fourteenth of August. I was anyway. I have not been to any place for a long time. Joe says that we have to go on a Saturday because he is not working that day and Manong Julian too, he is not working that day. You know I can hardly wait for the 14th, I feel happy about it. We 3, we talk and laugh. Manong Julian and Joe did most of the talking. I just listen. Joe, I think talk more than my brother. Joe went home late, about 11 o'clock.

Hall St., Honolulu, Oahu, T.H.
August 3, 1926

I just got home from the club. As usual we had a wonderful time. We bake a chocolate cake today. Mrs. Bessinger and Mrs. Patterson taught us how the cake is made. Today, just Sophia, Amparo, Victoria, and myself were at the club. Mrs. Patterson gave me 1 set of table cloth and 12 napkins to hand-roll and gosh, they are linen white set. When I took them from Mrs. Patterson's hands, I told her I'll try and keep them clean. She said, "Oh that's alright, I can always wash the table cloth and the napkins if ever they should get soiled." That was really nice of her to say that to me. Anyway, I am going to try and work on the table cloth carefully, so I will not get them dirty. When we have finished eating our cake and our milk, Mrs. Bessinger told her wonderful experience in the Philippines, at Manila where she learned how to speak Tagalog.

Hall St., Honolulu, Oahu
August 15, 1926, I'm in bed—

We, Joe, Manong Julian, and I went to Waipahu yesterday morning. We told Dorotea and her husband (they are the people we are staying with) that we are going to Waipahu to visit our cousins and Uncle and Auntie Mindoro. In case Tatay should come home unexpectly, they could tell him where we went to so Tatay would not worry. Anyway, we had fun over at cousins' place. We played on the beach 'cause their house is very close to the beach, near the train track. We sang songs and we danced and my cousins, Manuela, Incarnation, and Maria like my flowered print dress, it was tailored made for me, it was my favorite dress. They want to trade my dress. Cousin Manuela who is a year or so older than I am, and Incarnation is 2 years younger than I am, but looking at her I know she can fit into my dress alright, but not Cousin Manuela. Oh, another thing we did at cousins' place was crab-fishing. You know it was fun catching the crabs and so easy. There's a long flatform, a pier that goes far out into the sea water. I do not know how far out, but there was room for many people to go fishing for crabs. I say "fishing" because Cousin Manuela taught us how to catch the crabs by using a long pole and tie a long-string at the end of the pole and on the other end of the string a piece of red cloth and weight tied securely to the string, and then you let this down into the water and believe it or not the crabs grab hold of the red rag and hang on to it—it won't let go and so, we caught a lot of crabs this way. The real small crabs we throw them back in the water so they can grow some more. We brought some crabs home. I know the people we live with will like them very much, and so we are going to have more crabs to eat tomorrow. We did not want to come home yet. We told Uncle and Auntie Mindoro that and Auntie told us why not stay another day. But we could not, because Joe and Manong Julian have to go to work tomorrow. Anyway we stayed until 6 o'clock and we had to say good-bye to Auntie and Uncle and to our cousins. They did not want us to go but we have to. We sure enjoyed our 2 days stay in Waipahu.

Hall St., Honolulu, T.H.
August 30, 1926

I finished the table cloth and the napkins yesterday and today—
this afternoon, we had our club meeting. I gave the finished table
cloth and napkins. Mrs. Patterson really like my work. She
praised me highly and she said she had one more set and if I
would like to do it. I told her that I would. "Okay, I will bring the
table set on our next meeting." And Mrs. Patterson say that she
will keep the money and when the time comes for us to go camping, she will take care of me. I told Mrs. Patterson that whatever
she wants to do, it will be alright with me. Oh, Mrs. Bessinger
and Mrs. Patterson taught us how to prepare a light lunch. Some
salad and sandwiches and we had milk with our lunch. Mrs.
Bessinger had brought with her slices of ham, lettuce, mayonnaise. She told us spread some mayonnaise on one slice of bread,
put lettuce on it, and put the slice of ham on it, then put another
slice of bread on top of it and cut it length-wise and place the
sandwich in a small plate. That is the way we made our "sandwich." It was good.

Hall St., Honolulu, Oahu, T.H.
September 6, 1926

School opened today, and o boy, I thought I was put back to the
fourth grade, because when the teacher call the roll call, my
name was not called out. Actually, I felt my heart sank, I felt left
out. That's what happened. The teacher skipped my name.
Emmaline Ku told her I was suppose to pass like the others, so
the teacher read the roll call again, finally she called my name,
and so my classmates were really glad we all passed. Emmaline
Ku is a pretty Hawaiian girl. I sure like what she did for me. We
didn't do much today in class. We just talked and getting to
know each other all over again. And we talked about what we
did all summer. Yes, we have fun today. We did change rooms
today and we did all what we did last year in the fourth grade—

move from one room to the other, each room 2 subjects, like in our own room, it's or rather we have reading and spelling. Our teacher is Mrs. Pogue. The room to the left of us—is Mrs. Peterson and she teaches language and geography. Next room is Miss Yap. She teaches history. The next room to Miss Yap is Mrs. Cabrall; she teaches hygiene and civics. And the last room we go to Mrs. Ferguson; she teaches arithmatic only. Then before we go home, we go back to their own room and teacher. Our Teacher is Mrs. Pogue. She lectured us on our behavior that we should always remember our manners—be courteous at all times, even when it hurts. The school bell rang at 2:30, that meant everyone go home. We all said good-bye to each other. I'm really glad that school is open again.

Honolulu, Oahu, T.H.
October 8, 1926

You know what? Joe asked me to marry him, me. Marry? Oh my, I told Joe, I do not want to get married, I am only 14 years old, and getting married had not entered my mind. "Gosh," I told Joe, "I want to enjoy my girlhood days first—I do not want to start taking care of babies." Something went thru my mind. I remembered my mother, she had a baby every year—and I took care of them. Those days I'll always remember, they were oh so much work. Joe is 20 years old, as old as my brother. Anyway, Joe just smiled, and said, "Oh, that is alright. I guess you are young yet to get married."

Honolulu, Oahu, T.H.
October 18, 1926

You know, I got a surprise today, a wonderful surprise. Remember, I wrote about a couple that lives around here—across from where I live. Well, Mr. Mariano told me to come with him to the shoe store, he says his woman says it's alright that I go with him. At first I just looked at him, then as if he was reading my mind, he said, "It's alright, Angeles, I would not hurt you. I just want to buy you some shoes." So I went with him and there was a nice shoe store close by. We did not have to walk far. We went into the store. Oh there were so many shoes, pretty ones. He told me to pick the one I want so I pick a white sandal-low heel, for school. Mr. Mariano told me to pick out another pair. I saw a yellow high-heel that ties in a bow at the front. I tried it and I like it. I felt taller too. I really like the shoes. I have to have a nice dress to wear it with. Mr. Mariano asked me if I really like the shoes I had picked. I said that I did. "Okay, Angeles, they are yours." The store keeper put the 2 prs. of shoes in the bag and Mr. Mariano paid for them (I was really happy inside), and he turned to me and gave me the bag of shoes and told me to go home. I said thank you to him. I shook his hands. I turned and come on home with the 2 prs. of shoes that Mr. Mariano bought for me. I guess Mr. Mariano and his woman felt sorry for me because I walk around the place barefooted many times. I guess they figured a 14 year girl should not be walking around without any shoes. That was really nice of them to buy me the shoes. Yes, I was really surprised but a very happy girl at that. No one bought me things before. Except Mr. Navarro, he had a made to-order-dress for me in payment to me because I took care of his daughter for 2 weeks or more. I'll wear my white sandals tomorrow. When Tatay comes home, I'll tell him what those nice people bought me.

Honolulu, Oahu, T.H.
October 25, 1926

Boy, it is a good thing I worked on the table cloth and the napkins. I finish them just a few days ago, and Mrs. Bessinger wrote me a short letter, telling me that we have a meeting October 25 instead of the 15th of November, as we have planned. She went on to explain that her and Mrs. Patterson are going to be busy the next 2 months—so that is why we meet today. I gave the finish table cloth and napkins and Mrs. Patterson told me now she will keep the money, $30.00, all together and she will take care of my camping needs next year. I thank her very much for doing all this for me. Mrs Patterson taught us how to bake custard pie. We were taught step by step and I'm sure we will remember how it is done. We have the recipe. Custard pie is so good, I like it very much. I think I like it best, better than apricot pie. We ate the pie. There was enough for six person, including Mrs. Bessinger and Mrs. Patterson. We had a glass of milk with the pie.

Hall St., Honolulu, Oahu, T.H.
November 6, 1926

Joe and my brother and Rose and myself went to the Princess Theatre on Fort Street, to see the moving picture called "The Black Pirate," featuring Douglas Fairbanks Sr. Joe payed for tickets for all of us. This is the first time that I have been in this theatre, the same with Rose. It is big and beautiful and they play organ music. I like organ music, it's beautiful. It was really nice of Joe to treat us last night. The moving picture was very good. I always like Douglas Fairbanks Sr. We took Rose home because it was late and she thank us—especially Joe. And Joe said, "We're going to do it again, if there is a good moving picture coming." Rose and I are looking forward to go and see another moving picture at the Princess Theatre.

Hall St., Honolulu Oahu, T.H.
November 16, 1926

Tatay come home last night. Some of his friends at where he works brought him home and they are going to pick him up in a few days. Anyway Tatay only comes home to take care of our needs. I feel glad when Tatay comes home. Tatay says he will be home next month. I don't know when, but he will be home for a couple weeks in December. He says work is slowing down.

Hall St., Honolulu, Oahu, T.H.
December 15, 1926

I received a nice and wonderful letter from Igsoo. I am so glad to hear from her. I did not receive a letter from her for a long time, it seems. I was wondering if she has forgotten about me. So when I receive her letter, I really felt glad, that she did not forget me. She just got lazy for a while, she said. Anyway, she enclosed some pictures of her and one with her mother and father, she really looked very nice, so grown up. I showed the pictures to Manong Julian and to Joe and Rose. And they all agree with me that she's very grown-up and very nice-looking-lady, at that. Going to America really have changed her appearance.

1927

Hall St., Honolulu, Oahu, T.H.
January 1, 1927

Wow! did we have fun last night. As usual we the "four Muska-teers." Rose came to the house and I did not recognize her at first because she dressed up like a boy. She wore a mask and wore one of her brother's cap on and she came close to me and slapped my *behind* and said in a very low voice, "Happy New Year!" I turned around I was about to slap the boy when I noticed the curly hairs sticking out from under the cap. I said, "Rose?" And she burst out laughing, and said, "I nearly fooled you, huh?" and I said, "Yeah, and you nearly got slapped" and she said, "I know." So, dressing the way she did, I told her I am going to borrow my brother's pants and shirt and one of his caps. I told Rose, I am going to be a "copy-cat." Rose, just laugh and said that's a good idea. So she and I walked out of the house dressed like 2 young boys. We walk up Liliha Street just a short way and then we walk back heading towards King Street and went into some stores. The stores were still open, so we bought good things to eat, like chestnuts. (They are already cooked.) I like them very much. Rose, Joe, and my brother like them too. I ask Rose if she would like to spend the night with me and she said "sure" but, she said, "I better go home and ask my mother if I can"—so we, Joe, Manong Julian, and I, went with Rose to ask her mother if she can spend the night with me. Rose's mother gave her a "Yes" answer, she said to me, "Yes, Rosela (that's her real name and her mother, her stepfather, and her brother call her by her real name, "Rosela") can sleep with you to night but she comes home tomorrow before it gets dark." And I said to her, "Do not worry, Mrs. Caballero, Rose will be home by 5 o'clock." So we all walk to Aala Park, seems like everybody were walking out in the street, so many. The stores are lighted up but pretty soon the stores will close their doors. You know we got hungry just walking around and so we went in to one of the Chinese chop suey house and we all had a bowl of Chinese pork noodles. Noodles always taste good to me. We were talking while we were eating our noodles, Joe and Manong Julian did all the talking. Oh, I nearly forgot to write down here that we bought a "bang" stick— that's what I call it, because at one end there's a metal thing where we put 1 cap and we hold the stick upright and the metal side close to the sidewalk and we just bring the stick down hard and it really makes a loud bang sound. We had fun with the "stick" and scared quite a few of our friends. You see, we would do it behind them and when they jump and turn around we all say "Happy New Year!" and we all laugh. Before 11 o'clock we started to walk home. Do you know that my friends recognize me, even with a disguise? Maybe the way I walk or the way I talk. Rose got away with it, but I did not. I saw Willie and he pass by and said, "Hello, Felix." Oh, gosh, how can he tell anyway? It is a good thing Rose, Joe, and Manong Julian were busy

108

looking into the store window and did not hear, besides some people were talking loud.

We reached home we took off our masks. Just Rose and I wore masks. Joe and Manong Julian did not wear their masks long, they took them off after a while. But Rose and I wore ours until we got home. It was only 11:30 when we reach home. So we sang songs till 12 o'clock, then the real noise started. "Bang, bang, bang," whistles blow, car horns were blowing and firecrackers were really popping and people around—our neighbors and friends all saying "Happy New Year, Happy New Year!" and we all joined in. My brother hug Rose and Joe hug me—that was all, Joe could not kiss me much as he wanted to. He just gave me a tight hug, and let me go. The people I'm staying with made some Bee-Bing-ka, Maruya. So we all had some good things to eat. We talk and sang all the songs we know. Tatay and the people I stay with were playing cards. I hug Tatay and said, "Happy New Year, Tatay" and I hug the people I'm staying with and they say to me, "Happy New Year, Angeles!" Gosh, oh gee, we were all so happy, I felt so happy, because Tatay was home with us. The older people were all telling stories and jokes. They were really having fun themselves, like we are. It was 2 o'clock before we all said good-night. Joe spent the night with his aunt and uncle, who lives just 2 doors away from us. Rose and I said good-night to Tatay and Manong Julian and to Dorotea and her husband. I woke up early this morning to take a bath. I should take a bath at night 'cause I get dirty during the day time, but anyway, sometimes I do, on Friday, Saturday, and Sunday nights. I took a bath early before Rose and everyone else in the house wakes up. Rose was still sleeping when I finish taking my bath. Rose finally woke up and we talk for a while. I told her that I have already cleaned up and have taken a bath. So Rose took a bath too. When she finished, we went to a Chinese "coffeeshop." I bought some rolls with butter on them and a large pitcher of coffee. I carried the pitcher of coffee and Rose carried the rolls. They were still hot. The Chinese man told us they just came out of the oven and they are so good when the rolls are freshly bake. Really, Rose and I, my brother and Joe, we enjoyed our breakfast together. We really had a very good day—and a wonderful New Year—the New Year 1927. Before the day was over, I walk Rose home and thank Rosie's mother for letting Rose spend the night with me. I told Rose's mother that we had a good time. I said "Happy New Year" to her and she wished me a "Happy New Year" too.

110

1335 River St., Honolulu, Oahu, T.H.

February 2, 1927

We are back here at River Street. This time, we are staying downstairs. 2 years ago, when I was sick we live upstairs with Nanay and her family. Only now, Nanay and her other family are living in the Philippine Islands—where, I don't know. I feel sad when I think not to see her again. Anyway, Tatay, Manong Julian, and I moved in with Esperanza and her family. She is now a married woman and she had a baby boy named Robert Romero. Yes, Esperanza is now Mrs. Jose Romero, and she is only 17 years and Mr. Romero is over 30 years old. Esperanza have 3 stepdaughters, oldest Sally (she is in the convent), Rosario who is 12 years old, and Betty is 10 years old and I am older than they are. I am 2 years older than Rosario, and she is 2 years older than Betty. You know it was Tatay who met Esperanza and her husband Jose Romero and Tatay talk to them about us moving in with them. Beside Esperanza and her husband told Tatay that they are going to America next month to work over there. They say that there are plenty of work there. And do you know that Manong Julian is going with them—of course, he is going to pay his own his passage way, which is $75.00 dollars one way. It's a good thing Manong Julian has saved his money, otherwise he would not have been able to go. And Manong Julian says we can follow later, when he has some money saved, but I know Tatay will save some money too. And do you know that Esperanza is only 3 years older than I am. When we first knew each other she was fifteen and I wasn't quite twelve years old and when we got to know each other, her father decided to move away—and now we meet again 3 years later and she is a married woman with a baby boy. Me? I am still single and not married. I am not interested in getting married, not yet. Besides I am only fourteen years old. Gosh, oh gee, I have many years ahead of me still.

1335 River St., Honolulu, Oahu, T.H.
February 20, 1927

Manong Julian and Mr. & Mrs. Romero and their family are leaving for the United States of America on March 3, 1927—gee, that is not too far away, huh? And then, we'll be by ourselves. Oh, I forgot there's a single man here living with Esperanza. He is helping pay the rent. I suppose Tatay and Kenting (that's the man's name) will pay the rent half and half like he did with Esperanza. Anyway, I do not bother with that, it is not my doing, they are going to take care of all of that. Kenting is Tagalog and he is a taylor, and I am a little afraid of him. I avoid him as much as I can. I tell Esperanza this, how I feel towards the man, she just laughs at my fears and says to me, "Oh, Angeles, do not be such a baby. Kenting is okay, he would not hurt you." To myself, he may be okay to you but I do not like the way he looks at me with those eyes of his. They give me the shivers.

1335 River St., Honolulu, Oahu, T.H.
March 3, 1927

Bro and Esperanza and her family sailed for America this afternoon. The steamer start pulling out to sea after 5 o'clock. The band was playing "Aloha Oe" and Tatay and I waved good-bye to them until we could not see them on the deck of the steamer anymore. We stayed on the pier until we could not see the steamer anymore and Tatay and I walked home. Tatay and I stopped at a chop suey house and we had pork noodles. When we arrive at the house, Kenting was busy sewing. He said he was making a suit for someone. Tatay talk to him but I went to the bathroom to clean up and went straight to bed. I told Tatay that I was going to do my homework and go to bed afterwards when I finish my homework.

112

1335 River St., Honolulu, Oahu, T.H.

April 2, 1927

I saw a skirt on a pretty Japanese girl today and I like the style. I call it tomboy skirt, because it is belted and there's a pocket on the right backside of the skirt. It is a pretty skirt and I like the style. So I gathered enough nerve to ask Kenting if he can make the skirt. I drew him a picture of the skirt and I told him that I have one of my mother's skirt to make it out of. And he answered, oh sure he can make it. I ask him how much he is going to charge me—he answered me that he would not charge me because we live in the same house and another thing he says he like me. He told me that he will take measurement of my waist and my hips and he will start sewing the skirt right away. I do not like the way he said he is going to take the measurement of my waist, my hips, and the hem of the skirt. I am going to make sure Tatay is home when he takes my measurements.

River St., Honolulu, Oahu, T.H.

May 6, 1927

Gee, men are terrible—I hate Kenting. He is the Taylor who is making my skirt (when no one is home Tatay is still working at the pier, as a stevedor, unloading cargos from the ship). When I came home from school, Kenting was in his room. I put my books hurriedly in my bedroom. I didn't bother to change into my home clothes. I went into the kitchen to see what we have to eat—there was only cooked rice and shoyu. I was hungry, but I did not eat, I wanted to get out of the house right away. As I walked out Kenting ask me, "Why don't you eat?" I answered, "I'm not hungry, besides there's only cook rice, there's no cook fish or cook-meat," and I walked out onto the front porch and start talking to Ah Sam, and the lady's daughter. She is Chinese. Very nice people and the landlady is or rather she has very small feet. Sometimes I wonder, how she can walk having such small feet. Anyway about 10 or 15 minutes I was on the front porch I saw Kenting with his hat on walk out of the house. I did not know it was a trick. So I went into the house and I went straight to the kitchen, and got a plate and dish out some rice and just springle a little shoyu on it. I just wanted to eat a little bit to stop the growling in my stomach. I had my back towards the door. Just when I was finishing up the rice, I heard Kenting's voice back of me. He startled me. I nearly choke on the rice. I had to drink some water to swallow down the rice. Kenting said in Tagalog, "I thought you said you are not hungry." Anyway, he said, "When you finish eating come and get your skirt. I finish sewing it." I said "okay." Kenting knows I don't like him and he must know I am afraid of him too but I wanted the skirt. I have been waiting for about a month for him to finish my skirt. When he took my waist measurements, I made sure Tatay was home. Kenting took several waist mesurements of my waist. I finally told him he better take my waist measurement or I'll tell my father what he is doing. Then he said, "Alright I'll take it now, just stand still." He finally finished taking all my measurements, including my hemline. So when I finish eating I went to the door of Kenting's room. I saw the skirt all folded on top his sewing machine on the far side of the room and Kenting was saying and making signs to me to come and pick up the skirt. I was thinking of walking calmly to the machine and pick up my skirt and dash out but Kenting was thinking his own thoughts too. When I finally gathered my nerves, I walk to the sewing machine and pick up the skirt and when I turn to dash out Kenting had closed the door and was coming towards me and grabbed me and kissed me. Boy, did I struggled to get free. I finally broke his hold on me and push him as hard as I can.

114 I ran towards the door. The door was unlocked. I was crying by now, and I went to get out of the house and ran into my landlady's porch, and crying softly and my landlady come to me and ask me, "What'sa matter," so I told her. Just then Kenting come to the door and spoke to me and said to me in his dialect Tagalog, "Come back in here, you fool. You're making me embarassed!" Gosh, he sure had some nerve to tell me that like I was his wife or something. The landlady told him in broken English that if he does not leave me alone, she is going to call the police and she was shaking her cane at him. He finally told the landlady that he is going to leave me alone. In truth, I think he got scared, 'cause I told him I was going to tell my father when he comes home. So Kenting moved out of the house before Tatay came home that night. Since Kenting moved out I did not have to tell Tatay what happened that afternoon. I sure had a frightening experience. I hope nothing like that will happen again. I am afraid of men, but I think I will fight like a wild animal if they are going to do something to me, as long as they do not knock me down and out, I can still fight to get free, like I did today.

River St., Honolulu Oahu, T.H.
May 9, 1927

We have unexpected meeting today, because in our last meeting, I told Mrs. Bessinger and Mrs. Patterson that my father and I are leaving for America (California) sometimes in July, and so today is my last time to come to the meeting. So before we went home, I said good-bye to Mrs. Bessinger and Mrs. Patterson. I thank them for being so good to me and the girls. Mrs

Patterson called me to one side of the room and put something in my hand and told me that it is the money I earned for hand-rolling the table cloths and napkins for her. Somehow I have forgotten about the money. Anyway I thank Mrs. Patterson for paying me. Truthfully, I told her that this is the first time I have received payment for my work and this is so much money. I was really surprised but happy because this money will help us. I gave the $30.00 to Tatay to help pay our tickets to America, $75.00 each one way and this takes care for each of us with food—six days and 7 nights—1 week. I felt a little sad to say good-bye to them. I told them, I wonder if we will meet again someday. They just smile and said, "Good-bye, Angeles," and said, "Maybe, if God is willing."

River St., Honolulu, Oahu, T.H.
May 10, 1927

It has been over a month, close to 2 months, since Manong Julian left for America and do you know Joe has not been around to visit? Anyway, that I do not care, if he does not want to come around and visit us anymore. Oh, another thing. I receive a letter from Manong Julian and I also receive a letter from Igsoo. Gosh, oh gee, I really was glad to receive 2 letters at once. Manong wrote a short letter. He says hello and sends his regards to Tatay and me. He says he's busy working, picking apricots, that's why he did not write right away. Anyway he says he'll send some money as soon as he can. And he says to tell Tatay that he is alright. They are working every day and they are working piecework. He says if you are a fast picker and fill up boxes, you can make money. He did not tell me how much he gets paid for a box. Anyway I'm glad he is working. In the meantime Tatay is working too at the pier as a stevedore and he gets $2.00 a day and he's saving his money too. Tatay is very careful how much he spend for our food and he always pay our rent first of the month.

River St., Honolulu, Oahu, T.H.
May 18, 1927

Rose came over to visit me. I feel sorry for her because she feel sad today because she says pretty soon we are going to leave for America and she is going to lose a friend. I said, "Rosie, we do not know when we are leaving, so please do not think about us leaving yet." So we start telling some stories. I tell her my girl-classmates beat the boys in our class in playing indoor baseballs today. We do not win too often and when we win, we are very happy about winning. And so Rose and I try to enjoy each other as much as we can and not try to think that one day Tatay and I will be leaving for America.

River St., Honolulu, Oahu, T.H.
May 22, 1927

Well, well, who do you think came today? None other than Mr. Joe Flores. I was sitting on the river stone wall, just thinking about Igsoo, my brother, Rosie. I was wondering if my brother will be able to send Tatay and me enough money to buy 2 tickets to go to California? As I look up I saw a car stop on the other side of the street with its top down and I saw about 4 or 5 young men in it. One jump down and I know him—it's Joe. I thought he came to visit me, but no—all he wanted was my brother's address in California, so I gave it to him. As soon as he wrote the address down he said good-bye to me, so I said, "Good-bye, Joe." I meant it, because I was thinking, this may be the last time I will see him. As they drove off, he wave good-bye to me and I wave back. I suppose he was ashamed to introduce me to his friends, 'cause I am not pretty at all, I look so plain—and I just clip my long black hair back. My hair combs to my waist-line, but I don't care. Joe does not like me anymore, I know that to be sure. I still have Felix—who I do not see too often, either.

River St., Honolulu, Oahu, T.H.
May 28, 1927

Oh, what fun we had today. Mrs. Pogue took the whole class-room and we went to Waikiki Beach. You know we nearly fill up the streetcar going to Waikiki Beach. We swam, we played base-ball against the boys and we lost, but we did not care, we had fun. Elsie, one of the girls, nearly drowned. She went out a lit-tle too far and when she was okay, she told us that she would not go swimming anymore, and Emmaline and I told her that she is just saying that now, because she was scared. We told her that she'll change her mind 'cause swimming is fun. Anyway we all had fun, even our teacher. We thanked Mrs. Pogue for an enjoy-able day at the beach. We came home at 4:30. Since I have been going to school here in Honolulu, I have been having so much fun, my schoolmates, my classmates are all so nice, even the teachers, and I used to be scared of having new teachers and meeting new classmates. I was wrong in thinking the way I did. Anyway, my head tells me to be careful, so I am going to listen to my mind. I remember Nanay, her words are in my head and I am going to remember them always.

River St., Honolulu, Oahu, T.H.
May 30, 1927

Today is "Memorial Day""and Emmaline Ku, my Hawaiian classmate, and I went to Waikiki Park where there are so many rides. There is the dipper. This is a very exciting ride also dan-gerous, you do not stand up when this is going because you can get thrown off, but I like it. I really hang onto the bar that's in front of us. Emmaline and I share the same seat and we really had fun riding the dipper. I think we spend more on dipper-rides. There are the ferris wheel, there is the merry-go-round, "the whip," also the "caterpillar." I met Rose and her mother. I did not expect to see them there, but anyway, I was really glad to see them. I introduce Emma to them and told them that she is my classmate. Rose and her mother were glad to meet Emma. Rose joined us in the rides, but Mrs. Caballero did not want to join us. She is afraid to ride those "things," as she calls them. She told us to go ahead and ride those things, she will stay on the ground, and she laugh and we laugh with her. Oh yes, I really had fun today.

118

River St., Honolulu, Oahu, T.H.
June 2, 1927

We had tests and examinations all this week and last week. Oh, I hope I pass all the tests, we would not know until tomorrow. My classmates and I are all waiting anxiously for tomorrow to come. We are wondering if we pass our tests or not. Rose came over this evening and she told me that they had their report cards and that she passed—she will be in the seventh grade next September 1927—I am so glad for her. She ask me again if we are really leaving Honolulu. I told her that Tatay and I will leave if Manong Julian will send us the money to buy the tickets. Tatay have some money but not enough to buy our tickets to go to America, but just the same, I am going to take my report card before the school close. I already told my teachers that I am leaving for America maybe next month. They were all glad for me, they say that they are going to miss me. I answered them that I am going to miss them too, they have really been nice to me and have help me with my schooling.

River St., Honolulu, Oahu, T.H.
June 3, 1927—at night

My classmates and I all passed to the sixth grade. I am so glad we all did. We all jump up and down and said, "Hoo-ray." The teacher did not mind our outburst. She knows how long we have waited (not too long, really) to know about our marks. I have 3 "A"s that's for spelling, arithmetic, and reading—on the other subjects, I received "B's & B+." I am so glad. And do you know I just receive a letter from Manong Julian today telling us that we can be sure of going to America next month. Oh, I am so happy. I can hardly wait to give Rose the good news. I know that she is going to feel sad. I wish that she will have the money to come with us because she wanted to come with us because of her stepfather—he is no good. Gee, when Tatay and I leave, we have to leave our trunk, my Singer sewing machine. Tatay bought the sewing machine for me, because I know how to sew clothes. I learned from Nanay, and we are also going to leave our phonograph and so many records. I do not think we will have the money to take them along.

River St., Honolulu, Oahu, T.H.
June 10, 1927—at night

Today was the last day of school—it is vacation time again, only for me, it is the last day of school here at Kaiulani School, because Tatay and I are leaving for America next month. I took my school report card and I said "good bye" to my teachers, my Principal Mrs. Frazer ask me if I am related to Robert San Jose, who took his report card too and he is leaving for America, too. I told Mrs. Frazer that we are not related to each other at all. Anyway, I said good-bye to all my classmates and they all wish me good-luck and "bon-voyage." I said "thank you." I felt kind of sad at leaving them, but I was happy, too, because I am going to America. I wonder how it is over there? My Igsoo says I will like it there very much; she and her mother and father have been there over 1 year already and do you know, she is not going to school anymore. She would rather work and earn some money than go to school. I am surprise at her.

River St., Honolulu, Oahu, T.H.
June 13, 1927

Oh, I am so glad Manong Julian sent us some money. I just received his letter this afternoon and enclosed is a money order for $45.00 and he said this is all he can send, so it's up to Tatay to make up the rest. Gosh, we need $105.00 more to buy 2 tickets. I do not know how much Tatay have, he'll never tells me how much money he has. I'll find out tonite when we talk. Right now he is not home yet, he's still working. He gets home at 5:30 tonight. Maybe we cannot go to America next month like we had planned. You know, I already went to The Dollar Steamship Co. I ask what steamer is leaving for America next month and they told me there is one "President Jefferson" steamer that is sailing on July 22 at 5 o'clock. I just finished telling Tatay that Manong Julian only was able to send us $45.00 and Tatay says by the first week we will know. Anyway Tatay said, "We will go to America next month. So you just do not worry." I felt so glad and relieved at knowing we really are going. I won't tell Manong or write him a letter until I bought the ticket or I think I had better write him and let him know I received the money, and also tell him the steamer's name and the date the ship sails for San Francisco next month.

River St., Honolulu, Oahu, T.H.
June 22, 1927

Rose and I try to spend as much time with each other now. She came over as soon as she finished helping her mother with the housework and the cooking. She had supper with me and Tatay. We had some fried fish and cooked rice and some vegetables and mangoes. We talked and laugh while we were washing the dishes—I was washing them and she was drying them. After we finish doing the dishes I told Tatay that we are going to sit on the river-brick wall outside, in front of the building. He said, "Go ahead." So, Rose and I just sat on the brick-wall and told each other stories. Rose knew we'll be leaving soon and she wished, oh, so very much, that she can go with us. We sat on the wall and talk and watch people and cars going by and children playing down the street. Before it got dark Rose says, "I have to go home now," so we said "good-night." She said "I'll come over tomorrow." I said "okay." I told Rose also that we are leaving for America next month. I'm sure it is going to be the 22 of July. I did not want to tell her, but I know that I have to. She looked down-hearted but she finally said, "I wish I can go to but I do not have the money." I answered her, "I wish I have the money to lend you, but I do not." So we walk silently for a while, then she said, "I'll come tomorrow, if I do not have anything more to do for my mother." I know the feeling, it is truly a lonely feeling, when a good friend goes away. I try not to feel for her too much because it is sad to leave a good friend behind.

River St., Honolulu, Oahu, T.H.
June 30, 1927

Rose and I went to the library to return the books. I did not read them all but it's best I return them now before I forget. Rose return the books she borrowed also. She told me, "I don't think I'll be going to the library after you're gone. I will feel sad. I feel sad now just thinking about it." Anyway we try and talk about something funny while we were walking home. We really enjoyed each other, you know. When my Igsoo left for America, I felt so sad and lonely again, but when Rose and I became friends, she kind of take most of the loneliness away.

River St., Honolulu, Oahu, T.H.
July 4, 1927

Rose, Tatay, and I went to a carnival this afternoon. We stayed until 6 o'clock and before we came home we went to the chop suey house because we got so hungry just walking around and riding all (Rose and I did, Tatay did not join us) the rides. Rose and I really had fun. When we reached home Rose and I took turn in taking a bath, we were sweaty, walking in the "hot sun" and besides the carnival was on the ground. We kick dust all around us as we walk about. Anyway I felt dirty and sticky and Rose felt the same way. Oh, Rose's mother knows she was going to spend the night with me, we asked her earlier before we left her house. She is going home tomorrow at seven after we finish supper. This is what I told Rose's mother and she told me it was alright, that she comes home at seven. So we have one whole day tomorrow to be together Rose have a very nice mother, her brother is nice too; but her stepfather is mean and bad, I do not like him at all. Rose does not like him at all.

River St., Honolulu, Oahu, T.H.
July 8, 1927

I washed all my dirty clothes today. All my good and nice dresses I am going to pack and take with me. Tomorrow I am going to iron them and pack them in my suitcase. Tatay has a small trunk and he can pack his things in it. We cannot bring much more. Gosh, I do not like to leave our big trunk. Nanay's and Tatay's picture, our group picture are in it, all my books and some of Nanay's Filipina dresses are in it, and many more things but I know we cannot bring it because we do not have the money to pay freight on it, the sewing machine, my Victrola and the Victor records. I like my Victrola and records very much. I love to sing and I play my records every day after school or when I am not playing outside with my landlady girls, 2 of them (Ah See and Ah Sam) or when I am not doing any homework, I play my records, when Rose comes over and play with me. Anyway, I'm bringing the things I want to bring. Oh, tonight, I'm cooking corn-beef for dinner. Tatay and I eat simple, with the corn-beef we have rice as always, with cook meat sometimes we have cooked vegetables.

River St., Honolulu, Oahu
July 18, 1927   **123**

I bought the tickets today early this morning. I was there in the office, just Tatay and me and 2 other ticket agent. The one that was selling the tickets asked me so many questions, I answered them the best I know how. He asked how many of us going? I said, "Just my father and I." Then he ask me our names, so I told him. He ask me if I was born in Honolulu. I said "no." I was born in Romblon, Philippines Islands, then he ask me what year I was born, what month, so I said, "I was born August 2, 1912" and as if to read what he was going to ask me I went ahead and told him that Tatay was born in Romblon, Philippine Island, on January 1, 1880. He just look at me and smiled. Then he ask me what Tatay and I are going to do in California, in San Francisco, 'cause that is where the ship is going to. So I told him, Tatay is going to work and I am going to continue going to school, that was very strong in my heart and in my mind to keep on going to school. And the man also asked me if we have relatives or friends in California. I answered that I have a brother, who lives in San Ramon, California, he is working there and we have friends in Salinas, too. And I told the man that my brother is going to meet us when we arrive in San Francisco. He finally gave me the tickets. Oh, I nearly forgot to write here, that a pregnant woman asked me to buy a ticket for her that she wanted to go to Stockton. So I bought her a ticket. I could not really understand her—why she was leaving her husband and her 3 children and she is going to have a baby? I did not question her and why she is doing what she is doing, I just bought her the ticket and told her to be at the pier early and she told me not to worry about her. She is going to take care of herself. And she thank me for bying the tickets for her; you see, she doesn't speak English very well, but, I think she knows how to make herself understood. I was thinking what if she is going to have a baby, when we are on the way? Oh, I hope not—

124
River St., Honolulu, Oahu, T.H.
July 19, 1927

Oh! what a surprise I have today. You know I went over to Rose's house this noon to tell her that I have bought tickets yesterday. And that Tatay and I are leaving Friday evening at 5 o'clock sharp and the steamer that we are going to be on is called President Jefferson. Rose cried and I cried too. She said she is going to miss me. I told her I'm going to miss her, too. I am just sorry that Tatay do not have the extra $75.00, she could be going with us to America. I told Rose that I will write when we reach America, in San Ramon, California, that is where Manong Julian is staying. When I came home from Rose's—oh, Rose walk home with me, because, it was still day-light—who do you think was waiting for me at the lane leading to the house. None other but Felix and Lew. This is the surprise I got this afternoon. So I introduce Rose to Felix and Lew. You can bet that I got excited, I was thrilled. Only Rose knew, maybe Felix and Lew know it too, I guess they can tell when a girl gets excited. Anyway, I tried not to show it. I shook hands with Lew first and Felix and oh boy! I just tingled all through me when he held my hand and he looked at me and I looked at him but I had to drop my gaze to our hands still clasping. For a minute there seems like we were the only ones there. Felix finally spoke and ask me (that's when I pulled my hand away, I was still tingling and my face felt warm, oh! what a feeling to like someone very much) if I was really leaving for California. I answered Felix, "Yes, my father and I are leaving July 22 at 5 o'clock in the afternoon, the ship, 'President Jefferson' leaves the pier at 5 o'clock," and I told him that my father and I will be at the pier at 2:30. I turned to Rose too when I was talking to Felix. I grab for her hand and gave it a squeeze, 'cause I saw her eyes were starting to water slightly and she just smiled at me and I told her I won't forget her and I said the same thing to Felix, and I just smiled at Lew. Oh, Lew is Felix's Porto-Rican friend, he is a nice guy. I see him at Aala Park on my way home from the library. When he sees me he waves to me, so I wave back. I don't know how long we stood outside. You know, Felix took my left **125** hand and held it all the while we were talking. Rose and Lew just talked on as if they have not noticed that Felix took my hand and was holding it—I like that. I know he wanted to kiss me. I can tell when he looked at me. Anyway, I told Felix that my father and I are going to see a good movie at the Palama Threatre on the 21st of July at night. I told Felix that it's the last night we are going to spend here in Honolulu; Felix told me, also, that he is going to be there, that he is going to look for me, so, I said to him, okay, I'll be there. He does not know my father. He has not met him or even seen him. Rose wanted to go and see the show with me but she could not. There was something she had to do for her mother. "Gee, Angeles, I wanted to go see the movie with you because it is the last time we are going to be together, but I cannot, I must not disobey my mother." So, I say, "It is my wish too, hoping that you can see the movie with Tatay and me, but whatever your mother tells you, you have to obey." Felix finally said, "We have to leave now, but I'll see you Thursday night." He then took hold of my right hand and face me he look at me and said, barely a whisper, "I'll see you Thursday night at the Palama Theatre" and he squeezed both of my hands and let them go, and I said to him, "I will see you at the movie house." He smiled and both him and Lew walked away. Rose and I stood there until they were out of sight. Twice Felix turned to waved at me so I waved back. It is so exciting and thrilling when you like someone and that someone like you too. Rose and I talked until it was time for her to go home. Oh, we talked about Felix and how long I have known him. She was surprised that he has not kissed me yet. I told Rose that we have not been alone at all, like I told her, that it was for the best, I think, that we could not be alone together and she smiled at me, as if I read her thoughts. I told her I will not give in to him, much as I like him. I will not be like my friends. Some of them have babies and they have to marry someone that they do not love. I told Rose we have to marry first before we do anything. Rose said, "Okay, Angeles, I understand."

126

Our last night here on River St., Honolulu, Oahu, T.H.

July 21, 1927

At last Fel kissed me tonight, his first and farewell kisses. We were sweethearts for a year and a half and he just kissed me tonight. We kissed a long time and I pushed him away and ran out of the alley we were in. I did not turn to say good-bye. He must have a surprise look on his face, I wondered afterwards. Anyway, I walk into the house. Tatay just look at me. (I stayed outside for just a few minutes to stop shaking—then I walked in.) You see, Tatay and I went to the Palama to see the moving picture tonight, the last one we want to see in the Palama Theatre, here in Honolulu. Tomorrow we are sailing away to California—to America, you know. I feel so excited and happy that we are leaving for America. When the moving picture was finished, Tatay and I started to walk home. I noticed someone following, but was far back from Tatay and me. I have a feeling that it was Felix. I think Tatay knew someone was following us but he did not say anything, we just walked. Finally we reached the house. I told Tatay I wanted to stay outside for a while. He said, "Okay." So, I stayed outside by the alley way. I stayed in view so he can see me. He finally came to me and took my hand and we walk to another alley—just a tenement away, because where we were, people come in and out, we can be seen. By the time we stopped walking, I was trembling, I think. I was excited and thrilled to have Felix so close to me that I was scared, too. Anyway, he kissed me. It was really thrilling being kissed by Felix. Since the first time I saw him I wondered how it would feel to be held in his arms and be kissed by him. Now I know.

It's very thrilling and I love it, but tomorrow I am leaving that all behind. I do not feel sad about leaving him. I think it was meant to be that way. Felix will easily find another girl to be his sweetheart. I think too, that he has many sweethearts, because he is good-looking and he must be 18 or 19 years old. He never told me how old he is. He knows I am 14 years old, 'cause Manong Julian told Willie Sarmiento how old I am, and of course, Willie told Felix. When I got into the house I wondered about Felix, I wondered if he is going to the pier tomorrow to say good-bye to me because I pushed him away from me and ran out and not say anything at all to him. I felt a little ashamed, but my getting scared of what might happen made me do what I thought was best to do, get away while I can. Anyway, tomorrow will let me know how things are.

On the President Jefferson Steamer,
sailing out of Honolulu Harbor, The Pacific Ocean
July 22, 1927

We are out of Honolulu Harbor now. I stood out on the railing as long as I can. I waved good-bye to Fel and Rosie as long as I can see them. The band played "Aloha Oe." It was sad for the ones left behind, like Rose. She cried and I cried while on the pier, about half an hour. Fel just held my hand for a long time. Rose was close to me, she held my left hand while Felix held my right hand. We had a chance to talk to each other before Tatay and I boarded the ship. Felix told me—oh first, I might write here, Felix bought me lot of leis, my left arm was full of leis and he put one beautiful one around my neck. He bought leis for Tatay too and Tatay said thank you to Felix and he just smiled back at him. Rose bought me some leis, too, 3 of them, one she put around my neck, she put the other on my left arm, and one she put over Tatay's arm. Rose talked to Tatay for a while, while I talked to Felix. Felix was telling me that I was a funny girl—because I left him the way I did. He did not expect me to ran away like I did. I told him the truth, I just thought something was going to happen, so I had to do what I did, "just to get out of your arms and ran." Felix laughed. He had a nice-man-laugh. Then I went on to tell him that after acting the way I did "I did not think that you would come today to say good-bye to me but you did come and I'm glad." He look at me, I at him, and he squeezed my hand. He wanted to kiss me and hold me in his arms but he smiled instead and said, "Good-bye, Angeles, my funny girl. I wish you and your father good luck in America. Maybe someday I will go there, too." He squeezed my hand and was holding them tight. Pretty soon Rose come back to us and Tatay was close by watching us and the porter on the ship, 'cause anytime now he will give the order to come aboard. I hug Rose. She was crying, inside I was crying for her. I am just sorry Tatay did not have the money to lend her for the fare. Soon we were told to go aboard, so I said good-bye again to Felix and Rosie. The band had already started playing—I hate to leave them but I have to. I carried my suitcase, Tatay had to carry a small trunk, and we walk the plank. The steward guided us to our quarters on the steerage department. We had to go down below on the steerage hold—the tail end of the ship, we had bunk beds. The steward told us to pick out the spot we want. Tatay and I picked our bed and put our trunk and suitcase under the bunk beds. As soon as we put our things away, Tatay and I went up to the deck, the whistle or horn or whatever it is called, made a big loud noise to let us know the ship will be leaving soon, and that all people sailing must be on board. I leaned on the rail. I saw Felix and Rose. I waved to them. I could see Rose's tears. I smiled at her and to Felix too, then the second whistle blow and the ship start moving. I could smell the engine and the oil. The band is now playing "Aloha Oe," it is really a sad song. I can just imagine how Rose is feeling. The ship is really moving now. I can only see the buildings small at that, and then I just saw Diamond Head, soon it was gone. The wind was blowing and I was feeling kind of cold.

Diary

Tatay has gone down before I did. I went down below, too. It
was 6 o'clock. The steward brought us our food. We had stew
and rice, it was good. I ate all my food, Tatay did too. After we
ate I covered my bunk with a blanket. I went to the bathroom
and clean up and went to bed. Tatay did too, since there was
nothing else to do. The others talk among themselves and tell   **129**
stories and some played cards. Me, I write, I am writing this,
oh, I'll try and write as much as I can of this trip we're taking.
I think there are 36 of us here in steerage, there are 8 couples,
man and wife, 8 unmarried woman, 1 pregnant woman (she is
the one I bought a ticket for), 2 young girls like myself, I make
3 young girls, two of the couples are the parents to the 2 young
girls and 3 small boys belonging to one of the married couples
too. And the rest are all single young man in their twenties or
over—and we are all Filipinos, most of the young men are Ilo-
canos. I think I will write again tomorrow. I am tired, I had better go to sleep. I can really hear the ship's engine going full blast.
The noise and smell did not affect me. Oh we have shower
rooms and toilet facilities.

Out on the Pacific Ocean, the Big Pacific Ocean
Saturday morning, July 23, 1927

I got up early, about 6 o'clock this morning. I went to the bathroom, combed my hair, and cleaned up and brushed my teeth.
I thought I had better use the bathroom before the people all
wake up and want to use the bathroom at the same time. I got
dressed. Tatay got up early too, I think, then the steward
brought us our breakfast. We all had fried eggs and toast, coffee, milk, and oatmeal. I ate my fried eggs and toast and a cup
of coffee. About 9 o'clock I went on deck. I told Tatay I would
be alright. Some of the women got sick sea-sick, one of them
could not get out of bed. To me, it seems you have to fight the
sea-sickness off, by not letting it get you down. That is why I
got up early, and from today on until we reached San Francisco

I am going to get up early. I went to sleep with the ship engine going full blast. I think the hum of the engine put me to sleep. Anyway, since Tatay and I got on board the ship, I just feel all excited, and I feel the same way when I got up this morning. I just feel wonderful. I am writing this on my lap in bed, this way, no one will read and watch over my shoulder. When I finished my breakfast, since I was not going to wash any dishes, I went up on deck to watch the ocean wave—the sea was blue and calm and all I can see around me is the blue Pacific Ocean. There was somebody on deck besides myself. I think he was keeping his eye on me. Must be someone working on the ship. I think he wants to make sure I do not do anything foolish on deck. I went to the ship's railing. I hung onto the railing and look all around me. I feel so good and excited. I look up on second floor of the ship. I saw people up there, ladies and men together, and I know they were watching me too, 'cause I was the first one they saw come up from the steerage department. The wind was blowing but I did not feel cold at all. I like the breeze. I stayed on deck for 1½ hours, I think. I don't know how long I was on deck, when 6 young men came up too but they went to the other side, opposite from where I was. I like that because I did not feel like talking to anyone. I just want to be by myself and look at the beautiful blue ocean. I did not see any whales or any kind of fish. About 5 o'clock this afternoon I went up on deck but I did not stay up long because we have dinner or supper at 6 o'clock. We had a nice supper, I like it. We had roast chicken, with buttered toasts, gravy, mashed potatoes, and peas. About 7 o'clock P.M. I went back up on deck and it was kind of dark and the night air was cold. I look up at the second class people. I heard music, so there was dancing upstairs. The upstairs deck was lighted up. There were other people about 3, they were talking among themselves, telling jokes, because they were laughing. I stayed by myself. They were the young men I saw downstairs. Anyway, I'm glad that not one of them tried to make conversation with me. I

130

hung or hold onto the railing. All I see is ocean all around me, the moon and stars were out by now. Though I was alone I did not feel lonely. I was happy with the thought that Tatay and I will be in America in the next 5 days. I stayed up on the deck for a while—until I start feeling a little cold. I do not have a coat or a jacket. I wanted to stay up longer so I can hear and listen to the music coming from the top deck. I was thinking they must be having a wonderful time, dancing. You know, I just like to dance and sing. The orchestra was playing, "Bye, Bye Blackbird," "Drifting and Dreaming," "Five foot-two," and also "Who's Sorry Now." I was singing on deck, I was singing softly to myself. I do not think anyone heard me at all. Tatay told me that some women got sea-sick, they could not get out of bed at all. The ship's doctor told the sick women to just stay in bed and not try to walk around.

Out on the Pacific Ocean
Sunday morning, July 24, 1927

Our third day on the Pacific Ocean. I went up on deck right after I ate breakfast. I told Tatay I'll be alright. He told me to be very careful. I said, "I will." No one was on deck when I went up, I was all by myself. So I prayed. I had my back towards the upstairs deck. I thank God, our Father in Heaven to keep us all safe, bring us safely to America. I thank God for all that He has done for us, too. The morning was beautiful—I looked all around me, everything look just beautiful, the ocean looked so blue and I do not see anything on the horizon. All I can see is the ocean meeting the sky. I can see the big ship moving forward. You can tell from the waves it makes as it pushes itself thru the water and the rear of the ship well, that is where all waves says good-bye to the ship. Oh, we had pancakes for breakfast and coffee 1 glass of orange juice—that was nice. I put all the butter that was on my plate on my pancakes—the pancakes tasted very good with lots of butter and syrup.

Out on the Pacific Ocean
Monday morning, July 25, 1927

We just finished eating our dinner or supper, I call it, but the steward that brings our food calls supper dinner, so dinner it is. I'm writing this on my lap. I am in bed. I ask Tatay what time it is before I got in my bed, and Tatay told me the time was 7 o'clock. I went up on deck but it was cold up there, so I came back down here and just get in bed and do some writing. As I am writing, the people here, the older ones are telling stories, while the young men talk about their sweethearts back in Honolulu. Some of them says when he makes enough money and save he will go back to his sweetheart in Honolulu and get married. You know, I had to stop writing a while to listen to them. They cannot see me because I covered my bunk bed with a white sheet. I ask the steward if I can do that, he said I can. So Tatay climbs up on to the top bunk bed. Tatay did not mind climbing up there. I sit in bed and I can listen to their stories and we are all anxiously waiting for the day we reach San Francisco and that's about four days away. And that's going to be Friday morning. Oh, I can hardly wait for that day to come around. At last I am going to be living in America, a great land. I am sure I am going to like living in America. I just know America from what I have learned in school, from the fourth grade teachers I had in Kaiulani School, teaching me geography and history. Otherwise I won't have been able to know anything about America and its 48 States—and also about the other countries in this world of ours. Yes, education is a wonderful thing to know and have. Oh, I just write here the young men here do not speak to me, by this, I mean they do not start conversation with me. They just say good-morning or good-night to me and so I answer them the same way, so they do not think of me as a stuck-up-person. I overheard one of them say, "She does not talk much," meaning "me." Anyway, I am not interested in making conversation with any young man. To me I know why they do not talk to me. I am not a pretty girl. I look plain, I do not use lipstick—not yet, anyway; my hair is long, I just comb it straight back and clip my hair and just let it fall down to my waist, so I am not pretty so the young man do not talk to me. I do not care. I cannot help but wonder if I will meet a young man someday, who will love me for the way I look? We shall see, huh? I am going to sleep now, I feel sleepy, must be around 10 o'clock now. There is one woman here who is a wife and a mother and she has been sick since the first day we were out to sea. The woman could not get out of bed, she gets dizzy. I feel sorry for her. I hope that she will be alright when we reach San Francisco. We have four nights more and 3 days, because the steward told us we are going to arrive in San Francisco Friday morning, I really feel so excited and happy when I think of "Friday."

Out on the Pacific Ocean
Wednesday night at 7:30 o'clock
July 27, 1927

I'm in bed early tonight, it is too cold to stay on deck. I went on the deck as soon as we ate our supper; the ocean looked dark and beautiful especially where moon light shine on the water, the water looked calm. I see waves going back. I think it is because we are going forward, the ship, I mean and tonight is the last we have on the ocean. The steward told us at supper time when he brought our food that we are arriving in San Francisco tomorrow morning—early in the morning. Tatay and I, so does the other passengers are all excited and happy to hear about arriving in San Francisco in the morning. The young single men made the loudest noises of excitement. I just kept quiet, I gave a prayer of thankful to our Father in Heaven and I think Tatay did too. Tatay and I put our things in the suitcase, I put the one good skirt and blouse I have (I have no sweater) out on top my bunk bed at the foot-end of the bed. Tatay told me he'll wear the same clothes tomorrow that he is wearing now. He said his clothes are clean, so he is not worried about changing clothes. I told Tatay to wake me up early at 4:30 o'clock if I am not awake. I want to use the bathroom before the others wake up. He said, okay. Tatay and I are early-to-rise. As I am sitting here writing this, I feel oh so excited. My stomach feels funny. I can hardly wait for tomorrow to be here. We are all going to be in San Francisco Bay tomorrow morning, to see San Francisco at last. I have heard so much of San Francisco. I hope and pray that Manong Julian has not forgotten about Tatay and me, and that he will be at the pier tomorrow morning to meet us.

In San Francisco Bay
Thursday morning, July 28, 1927

San Francisco at last. The steamer just coming into the bay, there are many small boats around us. I won't be able to write any more until we arrive at our destination, San Ramon, that is where we are going to stay for a while, that is where Manong Julian is working and I think Tatay is going to work there too. A beautiful sight met my eyes this morning when I went up on deck to watch and see the boats and tug-boat and the ferry-boats, these boats was explained to me. The sun was shining on the buildings of San Francisco and the buildings just glitter like "gold" in sunlight and that truly made a beautiful sight. I was really thrilled and so excited. I think that is why it is called "The Golden Gate of San Francisco." Oh, I'm so happy, I told Tatay so, and he just smile that knowing smile of his. He does not talk much. Anyway, I shall write more later on. I have to put you away now. I have to go to the purser Office and answer some questions that concerns our trip (Tatay's and mine) here to California.

San Ramon, California
Friday night, July 29, 1927

This is the first chance I have to do some writing. We arrive here about 5 o'clock yesterday. Manong Julian was at the pier to meet Tatay and me. We did not get out of the steamer until 10:30 A.M. I was in the purser's office for half hour maybe less time, maybe 20 minutes, but anyway, the purser ask me questions, like he ask me, why Tatay and I came to California. I answered, "My father came here to work" and I told him I wanted to continue my studies here. Oh the "purser" asked quite a few other questions. He asked me if my mother was with us. I said, "No." I went on to tell him that Nanay went back to the Philippines. He asked me if there is anybody else in my family. I said I have a brother, living here in California and who is meeting us this morning. He also asked our address, so I gave him Manong Julian's address, Harlan Ranch, San Ramon, California. Oh, he also asked how old I am, I said I am 14 years old but on August 2, I will be fifteen years old, and he asked Tatay's age, too. Tatay was 46 years old. The purser was still writing and he finish by telling me that our suitcases will be searched and he told me to tell my father the steward will let us know when we can leave the steamer. It was not long that we have to wait. Soon the steward said we can leave and he directed where to go to get our suitcases check over. And then we were free to go, as they finish searching one's suitcases that person's allowed to leave. As Tatay and I were walking down the gang plank I look down. There was Manong Julian. I turned around to tell Tatay—Tatay just nodded his head and smiled. Gee, I have so much to write here. First I must tell you Manong Julian took us to a friend of his, a family, who lives in San Francisco. Her husband told us to stay a while and have lunch with them, because it is close to lunch time. Manong Julian told the man and his wife that he is going to take us to Market Street, he did not say why. Anyway, the man of the house told us, they are going to wait for us for lunch. So we left, Manong Julian went into a store at Kearney Street, a man store, he bought Tatay a heavy sweater, he told Tatay that's the best he can do now until he has more money later on to buy him a better one, like a jacket. Manong Julian was wearing a leather jacket but they cost a little bit more. From the man's store we went straight to Market Street. Gosh! it's a wide, wide street—we crossed it. We were walking on the left. We passed a clothing store, I noticed the name. It is called emporium store. I noticed a coat, a very soft brown plaid with a brown fur collar. It was on a manequin (I don't know if I spell the word right) and I like it very much. I look at the coat and Manong Julian ask me if I like the coat. I was looking at and I answered him that I do like the coat very much. So, Manong Julian, Tatay, and me went in and the store lady came to us and ask if she can help us and so I spoke up and say that I'd like to try the brown-plaid-coat that is on display at the window? She said, "Certainly." She came back with the coat and said, "This is small, but I am certain that it will fit you," and it did. The length was just right and so Manong Julian ask how much is the coat. The lady told him that the price of the coat is $35.00. I didn't think that Manong Julian had enough money to pay for the coat, but he did. I thank Manong Julian and gave him a great big hug. Oh, I was so thrilled with my coat. I wore it out. I told the lady not to wrap it, I am going to wear it. She just smiled and said "thank you," and we left and we went back to the house we came to from the pier. We ate there, the people won't let us leave without eating, So, Manong Julian bought some cooked meat (pork and chicken) in Chinatown, which was close by, it was walking distance. And the lady cooked some rice and vegetables. We thanked the nice people. Manong Julian explain to them we have a long ways to go. We left. From the house we took a cab to take us to the ferry-boat terminal. This is the first time I have been on a ferry-boat. And this is the boat I saw when the big ship was coming into the bay this morning. It carried people and cars from one side of the bay to the other side of the bay. You know every thing is so thrilling and wonderful and I feel oh, so happy and wonderful inside. It feels so good to be alive and well and to be here in America. I like everything around me, the people, the wonderful windows of stores where they sell so many beautiful and wonderful things. And when we got off from the ferry-boat, we took a train. We passed many little towns. Soon we stopped at San Lorenzo, and Manong Julian took us to a house and it was Jose and Esperanza's place. I was glad to see them, also Rosario and Betty. We had supper with them and as soon as I, Sayong, and Betty finish washing the dishes and pots, we put them away and we all sat around and we were all enjoying each other company. We talked and laughed for hours, and Mr. Materiano, Esperanza's compadre, told Tatay and Manong Julian that he will take us to San Ramon tomorrow. He says that he is not working tomorrow, so he can bring us and so for tonight, we sleep at Esperanza's. Tatay and Manong Julian will sleep on the floor, Esperanza have a mattress that they can sleep on and they'll use the blankets that Manong Julian had bought for Tatay and me, and me, I sleep with Sayong and Betty. Oh, we had fun together. We went to the bedroom, took off our shoes, and sat on the bed and tell what we had been doing—and we can hear Tatay and the others talking and laughing. Before we know it, it was 12 o'clock, so we all said "good-night." Before I went to bed, I had to wash up. I used cold water and it was cold, the water doesn't feel warm like in Honolulu, and I had to pump the water up. This is very new to me. I have not pump water before, but still, I feel excited about some new ways here in America. We have to heat some water to get "hot" water. Anyway, I just use cold water to wash my face arms and legs. Sayong and Betty did not clean up— they say it's too cold to wash up. After I cleaned up I combed my long hair and braid it, so it would not tangle when I wake up in the morning. Sayong and Betty just watch me. I finally went in bed with them. I sleep in the middle, and they asked me "Do you always do that?" I said, "Yes." As if reading what I was thinking, they went on to tell me that they do clean up sometimes, not all the time. I told them I have to clean up every night before I go to sleep, it is a habit I have learned since my mother taught me when I was a little girl. And so this morning Mr. Materiano brought us here to San Ramon. You know, where we are? On Harlan Ranch a few miles out of San Ramon, this place is out in the country. And you know what, San Ramon has 1 small post-office, 1 grocery store and general store and that's San Ramon. I expected to see a city but I was wrong. Oh well, there's nothing we can do about it. Mr. Santiago talk to us and told us that I help his wife in the kitchen, like washing the dishes and the pots, sweep the kitchen floor, and clean the dining room table after every meal. This way I get free, 3 meals a day. Tatay or Manong Julian did not have to pay for my meals. To this, I agree. I am getting sleepy, I will write more tomorrow or the next day. Tomorrow, I am going to look around.

138

Harlan Ranch, San Ramon, California
Tuesday, August 2, 1927

I am 15 years old today, and I feel very happy about becoming fifteen years old and I am glad that I am here in California now, but you know, this place is so far away from the city. When Manong Julian and Tatay, The "Boss" who is Mr. Santiago, and another older man as old as Tatay, I think, went to work. They come home to eat lunch. After we eat lunch, I finish washing the pots and dishes and cleaning the table. I am left to myself 'cause Aling Edad takes a nap at 1 o'clock, so I look around the place. I saw some fruit trees like peach trees, apricot trees, there are a few apple trees and oh, there are some pear trees and walnut trees, too. There's a big house near by, "The Harlan" house. Nobody is living in it, it looks kind of "spooky." I just went around it once and then I went to the "bunk house" and got Manong Julian's ukulele because I can play "by ear" only, and came back 'cause there's a big tree near Aling Edad's house and there's a spot where I can sit down and play the ukulele. And from this I can see the highway and the few cars that go by. Further ahead I can see hills and white houses here and there, and I was thinking, we are so far away from the city I kind of feel a little sad and lonely, but I said to myself, I must not feel lonely, so I started singing. I think I sang all the songs I know and I accompany myself on the ukulele. I sang "Hawaiian Love," "I Want to Go Where You Go," "Me and My Shadow," "I'm Sitting on Top of the World," "I'm All Alone," "Who's Sorry Now," "Moonlight and Roses," "Bye, Bye Blackbird," "Linger Awhile," "Five-foot-Two." I stop singing for a while and just looked and looked all around me and far ahead of me; and I thought of my friends in Honolulu and I thought of my Igsoo. I have not written to her yet. So tomorrow, right here I am going to write Rose, Igsoo, and to Felix and my classmates that gave me their address, also to Ah Sam, my land-lady's daughter. I better stop writing, 'cause, I'm sure, Aling-Edad will call me to do something when she starts cooking. Oh, I want to write here, the mornings here are colder than in Honolulu, but I do not mind it—I like it, I like the cold mornings, but towards the afternoon the days starts to get warm it gets hot out. These past few days it has been hot. It's a good thing there is a big tree here. This is where I sit and write— and I sit here and sing, too. When I have breakfast, I like the toasted buttered raisin bread very much with my coffee. This is what I like every morning nothing else. Our lunch and supper are typical Filipino cooking. Aling Edad, cooked sinigang Isda last night for supper. I do not know what she will cook for tonite.

San Ramon, California, Harlan's Ranch
Wednesday, August 3, 1927

Gosh, I wrote so many letters, my hand is tired. I have written 5 letters, I sat under the tree, I did not sing or play the ukulele this afternoon. I did not have the time. I want to finish writing all the letters I have in mind to write so I can mail them out tomorrow. Aling-Edad asked me what I am doing so I told her I am writing letters to my friends, and she smiled. I don't know what she was thinking when she smiled at me, but I just smiled back and start my letter writing. I wrote first of all to my Igsoo and told her just where we are. And I wrote to Rose and Felix, I wrote to Emma, I wrote to Mrs. Bessinger and Mrs. Patterson, they were very good to me, I shall always remember them. I hope they will answer my letters, all of them. When I finish writing, I put the letters in my bed in the bunkhouse and I'll mail them by putting them in the mailbox, by the side of the highway and raise the red-flag up, so the mailman will know that there are letters in the mailbox. It's different this rural mail deliveries here in America. In the city there are big mail boxes.

San Lorenzo, California
August 27, 1927

Tatay and I are staying for a while with Jose and Esperanza here in San Lorenzo. We are going to work here, in the Japanese carnation nursery. Mr. Materiano got us this work. We are going to pay board and room to Jose & Esperanza. Tatay gets paid $2.50 and I get only $1.00 a day, because I am only 15 years old and I am a minor. And I only help arrange the carnation flowers and put them in water. We cut carnation in the mornings and I thin out the carnation buds in the afternoon until 4 o'clock, that's the time we stop work. We start 8 o'clock in the morning. Tatay works somewhere in the nursery. He does heavier work. I do not know how long this work will last for Tatay and me. I'm glad and Tatay is, too, that we can work here. We are grateful to Mr. Materiano. Esperanza them were glad we would stay with them, help some on the groceries. Anyway Rosario, Betty, and myself are glad to be here, we have fun together. I wash the dishes and pots and the girls dry them. We talk most of the time when I come home from work. I take a bath first the hot water is ready, there is a bath house outside where Esperanza has heated the water, so Tatay and myself can take a bath before we eat supper.

Don't misunderstand me, I take a bath first and when I finish Tatay takes his bath. I felt good and clean after I have taken a bath. While Tatay was taking his bath I have a chance to comb my hair. I don't like wrapping up my hair when I am eating. I just comb my hair good and I brought both sides up to my head and stuck a comb on my head to hold my hair with my combs. **141** After we eat our supper and the dishes and pots are all washed, cleaned, and dried up and put away, Sayong, Beatrice, and me we just talk. Oh, we sang some songs we know. There's a new song we heard and we are trying to learn it. It is called "Me and My Shadow." We go to sleep at 10 o'clock, 'cause we all have to get up early tomorrow. I won't be writing much while I'm here because Rosario and Beatrice will be asking too many questions and I do not want them to know I have a book like this. I know they would like to read what I have written down in these pages, which I do not want them to know.

San Lorenzo, California
Friday, September 2, 1927

You know what? I have a big "boil" on my left shoulder. I got a sore spot on my shoulder a few days ago and I did not pay any attention to it. This morning I was really hurting. I told my boss I was going to the doctor and when I get home from the doctor, I will come to work. She told me it was alright. And do you know that Mr. Materiano took me to his doctor. I know why. Mr. Materiano is in love with me and he is doing everything he can for me. I went with him, and his doctor saw me. The doctor lensed the boil. First I felt the doctor cleaning or putting some kind of solution and then lensed it and he scooped out the boil and put some medication on it and put a bandage on it. He told Mr. Materiano to bring me back next week Tuesday, Sept. 6. Materiano told my father everything. My father told him he will get his money back and he thanked Materiano for the things he had done and that he appreciate everything he did.

San Lorenzo, California
Tuesday, September 6, 1927

I just got back from the doctor. He says, by next week, I should be alright, nothing to worry about. I went to work as soon as I have changed into my work clothes. I worked 2 hours this morning from 8 o'clock to 10 o'clock. It took Mr. Materiano 30 minutes to get to San Leandro and to the doctor's office, and when we got back home, Esperanza already have lunch cooked, so we had lunch. I told Esperanza to tell my father I had lunch already and that I am going to tell him about my last visit to the doctor tonight. You know, we have been here more than 1 week now. Maybe I do not have much more days to work here. I told Tatay what the doctor had told me. He paid Materiano what we owe him.

San Ramon, California
September 12, 1927

Tatay and I are back here in San Ramon. Jose Romero, Esperanza's husband, brought us back here this morning. I did not want to stay in San Lorenzo anymore because Materiano was really getting crazy. I was sleeping between Rosario and Betty but yet he kiss me. I was sound asleep. I felt someone holding my face and I was being kissed. I shoved him off and screamed. I woke up the whole house. I got so scared, I was shaking, I was crying. I was angry at Rosario and Betty, for letting him kissed me, they could have waken me up. I'm afraid of men. I think Materiano thought just because he helped me, he thinks he can kiss me, just like that. I know that he "loves me," he told me that many times and I just met him last month. I told him that I don't love him, I just want to be a friend. Anyway, we are back here and I'll try and pick tomatoes with Tatay and Manong Julian.

San Ramon, California
September 13, 1927

I just finished answering letters—5 of them. I was so happy to receive the letters. Manong Julian had kept them for me. I sat at my usual spot here near the kitchen to read my letters and answered them. It was so good to hear from my friends in Honolulu and I received a letter from Igsoo. They are still living in Salinas, but when her father finish working there they are going to move to Stockton sometimes in October. I received a very nice letter from Rose in Honolulu. She miss me she says—I miss her too. As for Igsoo, she wrote or rather I received a 1 page letter from her. She was very glad that Tatay and I are here now in San Ramon, Calif. She wrote me that she is working, but she would rather work in the pool room because she has more fun. She says also she hopes to meet me in Stockton and that we can be together again, like we use to in Honolulu and Waipahu. Anyway, I finished writing all five letters and I'll put them in the mail-box tomorrow. You know what, I missed the buttered raisin toast for breakfast. I just like the toast with coffee, they tasted so good together. While Tatay and I were staying with Esperanza in San Lorenzo, we did not have any. I guess Esperanza and her family do not like raisin bread. Oh, I am to work out in the fields starting day after tomorrow. I am going to pick tomatoes. I am going to help Manong Julian and Tatay because the work is piecework. You get paid according to how many boxes you fill up. So if I can help, we'll make a little more money.

San Ramon, California
September 15, 1927

I picked tomatoes today and did I get a scare of my life? I swear, I won't pick tomatoes again. I started with my first bush of tomatoes. I picked all the tomatoes that I see on the outer side of the tomato bush, but there were ripe tomatoes inside the bush, so I lift up the bushy part of the plant. As I did so I saw a snake around the plant, it was a big one. I drop the bushy leaves and ran out. I told my brother that there's a snake in the tomato bush I was working on, and I told Tatay and Manong Julian I won't

144 work out in the tomato fields anymore, not where there are snakes around. I'd rather work in the kitchen even if I just work for my meals. I told them I'm sorry that I could not earn money to help them out. Tatay told me it's alright if I do not work.

Harlan Ranch, San Ramon, California
Wednesday, October 5, 1927

Oh, I met the most wonderful man today from Stockton and he is a salesman for made-to-order-suits. Gee, he is really someone I could fall in love with, if he could only fall in love with me, too; but I have my doubts. No good-looking fellow like him could or would fall in love for a "country-mouse" like me. Beside, I'm homely, I have no business falling in love with a "city-bred-fellow." Here's how this young man I'm writing about happen to wander to this camp. There's a fellow that use to come here before and he went to Stockton to live. He is the one that brought these men. I say "these men" because there were three of them in all and it was "Mr. Villamore" that introduce me to him and to the other fellow. When I first saw "Ray" I did not fall in love with him—yet, I just look him over. I bet he was doing the same. Anyway, the others were heading towards the house where Aling Edad lives while Ray and I were walking slowly behind. We talked, he asked if I am a newcomer here in the States and I answered "Yes." He asked me how I like it here, I answered, "I like it fine here," and I asked him how long has he live here in the States. "Oh," he says, "about 7 years, I came here straight from Manila," and that he is Tagalog. I told him, I'm Visayan, from Romblon. I was born there but I grew up in the Hawaiian Islands. We finally reached the kitchen and sat with the others. Aling Edad gave them some lemonade, 'cause it was a warm day. And we sang songs. Aling Edad told them I can sing. I tried to get out of it, but could not. So I finally sang and accompanied myself with my brother's "uke." Oh, the men sang too. Ray had a nice voice, he sang a Tagalog love song. I don't know if he meant the song for me, I hope so. Anyway, while the others were busy talking he looked at me and I looked at him, and gosh, that's when it happened, seems like I saw stars explode in my mind. I had to close my eyes, so he won't see how I felt. My heart was beating like a hammer. I did my best to hide my true feeling. I was speechless for a minute. Pretty soon I look at him, he was smiling so I smiled back.

Aling Edad told them that she thinks the men would not be interested in ordering suits. And so Mr. Villamore and Ray and his friends decide to leave because they have a long ways to go. Before they left, Ray told me of a benefit dance sometimes the end of October. He asked if I can attend the dance? I answered him, "I don't think so, because we are living far from Stockton." Deep in my heart I wish I could be at the dance—it would be so wonderful to dance with him. We all shook hands. He was the last I shook hands with and he squeezed my hand ever so gently. He held it for a few seconds and that did something to this heart of mine. It's all I can do to keep calm. I smiled at him and he said to me, "Hope we will meet again." I felt sad some- how when they turn and walk down the road. He turned once to wave good-bye and I wave back. I heard the start of the car and then they were on their way to Stockton. I watch the car until it became just a speck and then it was out of sight. I ask myself will I see him again? Just Fate knows the answer. I believe in Fate. I just heard his first name "Ray" so his full name must be Raymond. I have really fallen in love with him. I wonder if he has a "sweetheart," he must have a sweetheart—a good- looking-fellow like him could not help and have a sweetheart. Anyway, I have fallen in love with him secretly. No one will know except what I write here. Even "Ray" won't know. You know I am writing this on top the bunk bed. Manong Julian thinks I am writing letters. I did write some letters, 3 of them. I do not want him to know. No one is going to see or read this book, except someday, when I die, I suppose someone is going to read what I have written here. I hope when I go to sleep tonight, I hope I'll dream of him. I would like that very much. I just hope that they will be beautiful dreams of him.

146

Harlan Ranch, San Ramon, California
Thursday, October 6, 1927

I did dream of Ray last night and they were wonderful dreams—I dreamed that Ray plays the violin. I wonder? if he can really play the violin. He looks just as handsome in my dreams as he was the last time I saw him. Ray was in my thoughts all day. I tried oh so much not to let anyone around here know, even my dad and my brother, that I have something in my mind. It is a good thing that they are working all day. Aling Edad and myself are the only ones homes and I don't see her until it's time to cook dinner or supper. I see her at breakfast time and lunch time too. At 3:30 in the afternoon I start to heat the water for the men's bath. The water has to be real hot and ready when the men come home from work because they take a bath before they come in the kitchen to eat. I don't go to work but I take a bath every day, I take one before the men comes home. The days now are really warm. I perspire so very much, I have to take a bath. After my bath, I go to the kitchen and help Aling Edad cook the supper. I cook the rice and she cooks the meat. Every day is the same, only now I am thinking of romance and love. When I finished my kitchen chores, I said "good-night" to Mr. Santiago and Aling Edad and I go to our bunkhouse. I put on a pair of pants. I had ask from Manong Julian to give me a pair of pants that is small for him. He had 2 small pants so he gave them to me and I wore one of my old dresses that I had made in Honolulu for shirt. This is what I wear and use as my "night-clothes." I feel safe in them. I am a light sleeper. I wake up very easily. So if any-one tries to "get me" I can kick or push them down fast. I'll put this away, it's already 9:30 P.M. Tomorrow is another day. Since we came here, I have been going to bed dressed this way.

Harlan Ranch, San Ramon, California
Friday night, October 14, 1927

Today is the ninth day since Ray has been here, and I have been thinking and I have been dreaming about him. I have really fallen in love with Ray. With all my heart I want him to be my life partner in this world, in other words I want him to be my husband. Yes, I feel very much that way about Ray. I never feel this way about Joe or Felix before. Though, I feel this about Ray, I do not think he will fall for me. I do not use any makeup and right now living out here in the country I braid my long hair like I always when I was in Honolulu. I did not know how to fix my hair pretty like some girls do, so I fix and comb my hair the best way I know how. Maybe someday I will learn how to fix my hair pretty, I will try and learn. Anyway, I am hoping that Ray will come back and visit—I wonder. Even if I do not see him again, I do not think I can forget him.

Harlan Ranch, San Ramon, California
Saturday night, October 22, 1927

I heard good news today. Manong Julian and Tatay told me today that they have finish the work here in San Ramon with Mr. Santiago and so we are going to Stockton tomorrow to look for work. Maybe I can work in the pool hall like Igsoo. You know I have not heard from Igsoo. I wonder if I am going to meet her in Stockton. And I am also excited, oh so very much, because I hope I will meet Ray in Stockton again. I can hardly wait for tomorrow to come. Tatay and Manong Julian was able to buy a second-hand car and it runs pretty good. I hope and pray that it will not give Manong any problems 'cause he is going to drive; Manong Julian learn how to drive at a car wash where he use to work while we were still living in Honolulu, Oahu, T.H. I hope I can go to sleep because we are going to get up early because we have a long ways to go. Oh gee, but I am excited thrilled and oh so happy that we are going to Stockton. Oh, I hope so very much to see Ray again.

148

Harlan Ranch, San Ramon, California

7 o'clock Sunday night, October 23, 1927

We just arrive home about an hour ago. I got cleaned, got into my night clothes, and got in bed so I can write down all what happened today. Before we left Stockton we ate at a Filipino restaurant called Mayon Restaurant. The owner was very nice to us. Mr. Juaner. He's a short man as tall as I am or maybe an inch or 2 taller than I am. It was in the restaurant that I met Mr. Medallio, who is a barber and has his shop at Mr. & Mrs. Menda's pool hall. He was having lunch when Conching, whom I just met, went to the Mayon Restaurant for some lunch, too. Of course Tatay and Manong Julian were with me. Anyway Conching ask Medallio if he knows any pool hall owners are in need of a pool-table-girl. Medallio spoke up right away and said Mrs. Menda is looking for a pool-table-girl. So I told him I'm going with my father and brother to see her. I introduced Medallio to Tatay and Manong Julian. After we ate we all walked Conching back to International Pool Hall where she works. We told her that we're going to see Mrs. Menda. Deep in my heart I hope and pray that I get the job. Conching said to me, "Here, let me show you how to fix the balls, it's very easy." She gave me the triangle and said, "Make sure your 1 ball is at the top—next comes 14–15, next row come 13–12–11, next 10–9–87, and last row 3–4–5–6–2, that's how you are to remember," and she showed me where to place the triangle on the table and remove the triangle without scattering the balls. "Whoever is playing will pay you a nickel a game." That was easy. It's a good thing no men are coming in to play and Conching was able to teach me how to fix the balls. You know that was really nice of her and I thank her very much for showing me how to fix the balls on a pool table, I appreciate that very much. I was getting nervous inside. We left Conching and I told her we'll be back whether I get the job or not. I'm going to let her know how I made out. We found Menda's Pool Hall, 31 E. Market Street. She was at the counter. We introduced ourselves, I did, anyway, and I came to the point right away. She said, "Oh, yes, I need a girl." As if she read my thoughts she said, "You like work." I said "yes." "Okay, you work." I introduce her to my father and brother. Than I went on to explain to that I can't start until October 28 because we have to go back to San Ramon to get our things and then we have to look for a place to stay. We are truly in luck today. We met another Pinoy who happen to be sitting near us and he heard us mention about wanting to rent a place to stay. He told us he knows someone who has a room for rent. He said he'll take us there when we have finished talking with Mrs. Menda. Then I ask Mrs. Menda if I can quit work at 7:00 P.M. on the 29 of October, she ask me why, so I told her that there's a benefit dance that night and I'm invited and I don't want to miss it. And she said, "Oh, sure, you quit 7:00 P.M. and go dance." So everything is settled. I got the job and I'm going to the dance Saturday, October 29, 1927. I thanked and I hug Mrs. Menda, I was really grateful and thankful for the work. Oh, before we left, she said, "You look so young (I was only 15) when you come to work put a little lipstick on, fix your eye-brow by darking it." I have such scanty-eye-brow. She said, "There's a policeman that comes around and you can't work here unless you are 18 years old." So I'll do what she advised me to do, much as I dislike putting makeup on. Before we parted I gave Mrs. Menda my name, date of birth, gave her Tatay's and Manong Julian's name, and I start work on Oct. 28, 1927 at 10:00 A.M. We said good-bye to her and we or rather

Mr. Seriaco took us to Mrs. Sapanta house. We were lucky, she has 1 room to rent, $18.00 a month. It is a small room, I can sleep on the cot bed while Tatay and Manong Julian sleep on the bed. I'll fit in the cot bed very nicely. So we told Mrs. Sapanta we'll be back on the 27 and our rent starts on the 27 and Manong Julian paid her $18.00 in advance. So that part was settled and we said good-bye to Mrs. Sapanta. We went back to Conching and told her I got the job and also we found a place to stay for $18.00 a month. I thank Medallio for his help for giving us Mrs. Menda's name and we also thank Mr. Seriaco for bringing us to Mrs. Sapanta apartment. And I told Conching it was close to the place where I am going to work. Conching congratulated me for getting the job. I was so excited and happy, now I can help Tatay and Manong Julian with the rent and our food. When I saw Conching was kind of busy. I sat down on a chair by the window—I sat there looking, then I saw Ray passed by. He happened to look in. I waved at him. I thought he did not see me wave, but he did. He turned back and came into the pool room, come straight to me and we shook hands. Oh, it was so good and thrilling to see him. He has such a nice smile so I smile back and he said, "Hello, Angeles, how are you?" I answered, "I am fine, thank you." He asked if we are now living in Stockton. I said, "No, not yet, but we will be on the 27 of this month." I told him that we have to go back to San Ramon and get our belongings and come back on the 27 of October because I have to start work on the 28th of October. Then he said, "Oh, you got a job working in the pool hall." He was not surprise. Anyway, he went on to say, "Than you are going to the dance on the 29?" I look at him and smiled and told him, "Yes, I am going to be there." And he was in a hurry so he said, "I have to go, I'll see you at the dance," and my parting words, "I'll see you at the dance, bye." He look so good, he wore a pr. of brown tweed pants, white shirt open at the throat, and rolled his shirt-sleeves 3/4 rolled-up. He looked so good-looking, well and good physic, tall and in a dark way, he has thick wavy-hair, black of course. Did I tell you he is Tagalog? I like the way he speak in other words, I just love to hear him talk. I felt kind of sad when he said, "I have to say good-bye." Anyway we are going back to Stockton on the 27, so I have a good chance of meeting him again. Tomorrow Manong Julian and Tatay will talk to Mr. Santiago if we can stay until the 26 of this month and we are leaving early on the 27th. You know, I can hardly wait for that day to come around. Tomorrow I am to wash all our dirty clothes, starch and iron them the following day. This way we do not have so many dirty clothes. Our clothes will be pack all clean. So I better go to sleep now and put this away before Manong Julian comes in. As always, I put my book at the bottom of Tatay's trunk. Tatay gave me a key. He knows my book, and he never question me about it. Tatay never learn to read and write but can write his name Enarciso Monrayo but most of the time he just makes the sign of the cross like so, †.

Harlan Ranch, San Ramon, California
Thursday at 6:00 in the morning, October 27, 1927
I am up early, Manong Julian and Tatay are still sleeping. I could not write long. I'll write later. We have everything packed. I have my dress on already and I wash my face and combed my hair. Now as soon as Tatay and Manong Julian wake up, we are going to eat breakfast of course. I'll have to wash the breakfast dishes and sweep the floor and clean the table. I do not mind, because it is the last time I'll be doing that. I know as soon as we have finished eating, we are going to leave. You know I feel so happy at leaving this place. I hope we will never come back here. I sure would not like that so I pray that our Father in Heaven would help me keep my work at the pool hall—I hope I will not be fired and taken away from my work. Oh, I will work hard, I will learn the job well. I won't be able to write as often in this, but I will see. I will write every chance I get. I must put this away now. From now on, I can keep this lock in my suitcase. Tatay found

the key among his keys so now, I can keep my book in the bottom of my suitcase.

25 E. Market Street, Stockton, California

October 27, 1927

152

Manong Julian finished bringing up our suitcases and Tatay carried his small trunk upstairs. I have a chance to write. Tatay is sitting across the room fixing the blankets on their bed, while I am writing this on my bed. Oh, Manong Julian left as soon as he finish what he was suppose to do. About noontime we arrive at Mrs. Sapanta's apartment and we talk to her for about an hour. She showed us our room. It's upstairs, 1 small bed for me and one big bed for Tatay and Manong Julian. We all sleep in one room. We can't afford to rent another room for me. Oh, it would be nice if I can rent 1 room for myself, but that is not to be. Mrs. Sapanta is a very nice person. She told us we have to share the kitchen, if we would like to cook. We share the bathroom, too. Yes, this is going to be just like one big family. She told me she has 3 young men renting from her and 1 woman—not married. Right now the young men, she says, are working in the camp. After she had finished talking to us, she told us that our rent won't be due until the 1st of December. She is giving us a few days free, that was very nice of her. She did this for us. Tatay and Manong Julian are not working. Then she looked at me and told Tatay that I was lucky to have the pool hall job. Oh yes, I joined in, I am truly lucky to get the job and I start working tomorrow. I feel so excited inside and thrilled and oh so very happy that I can work and help Tatay and Manong Julian now, while they are not able to find work yet. I hung up the dresses I have. I do not have too many dresses. It is a good thing there is a big closet in this room. I will put my suitcase up on the shelf and put our shoes and the charcoal iron I will keep that in the box. Tatay bought me 3 heating-irons, these you put on top the stove to get hot. Mrs. Sapanta told me to use the stove when it's not being used. You know, it is a good thing the weather is still warm. I can still wear my cotton and voile dresses. I have no winter clothes, except the brown-tweed coat with the fur collar that Manong Julian had bought for me at the emporium store at Market Street in San Francisco. I ask Tatay if I can keep 8.00 dollars from my pay to start buying a few clothes and I give Tatay $10.00. He said that is alright. Tatay know I need clothes, I need a new pair of shoes and I want high-heels at that. Tomorrow I'm going to get up early, clean up and go up Main Street. I know where it is. The stores open at 8:30, some open at 9:00 every morning from Monday thru Saturday. I am going to look around. So the first chance I get to buy some clothes, I know just where to go. I have to put this away now, I have to take a bath. Tatay and Manong Julian went to El Dorado Streets to make friends.

153

25 East Market St., Stockton
Friday at 6:00 P.M., October 28, 1927

I just came home for supper. I go back to work at 7 o'clock and stop work at 12 o'clock tonight. Yes, I started to work today, this morning at 10 o'clock. Mrs. Menda watch me as I fix my first rack of balls, I was slow at first. When I finished, she said to me, "You will be okay." I felt good inside. I did not get busy until 3 o'clock. I noticed quite a few men were coming in to play. And there are only 6 tables but I like the work, it was fun. The men were all nice and most of them smiled and talk with me when I fix or rack the balls. I will write more tomorrow if I have time. I just have a donut and a cup of coffee. I ate in our room. I bought the donuts at a bakery close by. Maybe later I will have some fresh milk. I have to hurry up, brush my teeth, put lipstick on and a little powder on so I'll look more grown-up and get back to work in time. Tatay is here, having donuts and coffee with me. Manong Julian is somewhere, anyway we do not worry about him. Tatay told me by 11 o'clock he will be at the pool hall and wait for me and we will come home together. He does not want me to come home by myself.

Stockton, California
Saturday at 6 o'clock in the morning, October 29, 1927
I am writing this early. I just finished washing my face and brushing my teeth. I fix my face putting lipstick and all that so that later I just put on my dress. I noticed a small coffeeshop across the pool hall where I work. I will eat breakfast there before I go to work. Tatay and Manong Julian are still sleeping. Oh, before I go to work, I'll see Conching. She lives upstairs back of the International Pool Hall where she works. You know, she's going to lend me a dress to wear tonight to the dance, because I do not have an evening gown. I told Tatay and Manong Julian I am going to the dance with Conching tonight and that she will bring me home after the dance, so they have nothing to worry about. Tatay says "alright I can go." I am so happy about going to the dance and I am hoping that "Ray" will be there.

Stockton, California
Sunday morning, 6 o'clock, October 30, 1927
I have a wonderful time last night and I am so happy. Ray loves me and he kissed me, on the stairway. I was truly in heaven. Oh, but I love Ray. I know now he is the one for me. He did not dance with me until 11 o'clock. I was thinking Ray does not care, but when the orchestra started playing a popular song (I know the song well) called "Always." As if to answer my wish, I saw Ray coming towards me and I look at him and he ask me if I would like to dance, I just nodded my head. He put his arm around my waist, oh, I seem to melt in his arms. As we were gliding over the floor, he ask me if I knew the song the orchestra was playing. I said, "Yes, I do." He asked me if I know the first sentence of the song, and I said that I do. Ray asked

me to say it so I did. I said, "I'll be loving you always," and he then asked me if I meant it. I said, "I do," and then he said, "I love you, too, dearly," Oh, that was heaven just to hear him say, "I love you, too." And we danced without saying anything. He just held me a little tighter. When the music stopped, Ray asked if I want some refreshment. I said "yes." So he led me to the refreshment and got our drinks and then he led me to the stairway. No one was around, so we put our drinks down and Ray took me in his arms and he kissed me and kissed for a long time it seems. I just went limp in his arms. And it's all I can do not to lose my senses. I said, "We better go back, before my friend will think differently of me." Ray agreed with me. We went back to our friends after we finished our drinks which was just "Punch." Ray stayed with me until 1 o'clock. He held my hand most of the time when we are not dancing. Oh, he said for me to dance with anyone, but do you know, I just want to dance with him. But that was not fair to the other fellows. You know, Ray come home with us, he told Conching he'll come along when Conching bring me home. As soon as Ray brought me to the door, Conching left with her brother. I thank her before she left for taking me to the dance. I sure appreciate what she did and she knows what happened. I told Conching, "I love Ray and he loves me." And Ray kissed me long. No one was around, but we have to part. We said "good-night." I opened the door. Ray squeezed my hand and I said good-night and said I'll see you tomorrow. I went upstairs on wings. Oh, I was so happy. It's a good thing Tatay and Manong Julian were asleep. I don't want them to know about Ray. I have a feeling that they will not like him, and besides I want to keep this to myself for a while. Conching is the only one that knows about Ray and me. When Ray sees me tomorrow, we'll pretend as if there was nothing between us. If Tatay and Manong Julian goes to El Dorado and Ray comes to see me, we will be able to talk, but if they are around, we would not be able to talk to each other at all.

Stockton, California
5 o'clock, Tuesday night, November 1, 1927
Mrs. Menda let me have 1½ hour for supper, 'cause I start at 10 o'clock this morning. I did not stop for lunch, I was not hungry. She gave me 1½ hour for supper. I was hungry by 6:30 o'clock tonight. I passed by the "coffeeshop." I bought a chicken sandwich. I just love chicken sandwich. I told the man that I am taking the sandwich with me. So he wrap it and I bought some coffee too. He had a pint jar and he let me have it so I can have coffee with my sandwich. I told him that I will bring the pint jar back. I came to the apartment. I had my supper all to myself. I was able to write and let me tell you I've been busy all day. Ray was able to stay and played pool with his friend and we were able to talk to each other when my father and Manong Julian went to El Dorado with some friends.

Stockton, California
Wednesday morning at 12:30, November 2, 1927
Before I quit work, I was told that we are going to a fireman's ball. The dance is going to be at the Civic Auditorium. There's going to be just 3 couple going. There is Conching and her friend and her brother Joe and his friend and there is Ray and myself, and it's formal. The men are all going to wear "tuxedo" and the ladies are going to wear formal gowns. This means Conching will have to lend me her gown again. I know I am going to enjoy "The Firemen's Ball." I just love to dance, especially when Ray is going to be there too.

Stockton, California
Sunday morning at 6:00 A.M., November 6, 1927
Oh, I had a wonderful time last night. I know Ray did too. I think we all had a wonderful time. Conching and her manfriend, I don't know if they are "sweethearts" or not. There was Mary Can-

las, I just met her, there was Joe Conching's brother. He was Mary's escort. Oh there was Medallio. He didn't have a lady-friend but he danced with all of us and there was another couple that came with us—Mary's mother and her husband. We danced with our group only. Nearly all the dances, Ray danced with me. I was hoping he would dance all the dances with me. Oh, I'd like to write here that we were the only Filipino couples there last night. The rest are all white couples. They all looked so so nice and beautiful. We did too in our formal gowns & tuxedo.

Stockton, California
Tuesday at 6 o'clock in the morning, November 8, 1927
Mary and I are together again. We met yesterday and she got a job just a few doors down the street where I work. She gets the same wage I'm getting—$18.00 a week. And we are sharing 1 big room. Mrs. Sapanta charge us $36.00 a month. Since Igsoo's parents are not working and Tatay and Manong Julian are not working also, so Igsoo and I pay the rent, she pays $18.00 and I pay 18.00 = $36.00 a month. Igsoo and I sleep on a full size bed in one corner and Igsoo's parents sleeps in one corner to the left of us and Tatay and Manong Julian sleep to one corner. Oh, we are so glad we are together again. We had so much to tell each other, already she tells me about her sweethearts. She says she just got another sweetheart before we met. So, I asked her, so you have two sweethearts? She laughed, "No, Igsoo, I gave up the other one, besides he is not good-looking as Ralph (her new sweetheart)." I met Ralph. He is nice-looking but a short fellow —anyway she likes him.

25 E. Market, Stockton, California
Saturday, November 12, 1927
It is only 5 o'clock in the morning but I'm wide awake. I'm still in bed writing this. I can't do any writing when Igsoo is awake.

I do not want her to know I am keeping a "diary." This is some-thing I want to keep to myself. Much as I like Igsoo, I do not want her to know. I told her about "Ray," my one and only love. I told her he is the only one I ever will love. She look at me and smiled as if to say she did not believe me. Anyway whether she believe me or not, in my heart I really mean what I say. This past few days I was not able to write in my book because Igsoo and I are always together and I thought about getting up early before Igsoo wakes up. Ray came to the pool room last Wednes-day night. I was so glad to see him, seems like I have not seen him for a long time. All he can do was held his right hand over my left hand while I was about to pick up the 6 ball to put in the rack. His back was towards Tatay, who was sitting at the counter. It was just for a moment I look at him and smiled and he looked at me. Ray's friends was just watching us. While I was fixing or arranging the balls in the rack which takes me a few seconds, Ray was able to tell me "I love you" and he fol-lowed with "my friend and I are going to play pool for half hour and we are going to leave" and he added, "I'd like to kiss you—take you in my arms, but that's impossible, of course." I picked up the five-cents they paid for the last game. I just look at him and said, "Yes, that's impossible." I put the rack back under the table, and left them to fix another table. Since we became sweethearts, we've been careful, because Tatay does not like Tagalogs. Just for now, I think only Ray's friends know about us. You know, I have been here just a little over 2 weeks and already I am receiving love letters and proposals thru the mail. Even Mrs. Menda, my boss, said to me yesterday when she hand me 3 letters from the men who are coming here to play pool, "Angeles, you are popular. You have been working here only a few weeks and already you are getting letters." I told her I am indeed surprise. Since I have been working here the 6 pool tables are always being played on. I stay by the counter and when they are finish or they want the table rack, they tap the floor. I better put my book away before Igsoo wakes up.

5 o'clock in the morning,
Monday, November 14, 1927

I forgot to write here that Igsoo and I have Monday off—we do not work on Mondays. I am glad that we have one day off from work. I would not see Ray tonight because I will not be working today but I'll see him tomorrow. I hope he'll be able to come in the afternoon because we can talk to each other without being watched by Tatay and Manong Julian. You see, since we came to Stockton to live, Tatay and Manong stays in the apartment or go to El Dorado to talk to new-found-friends or Manong Julian will take Tatay to a movie. You know, there's one movie-house across from where I worked and there are 2 more on El Dorado. The only time Mary and I can see a movie is on Monday.

159

Stockton, California
Friday, November 18, 1927

My watch tells me it is only 5 o'clock in the morning and as usual, everyone is sleeping. Igsoo must be tired, she is snoring softly. Do you know that when we got home from work it takes us 10 minutes to reach the apartment and the other tenants were still awake and they were playing the phonograph and the record was playing "Charmaine" and they were dancing. They ask us to dance, so we dance with them. Bob ask me and Jose ask Igsoo, and Martin was dancing with the landlady. We were having fun but I was tired and I know Igsoo was too. So by 40 minutes after we told Jose and Bob and the others we have to go to bed, we are tired. We said "good-night" to all of them. We walked upstairs. Tatay and Manong were in bed already, same with Igsoo's mother and father. Mary and I tried to move quietly about but we can't help but giggle and laugh a little. It's a good thing there's running water in the bedroom. We do not have to go downstairs to wash up and brush our teeth. By 10 minutes after 1 o'clock we were in bed. We fell asleep right away.

Sunday, 5:30 in the morning,
November 20, 1927

I did not see Ray until last night at 7 o'clock. He came in with his friends to play pool. He told me why he did not come in to see me, because they have to work late. I told him that it was alright if he cannot come in to see me. I understand but anyway he says he would like for me to know. I told him that whenever he has the time to see me is alright but down deep in my heart I'm always wishing he can come every night even just for a short while. And oh my goodness, the men that comes in to play are all Filipino and they are about Ray's age, I think the most of them are, I mean have made love to me. All I can say to them or answer them I have a "someone" already. And they think I am lying, they tell me I am only saying that so they would leave me alone. And do you know, that since I have started to work here the pool room have been very busy. I'm glad because this proves I will keep my job. And do you know there's always a gentleman who wants to look good in Tatay eyes that would invite us to the chop suey. This is usually in the evening—6 o'clock supper time. You know, I have been here only 3 weeks, I have several proposals of marriage already? I give them my answer. I can't tell them yet that I have someone, who I really love and will love forever and ever. I better put you away now before Igsoo wakes up

Stockton, California
Friday, at 5:30 in the morning, November 25, 1927

I found a ten dollar bill yesterday—about 4 o'clock in the afternoon. I was walking toward the cash register when I saw a crumple piece of paper. I pick it up 'cause it look like money to me. And believe it or not, I stretch out the crumpled paper and it was a ten dollar bill. It was a really happy day for me and a lucky day. I bought a dress with it on my supper hour. Igsoo was glad for me too. I found a black-heavy-satin, flared skirt and a heavy lace-collar. It was beautiful really nice for dancing but I'll wear it for work sometimes, not all the time. Right now, I have skirts, blouses, and jackets to work in. Igsoo and I almost dresses alike, whenever we can. I do not have too many nice clothes to wear, but whatever I have I wear to work, just so long they look nice on me and with high-heels, I know I look alright. Anyway the men tells me how I look, they always tell me I have a "nice body." So, I say "thank you," and I add, "Every girl have a body like me, what is the difference?" They answer, "A big difference." I shrug my shoulders and walk away to put the money in the cash register. I know I do not have a beautiful face but they say I have a beautiful body, "a nice walk." They say this in Tagalog most of the time, "Ang ganda nang katawan." They usually make this remark when I walk away from the table, after I have fix the balls or rack up the balls for them. I pretend I did not hear them, but I must tell you, I do feel good and nice inside whenever I hear them make or say nice things about me. I am only 15 years old, 3 months. I weigh 110 lbs and I am only 5 feet tall without my shoes. My measurements are hips 32, waist 19, and my bust is 32. My boss says since I have work here, the pool room have been busy. She says I draw customers in. I am happy to know that. I told my boss that I like my work very much. Working and being in love with Ray, I am truly the happiest girl. I have never been so happy before. My world now is so different from my childhood. And I am glad that we came to this wonderful land of America. You know I like this land better than Honolulu. I hope I'll always like it here. I better put this away now before Igsoo wakes up. I have to get in the bathroom before any of them gets in there first. Those first days that Igsoo and I live together, she's always surprise when I am almost ready and dressed when she wakes up at 7 o'clock. I must tell you the room across ours is rented by 2 brothers, they are both nice fellows, nice-looking too, and they are Visayan from Cebu. Bob Alisna, the youngest of the two, chubby sort of a fellow, is the

161

aggresive one. The days that we moved here, he talk to me first and introduce himself to me. "Hello, I am Bob Alisna, my brother and I live here across from you." He put out his hand to shake hands with me, so I smile and I put out my hand and he took it and held it tightly, and I told him my name, "I am Angeles" and pull out my hand because I can feel he was going to hold my hand long. I do not want him to think that I love him 'cause I do not. I like to be a friend, like I am to the other fellows. We danced and that's the only time he can put his arms around my waist. There were times I go straight to my room, I leave Mary dancing with the fellows. Anyway, I get to our room and clean up and get ready for bed and while Igsoo is having fun downstairs I have a chance to write.

In the San Joaquin pool hall
Sunday, December 4, 1927

I have one hour for lunch—Tatay and Manong Julian went to eat. I told Tatay that I was not hungry, so they went by themselves. I stayed in the pool room, so I can write. I ask Mrs. Menda if I can stay and write during my lunch hour. She said, "Okay. You can use the farthest end of the counter," and she went on to tell me that "it's not too busy right now, so go ahead, you use that side," pointing at where I should write. I was hoping that Ray would come in at this moment, I put the thought aside. Wishing or hoping will not send Ray to me this way. Beside he is working today. I am hoping he will be able to come in tonight and play pool. Ray and I have a friend, I think he is around 40 years old. Ray introduced him to me. Seriaco have been delivering Ray's letters to me. Ray writes me short-love-notes whenever he cannot see me or come to pool room. Seriaco is always careful that Tatay or Manong Julian does not see him giving me something. Seriaco gives me the note at the counter if Tatay and Manong Julian is not at counter or he gives me the note when I'm racking up the balls. It's truly nice to have a friend who is really helpful. So whenever I see Seriaco come in the pool room, I know I have something from Ray. You know, I have been working here for five weeks only, seems like have worked here for a long time already, but I like my work very much. Not hard at all, though I am on my feet from 10 o'clock to twelve at night, that's 14 hours altogether that is why Mrs. Menda pay me $18.00 a week. I am glad I am working 'cause Tatay and Manong Julian are still not able to get work yet. I better put this away now. I have to start work soon, and too, Manong Julian and Tatay will be coming and also Igsoo will pass by before she goes to work.

> 31 E. Market St., Stockton, California,
> San Joaquin pool room
> *Friday, December 9, 1927*

At last Mac believes that I do not love him. We had a good friendly talk with each other. I finally made him understand that I have only a friendly feelings for him, that I have someone who I loved very much and he loves me. I told him who he is. And you know Mac told me? He said, "I had a feeling that it was Ray that you love, 'cause I saw you two looking at each other when you thought no one was watching you two. So I am talking to you now, so I can be sure." He shook my hands and smile. He wished Ray and I all the happiness, health, and plenty of good luck. I thank him for that and do you know where we talk? In my boss' kitchen, 'cause it's a room on the farthest end of the pool room. As soon as I walk in the pool room Mrs. Menda told me that there's a man who want to talk to me in her kitchen. She told me to be careful when I go in. Of course I felt scared. I went in the room, he stood up and said "good-morning." I said "good-morning." He came to the point right away. He told me what he wanted to say and I gave him the answers he wanted to hear and he was satisfied with my answers. Before he left he said, "I am going away from

Stockton and maybe I will not see you again" and he said good-bye and we both walked out of the kitchen. He just turned once to wave good-bye and out the door he went, that was the last I saw of him. When I have a chance to talk to Ray I shall tell him about Mac and today. And Mac is one of my suitors that treats us to the chop suey. Now there is one other fellow that brings us to the chop suey house. The young men or rather I still receive letters from them I have a shoe-box-full of love letters. I answer them all, I give them all the same answers.

San Joaquin pool hall, Stockton, California
Saturday, December 10, 1927

Ray took us to chop suey tonight. He had to borrow some money from his friend to take us to the chop suey. He proposed marriage to me. Of course, when he asked me to marry him, I said "yes," but I said, "You must ask my father," and Ray said he will after Christmas and he said if your father does not agree about us getting married, we elope, agreed? I said "yes." I did not expect Ray to propose marriage to me so soon, but I was in heaven when he said, "Will you marry me?" We were dancing, it's the only chance we have to talk with each other, and he held me oh, ever so gently but there was firmness when he put his arms around my waist. He danced me away from the booth where Tatay and Igsoo's parents were seated, and Ray kissed me. We were silent after that and we danced until the food was brought to the table. Igsoo smile at me and Ray, because she saw Ray kissed me. Ray planned all these tonight, even if he has borrow money to bring us to the chop suey house. We could not dance anymore after we ate. Ray took me and Igsoo back to work. We were walking ahead of Tatay and Igsoo's parents. Ray was telling me again that after Christmas, he will go to the apartment at midnight, because I stop working at 12 o'clock at night. By the time I reach the apartment he should be there first. I agreed to everything he had planned.

We walked a little faster than Tatay and Igsoo's father and mother. Ray and I got to the pool room early about 10 minutes before I start, but I started working anyway. First Ray took hold both of my hands and held my hands for a minute or so. I saw Tatay coming down the street so Ray let go of my hands and said, "Vidal and I are going to play pool for a while." So I rack and set up their table. I was racking the balls. Ray came close to me and said, "I won't be able to see you tomorrow, maybe, the next day." I just said "okay" softly while I was racking up the balls. Before I left the table, I thanked Ray for the wonderful chop suey dinner. I know Tatay was watching us, and Vidal was watching us, too. I happen to look up at him and he was smiling at Ray and me. Ray and Vidal played for over an hour 'cause Mateo came in. He is one of Ray's friend, he is Tagalog too, like Vidal, so he challenge the winner, and the loser pays for the game and of course there is always "betting" on the side. They had to leave, about 8 o'clock. Ray held my hand for a few seconds and said good-night in my ear. Vidal and Mateo sort of block Tatay's view. I said "good-night" softly to Ray. I looked up at him and he just squeezed my hand gently and let go. I turned. I smiled at Mateo and Vidal and said "good-night" to them and they walk out. I followed to put the money in the cash register. I was really busy after they have gone. All six tables going.

Stockton, California, San Joaquin pool room
Saturday, December 17, 1927

Oh, boy, Bro and I had our first quarrel last night, over Ray's letters. Tatay and Manong Julian know that Ray and I are in love with each other. I kept Ray's letter in my jacket pocket. I did not think Bro would be checking my jacket. He tore all the letters except one. Bro told me he's going to keep that one letter for evidence. Bro told me that they do not like him because he is a loafer, a black-hand and no good for nothing sort of a

165

guy. I know they are all lies. Ray is not anything of what they say he is. I know someone is telling Father all these lies. There is one fellow Tatay likes because he has a steady job. He is a "chef" at the Stockton Hotel and he is old enough to be my father. Even if he was younger, I could not love him anyway. I love Ray and no one will ever take his place in my heart. I know from now on Tatay and Manong Julian will be watching me. I told Ray about my brother finding his letters so he told me after I read his letters in the future I should tear up his letters and flush it down in the toilet. "This way your brother won't have a chance to read my letters."

Stockton, California
Tuesday in the pool room, 6 o'clock at night,
December 20, 1927

Mr. Sebastian Gravera who tells me he loves me very much and he tells me after Christmas he will go to the apartment and ask Tatay for my hand in marriage. And so I told him that if Tatay likes him then the two of them should get married, because "Mr. Gravera, I am telling you now that I do not love you and you are just waisting your time going to the apartment." To this he just laughed. We were playing pool. Mrs. Menda told me to go ahead and play because the place was not busy yet. I stop playing long enough to rack up the balls for the men to start playing, that is, if there's only one or two tables playing, otherwise I stop playing completely. Anyway, he ask me, while we were playing pool, what I want for Christmas? So, without hesitation, I answered I want a dress. "Oh, sure, we go at lunch hour." I spent my lunch trying dresses on at the "Livingston Dress Shop." It was fun. Igsoo went with me and Tatay, too. Him and Mr. Gravera were talking in Visayan. I know Tatay likes him very much and I know too, that Mr. Gravera was trying to make a good impression on Tatay. I picked a light-blue-beaded-evening gown because I do not have an evening gown, first beautiful dress I will own. The price was $29.95 cents. We did not stay too long. Mr. Gravera paid the dress and told the sales-lady to put it in a Christmas box. I thank Mr. Gravera for my Christmas. He did not walk us back to the pool room because he has to go back to work at 1 o'clock and from where we were it should not take him long to reach The "Stockton Hotel." And we went the opposite direction. Across from where I work there is a small café. So Tatay and Igsoo and I had chicken sandwiches and coffee. We ate hurriedly because Igsoo and I start work at 1 o'clock, too. Tatay was going back to the apartment, so I told him to please bring my pkg. home, and just put the package on our bed. "And please, Tatay, do not open the package for no one, not even for our landlady, Isabella. Just put the package on the bed." Tatay said, "Okay." "Boy! That was a Christmas present you got," Igsoo said. Then Igsoo ask me if I am going to tell Ray about it and I answered, "Of course, Igsoo, I am going to tell him everything." I am going to tell him also that Julian, I can't remember his last name, gave me a gold Elgin watch yesterday. And Christmas is just five days away. Oh yes, I will show and tell Ray everything. I am not going to hide anything from him, I am going to be honest with him because I want him to be honest with me. And I know now, Ray cannot buy me expensive present but that does not matter with me. All I want from him is his sincere love for me and I hope he come to the pool room on Christmas Day. Since Ray have told me that he was coming to the apartment to ask Tatay for my hand in marriage, I have been jittery, my stomach is acting funny, in fact all of me is jittery. I'll feel better if this will be over but until that time comes around I will have to try and act calm and do my work. I have told Igsoo that Ray is coming to the apartment on the 26 of December, and she said, "Really?" I said, "Really." Then Igsoo added, "You two are serious, aren't you." I answered that we are. Oh, I just found out, too, that Mr. Gravera is coming to the apartment on Christmas Night. Gee wheez, that Mr. Gravera just does not give up.

Monday morning at 1 o'clock,
December 26, 1927

I am writing this in a hurry. I excuse myself from Tatay, Mr. Gravera, my brother, Igsoo's parents, and our landlady. Mr. Gravera came to ask and tell Tatay he loves me and wants to marry me.

168   Mr. Gravera tells Tatay that he has money in the bank and also have a good steady work. And so with everyone around listening to what Tatay will say, Tatay tried his best to change my mind and marry the man. And so facing Tatay, my brother, and Mr. Gravera, I told Tatay I do not love him, I cannot marry him, not for all the money he had and for all the things he can give me. And so I said to Mr. Gravera, "You just wasted your time. I told you a few days ago my mind is made up." I said good-night to them. I know they'll be talking for a half hour or more, that's when I start writing this as soon as Igsoo went to the bathroom to clean up. Now, back to Mr. Gravera. I hope he understands. I do not think he'll propose again. Ray was able to come in the pool room and played pool with his friends. Tatay and Manong Julian were not around, thank heavens, and it so happened when Ray and his 3 buddies came in, I was not busy. They all said hello and Merry Christmas. He told his friends we'll play at the last table. My boss Mrs. Menda smiled at me. She seems to know that Ray and I are in love with each other. Ray and I talked while his friends played pool. I was always ready to rack up the table. There were only 2 playing besides Ray's table. Otherwise I would not have been able to talk with Ray. We talked more freely if Tatay and Manong Julian are not around. Anyway, before Ray left, he said, "Merry Christmas. I love you and I'll see you day after tomorrow 20 minutes after 12:00 Tuesday morning," because he knows it does not take me long to walk from the pool room to the apartment. I told Ray about the gift Mr. Gravera have bought me. He only said, "That was nice." I told him about the other present. "Julian gave me a gold Elgin watch. I think I am going to give that watch back to him." The slips and the bloomers I did not mention them to Ray. I told Ray of the scarf Tolio gave me.

He just smile. I gave Ray 3 beautiful embroidered initial handkerchiefs and a scarf, that's all I can afford. He in turn gave me 3 beautiful embroidered lady's handkerchiefs. I love them.

Tuesday morning at 3 o'clock,
December 27, 1927

Ray came to the apartment with Mr. Isidro Gonzales, Ricardo Trumbullo, and Pete Braga. 2 are Visayans and Ricardo is a Tagalog. They came to interpret for Ray because Tatay could not speak well in Tagalog, so he speaks in Visayan and this is where Isidro and Pete come to translate to Ray. Ray and his friends were already in the living room and it was full of people already. We walked in. Ray and his friends stood up and payed their respect to Tatay and Manong Julian. I know that they did not like Ray at all. You know, while the talks were going on people were coming in to see and hear what Tatay have to say. The stairway was crowded. I notice the doorway was full of people. I was thinking, why do they want to know everything—anyway, all three men try to reason with Tatay but to no avail. So Ray finally said to Tatay, "If you do not want me as a son in law, I love Angeles and she loves me and if she agrees, we are going to elope." Oh my, Tatay flew into a rage. Tatay answered, "Ray, if you do, if I find you I'll kill you both!" I was trembling slightly beside Ray. I did not want Tatay to know I was afraid of him. Ricardo ask Tatay why he dislike Tagalog so much. Tatay answered, "Because they are no good, they are loafers, they are bums, they're no good for nothing." Ricardo told Tatay that's not so, there are good and bad in every one of us. Tatay answered, "I don't care what you say. I do not like Tagalogs, and that is all I have to say." With that Mr. Gonzales, Mr. Braga, Mr. Trumbullo, and Ray said goodnight to Tatay and everyone. Ray talk to me even when Tatay glared—his 3 friends waited until Ray finished talking. He took my hand and said low so the others won't hear. He said, "We are going to do what we have planned, agreed?" I said, "Yes." "I'll try and see you tomorrow, good-night, I love you." And they left. I thank them before they left for coming with Ray to talk to Tatay. When they left, I felt downhearted because Tatay did not like Ray. I wanted so much for them to like Ray. Tatay did not ask me if I love Ray or not. I suppose whatever I say won't mean a thing. Anyway, I should not see or try to meet Ray. I know now they will be watching me closely. After Ray and his friends left, I said good-night to everyone that were there still buzzing like bees to Tatay about what happen in Isabella's living-room. Oh, another thing that Ray had planned is if Tatay will not agree to us getting married is to pretend that we have broken up and the reason is we broke up because Tatay does not like Ray; but deep within our hearts we still love each other and we are going through with our plans. When Igsoo went to the bathroom, I have a chance to write a few lines and I could not write much. I went to the bathroom to clean up and when I came out Igsoo and I talked for a little while. She said to me, "Too bad, Igsoo, that your father does not like Ray. Now I suppose you two will have to break up and not see each other again." I agreed with her. I could not tell her of our plans. I thought that I could not trust her, she will tell my Tatay and Manong Julian. Then we said good-night. I told her I was tired. So we turned our backs to each other and in no time at all she was already asleep. Pretty soon I hear Tatay and Manong Julian and Ninang and Ninong come in and they were still talking about the happenings earlier. I pretended to be sleeping. I tried to go to sleep but I could not. Then I could hear Tatay, Manong Julian, and also Igsoo's father and mother is snoring softly. When I look at my clock it was 3 o'clock, so I took this book out and write what happened earlier, and now I must go sleep. I have to work tomorrow and I hope Ray and I will have a chance to talk to each other. I know we could not talk to each other when Tatay or Manong Julian is around. It is going to be hard now to talk to each other. I know Ray will think of something.

170

Diary

Stockton, California
Thursday in the pool room, December 29, 1927

I saw Ray and we talked for fifteen minutes only during my lunch hour. Tatay and Manong Julian went to see someone at Cesar's pool room over at El Dorado Street. Ray told me that next day I'll receive a letter from him. Seriaco will be our "messenger person." Ray says he can be trusted. He told me also to give him whatever clothes I am going to bring when we elope. Ray says 1 or 2 pieces of clothes or 3 and pretend that you are sending them to the dry cleaners. Seriaco will give him my clothes and he will take care of them. Ray had already planned with friends. A couple will take or drive us away, who will be our Ninong and Ninang on our wedding—we are going to elope on the 15th of January, 1928. He told me to be sure and be at Market Street between El Dorado and Hunter at 12 o'clock sharp, because that is the time I will be picked up. I answered, "Ray, I will be there." All these time we were talking we were holding hands. I was inside the counter, while Ray was standing on the outside of the counter. My boss just smiled at us while we were talking. I was watching up the street 'cause I can see both sides if Tatay or Manong Julian are coming. Oh, he also told me that he was going to place the crown on the queen for the Rizal Day celebration on December 30, 1927, and I said, "That's tomorrow night," and he nodded his head and smiled at me. "Don't be jealous." I told him, "I am not." Anyway he went on to say the Filipino community asked him to do the honor of crowning the queen. Besides they say he is Tagalog and he is a "poet," a Tagalog-poet. I just found out. He asked me to try and come to the affair. There will be dancing too. I told him I have to ask my boss first if I can have the night off. I have to ask Conching to ask Tatay to let me go with her. I have to asked Ray to ask Conching to ask Tatay 'cause I cannot do it tonight. Ray said he will do it and he will tell her to pick me up here in the pool room and I will be ready. I am hoping very much to go to the Rizal Day celebration. I just talk to my boss, she say I can have the night off.

Saturday at 5 o'clock in the morning, December 31, 1927
I was able to go to the dance last night. At first Tatay did not want me to go but Conching changed Tatay's mind. She really convinced Tatay I would not see or try to talk with Ray. Ray was wonderful, crowning the queen. He spoke in Tagalog when he was crowning the queen. The crowning poem was beautiful even if I did not understand every word. The audience clapped. I really felt so proud, inside I was so happy that he is going to be my husband someday. We were able to be together most of the time. We danced most of the dances together. We are going to elope on the 15 of January 1928, that is next month, and that is not too far away. Ray told me to start giving more of my clothes to Seriaco, starting the second of January, 1928. Just to think of what we are going to do, my heart seems to beat faster and I get excited. I try so hard not to show it because I do not want anyone to know, especially Tatay, Manong Julian, and Igsoo too. I hope our Father in Heaven will help us by not letting Tatay know what Ray and I are planning to do. Since the night Ray went to the house to ask Tatay for my hand in marriage, we tried our best not to let Tatay or Manong Julian see us together.

1928

In the pool room, 31 E. Market St., Stockton, California
6 o'clock in the evening, Monday, January 2, 1928
This is my supper hour, but I am not hungry. I told Igsoo, Tatay for them to go ahead and eat supper. I am not going with them because I am not hungry. I told Tatay I am just staying in the pool room. I was hoping that Ray would come in the pool room while Tatay and Manong Julian are not here. I truly do not understand why Tatay does not like Ray. Anyway I am sorry he feels that way about Ray because we are going to do what we had planned of doing, elope. As I sit here I feel so excited, thinking of that day. Oh dear Father in Heaven, "please help us and don't let anything

go wrong." My wish came true. Ray came in, he got hold of my hand over the counter—'cause we could not go anywhere else and look at each other. I know my boss was watching us and Melanio the barber who has a shop across the counter but his shop is enclosed with glass, he was watching us too. But we did not care. They can watch all they want to. Mrs. Menda is a nice person. To her I told her that Ray and I are "sweethearts" and that some-day we are going to get married and I told her that Tatay does not like Ray. She smiled and said, "I understand." So from now on she'll be seeing us talk to each other when Tatay is not around. As for Melanio (he is in love with me) I told him I'm in love with Ray. I'm hoping he won't be such a tattle-tale and tell Tatay that he saw Ray and I talking to each other 'cause he know how Tatay feels about Ray. I think the whole world knows how Tatay feels about Ray. Ray told me that Seriaco told him that Tatay and my brother were eating in the Mayon Restaurant, so we talked for about 40 minutes and holding hands over the counter top—we were unmindful that eyes were watching us. Ray said, "We have 13 days more and we will be together for always. I hope you will not change your mind when that day comes?" I answered, "No, Ray, I will not change my mind. I'll be there, at the spot you told me to be." When we were planing all these, my whole being seems to tingle all over. Finally Ray said, "I better go now, before your father and your brother returns." We just look longingly into each other's eyes. I know he wanted to kiss me and I wanted him to, but we cannot in public. So he just squeeze my hands tightly and said, "Good-bye for now, and I will try and see you here whenever I can." With that he turned and out the door he went and all I can do was follow him out with my eyes. And about 10 minutes later, here comes Tatay. And Igsoo came in for a few minutes to talk with me. She was telling me about her latest "sweetheart." As for me, I do not tell her anything more about Ray and myself. She believe me that Ray and I have broken up. I told Ray before he left that I have a few dresses that I am going to give Seriaco, also a coat and a pair of shoes and that would be all. I would like to bring all my clothes but they are going to get suspicies so I had better not. I have been saving the five dollars I keep from my wage, because I give the rest of my wages to Tatay.

31 E. Market St., San Joaquin pool hall, Stockton
at night Friday, 6 o'clock, January 6, 1928

I stayed in the pool room and I ate my sandwich here. Igsoo and her parents, Tatay and Manong Julian are going to eat at the Mayon Restaurant on El Dorado Street. I told them I did not feel like eating at the restaurant. Tatay and Manong Julian kind of believe me that I am not seeing or meeting with Ray anymore. They have not seen him since the last week of December. Even Igsoo has not seen him since last month. There are only 8 days more before the 15 of January. Ray will be there waiting for me in the car. I am really excited and I am very happy in the thought that we are going to get married soon and we'll be together for all the time we are here in this world that God have made. I have not seen Ray since Wednesday, I guess he is working. I must be patient and understanding if he cannot come around and see me. It is a good thing that I am working, it keeps me busy.

Apartment
Tuesday morning at 4 o'clock, January 10, 1928

Five more days before the 15th. Everyone is sound asleep, even Igsoo snoring lightly. I am writing on my lap in bed. Igsoo has her back to me. I hope she does not wake up until I finish writing. I think I slept just 2½ hrs. I have been thinking about Sunday, the 15th of January. My heart starts beating faster it seems and louder. I just hope no one hears my heart beats so. I hope Igsoo does not hear it. Igsoo ask me yesterday where are my clothes? I told her that they're at the dry cleaners. I told her I have to give Tatay all my wage, but I am going to take most of them out of the "cleaners" by next week. I will have the money then. Oh boy, if she only knew what is going to happen next Sunday at noontime. I know Tatay will be furious; Tatay is a quiet man but he can be violent when angry. I have not seen Ray for 2 days now. I hope he is well. I worry about him, I love him so; please Dear Father in Heaven, don't let anything happen to him, please watch over him and please help us Sunday, do not let Tatay catch us, help us to get away. Amen. I don't know where we are going, I am leaving everything to Ray. I have not been told of their plans. They just told me to be sure and be at the spot at 12 o'clock or little after 12 o'clock. As soon as I finish writing I am going back to sleep if I can and get up at 6:30 to get ready and Igsoo and I eat breakfast at 8 o'clock or before that and as soon as we finish eating breakfast, which is only 1 fried egg and 2-buttered toast and Igsoo has the same thing. (You know sitting and writing this at fifteen years old, and being so in love with Ray, I feel so alive and very happy inside and everything so exciting and I am glad to be alive and in this world—and it won't be long now Ray and I will be together for always like our song, "Always.") Like I was writing, when we finished we go straight to Main Street stores. The stores open at 9 o'clock and look at the pretty dresses. This time I will not buy, I'll just look around. I cannot spend the money I have saved just $25.00, but this small amount should help Ray and I some—to start our lives together. I better put this away and try and get some sleep, now I feel sleepy.

Stockton, California, San Joaquin pool hall
Saturday, January 14, 1928

It is lunch time now but I am not hungry. Tatay and Manong Julian as always went to Mayon Restaurant to eat some Filipino food. Tatay likes "Adobo and Dinagoan." Mayon Restaurant always have those two on their "menu." I talked to Seriaco just a few minutes ago and I ask him about Ray; he told me that's why he came to see me. Ray says, "Don't forget tomorrow at

noon" and he cannot see or even try to see me today. I told Seriaco to tell Ray that I understand. I felt a little shiver go thru my
body thinking about tomorrow, the commotion I'll start behind
once Tatay finds out I have eloped with Ray. And there's an
installation and dance, the Gran Oriente Filipino is giving
176 tonight, and Tatay won't let me attend it. I know why. He says I
cannot go to the dance, but it does not matter now.

8 o'clock in the morning, Oakdale, California
Wednesday, January 18, 1928

Ray and I eloped last Sunday, January 15, like we had planned.
We are here in Oakdale. I don't know how far we are from
Stockton; I hope and pray that we are far, far away so Tatay
cannot find us right away until we are married. I could not
write in this book until today. We are staying with Mr. & Mrs.
Roxas until we can afford to rent a house. All the money we
have is $26.00. Ray is broke. Mr. & Mrs. Roxas are going to be
the best man and matron of honor when Ray and I get married. So they are going to be our Ninong and Ninang. They are
really good people to help us out this way. Ninang and Ninong
took Ray and me to Modesto last January 16, 1928, which was
last Monday, to register for our marriage license. The clerk did
not believe me when I told him that I am 20 years old. He even
looked at me thru the window—he shook his head and said, "I
do not believe that you are 20 years old." At this time I was
hanging on Hon's arm (Ray and I decided to call each other
Honey—Hon, for short) and my knees were shaking. I was
sort of scared that he will refuse us but he went on writing.
Hon and I answered all his questions. When he finished, he
told us to come back in 3 days and pick up the marriage license.
While he was talking to us he looked at me with a doubt look
on his face and shook his head once again. We thank him and
started down the stairway. And as we walk down I look at Hon
and smiled and he smiled down at me and squeeze my hand.

While we are staying with Ninong and Ninang Hon is able to work with Ninong pruning fruit-trees. Ninong has four men and with Hon makes five men. They have started to prune yesterday and Hon told me that they are going to work tomorrow till Saturday or Sunday until the pruning is finished. So this mean we cannot pick up the marriage license tomorrow. We have to wait till Monday and I am hoping very much that Tatay does not find us until Hon and I are married. I hope our Father in Heaven will take care of Hon and I and not let anything happen to us. He has help us the day we elope and I am hoping and praying that He will watch over us and we can get married next Monday.

Oakdale, California
Saturday, January 21, 1928

I washed all our dirty clothes, just Hon's and mine, this morning, took me 2 hours to finish my washing, then I hung them out to dry. I hope that the clothes will be dry before Hon, Ninong Roxas, and the men comes home. Ninang just smiled at me so I just smiled back and I continue my washing. After I finished washing Ninang said, "Come, let us eat." I washed the dishes when we had finished eating. After, I sat down and read, I just love to read. Ninang sat in her chair in one corner of the room, on her favorite corner, and start on her embroidering. When Ninang starts cooking supper, I get up too. I ask her to tell me what I can do to help her. She told me to cook the rice and so I did and she told me to peel a large onion and peel about 6 large potatoes cut-up. Without being told, I put them in cold water, enough water to cover the potatoes. After that there's nothing more to do until we finished supper. Hon, Ninong, and the boys came home at 4 o'clock, they have finish pruning this one place. No work, Hon says, until next week Tuesday, because on Monday, January 23, Ninong and Ninang will drive Hon and me to Modesto and pick up our marriage license so we can get married early Monday morning as soon as the justice of the peace opens Monday morning. While we were eating supper, Ninang told Hon especially, that I was busy this morning, washing clothes. Hon looked at me with a surprise look on his face, swallowed the food, he was chewing on

178

and said, "I didn't think you know how to wash clothes. I was going to do the washing tomorrow, being we finished pruning today." So I told Hon, "Of course I know how to wash clothes. My mother taught me how to wash diapers since I was 7 years old. And so from there on, I wash clothes. My mother made me wash the little things like my own clothes and my brother baby clothes and I know how to iron. We were still in Honolulu, I do the washing for my father and brother and wash my clothes besides." Yes, they were all surprised to know that I know how to wash. I know Hon was pleased, he gave me tight squeeze and when I looked at him he kissed me. I like that very much, but I got embarrass at the same time because he kiss me in front of them all. As if he read my thoughts, he said, "Don't feel ashamed, they know what this is all about, we are husband and wife." He hugged me again and said, "Come on let us eat" and the chatter went on at the table. I do the washing of the dishes while they all went and sat down on the dining-room benches and start playing cards. Ninang wanted to wash the dishes but I told her that I do the dishes as long as we are living with her and Ninong. Besides, I told her, you did the cooking. When I finished washing the dishes and pots and pans I sat down beside Hon while they played "poker," while Ninong and Ninang played Koonkian, a "Filipino card game." They played poker until 7 o'clock and being today is Saturday they went into town to see a movie. Oakdale is a very small town. Hon and I stayed home and we played the same card game that Ninong and Ninang were playing. We played cards until 8 o'clock, 'cause by this time Ninong and Ninang said good-night and we said good-night too. We went to bed too, since the men all went to see the movie. When Hon finally fell asleep I had a chance to write in this book. I am writing this on my lap here in bed. The men haven't come home yet, if I hear them coming I'll turn off the light. Until then, I'll try and finish my writing. Hon does not know I am keeping a diary. I keep this under the mattress on my side of the bed. I like to keep and write what's happening to me, Hon, or other things I would like to remember.

Oakdale, California
Tuesday, January 24, 1928

At last, Hon and I are married; we were pronounced "husband and wife" yesterday at 10 o'clock at the Hall of Justice here in Oakdale by the justice of the peace, Judge Woods. We were married January 23, 1928. Oh, I am so happy that we are married. Ninong and Ninang Roxas were our witnesses besides being the best man and the matron of honor. They both wish us a lot of good luck and happiness and every good wish they thought of. Hon gave the judge $5.00 and Hon paid $2.00 for our marriage license. From the Hall of Justice Ninong drove to a chicken farm here in Oakdale. We were there about an hour or longer, I think there was a very good reason why we stay at the chicken farm longer. By staying at the farm longer than usual saved our lives and also Ninong and Ninang's also because as soon as we got home our neighbor told us that Tatay has been here and he was furious, so very angry, that he wanted to kill Hon and me. Do you know he was 15 minutes late after we were married. It's a good thing we left right after the ceremony. By asking around he found out where we live. Our neighbor told us that Tatay and Manong Julian and some friends stayed and waited for us about half hour. Then our neighbor told us that my brother finally convinced Tatay to leave. My brother told Tatay to leave us alone because Hon and I are married now, there is nothing he can do but to leave us alone. Anyway, I'm glad that they were gone when we got home. Alonzo cooked the chicken. Hon killed the chicken and we plucked the feathers off, it was hard work plucking the feathers off. We got the chickens cleaned and since Alonzo is the cook, he prepared the chickens for our wedding supper for all of us, which was very nice of him. We were all so happy especially Hon and me. Tatay **180** was forgotten. Ninang put on the phonograph and we all danced to it. Alonzo danced with me couple times and he went back to his cooking. I sat out the plates and spoons on the table. Alonzo cooked a wonderful supper. We all enjoyed our wedding supper, it was really wonderful. Everyone toasted and wished Hon and me the best of health, plenty of good luck (we need plenty of that), and all the happiness in this world. After the supper, the men went to the movies in Oakdale. Ninang and Ninong Roxas went to the movies too. They left Hon and me to ourselves. Hon and I are going to the movies, too, but we are going not until Saturday, January 28—there is going to be a good movie "Ramon Navarro." Hon and I both like him. Ninang and Ninong and the men gave us a chance to be by ourselves for 3 hours. We took a quick bath together and went to bed. I am only fifteen years old and being in love with Hon seems to make my life complete. I love Hon so very much. I am so happy that we are married now and tonight we loved. This night and other nights like this and all other nights to follow, I'll always remember them, and I pray to God our Father in Heaven that He will always keep us together as husband and wife—for always. I fell into a deep sleep. I woke up with the smell of coffee perking. Alonzo was already up and was making coffee. I got out of bed and used the bathroom before the others woke up.

Oakdale, California
Thursday, January 26, 1928
Ninang Feliza is taking a nap. Hon and the men with Ninong Roxas are pruning somewhere at Riverbank. They have been

pruning apricot trees since last Tuesday. I washed this morning. The clothes are out hanging in the sun to dry. I swept the kitchen floor, the dining-room floor, and the living-room and now I can sit down and write. It is very quiet here. I do go out in the back yard and sit on the steps, that is what I did after I finished sweeping and washing. The sun got too hot so I came in to write. Pretty soon Ninang is going to wake up. I am going to cook the rice about half an hour after 3 o'clock so I won't be in the way when she is cooking. I try to help her as much as I can when she is cooking and I try to do the sweeping of the floors and dusting the furnitures, all the time.

Monday, January 30, 1928

Hon got paid last Saturday January 28 so we went to the movies. We invited Ninong and Ninang Roxas to come with us but they say they'd rather stay home because Ninong says he is tired. So Hon and I left for the movies as soon as I finish washing the supper dishes. We said good-night to Ninang and Ninong. Some of the men left for town already. We walked to the movie house. It was wonderful walking with Hon and to be his wife and I feel very happy. Now and then Hon would squeeze my hand and said, "I love you," and I'd whisper back looking up at him, "I love you, too." Before we reach the street lights, Hon kissed me. I returned his kiss. And then Hon said we better stop this or we'll never reach the movie house and we both laugh and we continue walking. Anyway the movie was very good. Hon and I like the movie. When we came out of the movie house, we stop in at a coffee and donut shop and bought a dozen donuts. When we got home, Hon put some wood in the stove. Ninang have an iron-cast-wood-stove and had the fire going and pretty soon the kitchen felt warm. (It was cold outside.) And Hon put five donuts in a pan and put it in the oven, which was hot inside by this time. I made some tea. Soon, we had some hot donuts and tea. Oh the donuts tasted so good. I ate 2 and 1 cup of tea, Hon finished the 3 donuts. We left the rest of the donut on the table. Whoever comes in later in the night are welcome to the donuts. Between each bit mouthful of donuts Hon would kiss me, but I would not let Hon kiss me until I have swallowed my mouthful of donuts. It is so wonderful to be in love and married. Anyway, Hon and I enjoyed our donuts and tea very much. It was past midnight before Hon and I crept in bed. Ninang and Ninong were asleep already. In the afternoon Hon and his men friends played a Filipino-football game called "Sipa." I sat on the front steps and watch them play. They play for 2 hours. I finally went into the house and start helping Ninang cook supper. Hon came in later and took a bath, because playing out there really made him sweat very much. It was close to supper time, so Hon stayed in the house and played card with the men. I set the table for supper. We had fried chicken for supper and we enjoyed our supper very much. Ninong and Ninang and the men, even Hon, were telling jokes. I just smiled as I looked around and kept on eating. When we finished supper, as usual, I cleared the table and wash the dishes, while they played cards. Later when I have finish with the dishes and had taken a quick bath, I sat by Hon and watched them play cards until 8 o'clock. The men went to town and Hon play a filipino card game called "Kung kiang." I do not know how to spell it, I am spelling it the way the word is pronounced, with Ninong. They played until 9 o'clock then Ninong said to Hon and me, "It is time to go to bed. We have to work tomorrow." So we all chimed in and said "good-night." This is the only time I can write in my book when Hon and the others are working. Ninang does not question me about this book. When I write, she just looks up and smile, and I smile back, we do not make conversation. I'd rather write than talk any time and I think Ninang Feliza feels the same way. She always takes a nap in the afternoon. She tells me to take a nap, too, but I told her that I do not take naps.

Diary

Oakdale, California

Monday afternoon, February 6, 1928

Today's the first chance I have to write in this book. I did my washing clothes this morning and Ninang did some sewing. At lunch time she called me to eat lunch. I wash the dishes and dry them and put them back on the shelf in the cabinet where Ninang puts her dishes. I have lots of time this afternoon. I want to write here that since Hon and I got married, I have been so happy, I have never been so happy before. Hon have been very loving and so very good and thoughtful to me. I have been so happy here with Hon that I forgot all about Tatay and Manong Julian somehow. What they think of Hon does not matter anymore. Someday, I hope, very much that they will learn to like Hon and think of him differently and welcome as one of the family.

Oakdale, California

Friday, February 10, 1928

This morning about 10 o'clock, Ninang and I went to town. First we went to a 5 & 10 store and look around. There were so many pretty things. The dishes caught my eye. I thought to myself someday when we have our own place Hon and I will come here and buy some pots and plates, spoons, and other things that we need. Right now we do not own anything— except for our clothes, a steamer trunk that Hon owns, and a suitcase. So someday we can start buying things that we need. From the five and dime store we went to a Piggly-Wiggly Butcher or meat store. Ninang bought some pork steaks, some stew meat, and she bought some pigs feet. Ninang bought some washing soap and vegetables. We both had our arms full of bags of groceries. Then we walk back home. I think we walk about 1½ mile to and back home. I did not mind the walk. I enjoy walking. I helped her put the groceries away. I put the meats in the wooden "ice-box." Hon bought a 25 lbs of ice a few days ago to put in the "ice-box." The ice lasts for about 6 days. It sure keeps the box really cold. Oh, tomorrow I am going to iron our clothes. I have to ask Ninang if I can use her heating-irons that is if she is not going to iron clothes herself. I have to iron right after they leave for work. This way it will warm up the room.

184   I'll try and finish my ironing in the morning. I sing when I'm ironing or sweeping the floors. Ninang do not say anything, besides I sing softly. When I sing, I sing all the songs I know. I hope Ninang won't get tired with my singing and I think of Hon when I am singing.

Oakdale, California
February 15, 1928

Ninang told Hon and me that the cannery here will open and start their canning season for spinach next month, March, and she told Hon when they start hiring he should be there and that I should go with her and apply for work there too. Hon and I answered that we will go with her when that time comes. I and Hon, too, was very glad to know about the cannery work. We're very anxious for the cannery to open. I am anxious to be able to work 'cause if Hon and I are working, we can rent a house sooner and that would be wonderful.

February 16, 1928

I do not have very much to do these days when I finish sweeping the house and dusting. I sweep the kitchen, dining and the living room floors. I do not have anything more to do but wait this afternoon when Ninang starts to cook our supper, then I help with the cooking but until that time I write and read and day dream about Hon until he comes home from work. Then we have each other for the night until dawn, then I fix him his breakfast. He likes fried eggs and toast but if there's rice left-over from last night supper Hon would rather have fried rice and some "toyu" fried, and a small saucer of little mashed garlic and vinegar so he can dunk his toyu in it. At least I am learning what he likes to eat. He loves fish, any kind of sea food, and he likes pig's feet cooked either "sinigang" or "adobado." I know I'll enjoy keeping house and cooking for him.

Tuesday, February 28, 1928

Yesterday was Hon's 25th birthday. Ninang cooked a nice supper. We sang songs, after we had supper. For Hon I sang "Always," our love song, and I also sang "Girl of My Dreams," one of the newest song I learned. But "Always" will always be my favorite song. Hon danced with me most of the dances, he danced with Ninang and our friends danced with me too. We sang and we danced until 8 o'clock. The men all left to go to town to see a movie. Ninong Roxas and Hon played "Kungkiang." I sat close to Hon and watched them play cards and Ninang sat by Ninong. They played until 9 o'clock and Ninang said, "We better go to bed, we have to work tomorrow." We all said "good-night."

Oakdale, California
Saturday, March 3, 1928

Tonight Ninong told Hon and me and the rest of the men here that cannery will open and hire workers this coming Monday, March 5, and he advised us to be there early and stand in line, otherwise we might not be hired. Hon told Ninong and Ninang we are going, we shall be there early. If Hon and I can work steady in the cannery we can rent the house next door. It is only $10.00 a month. It has a bedroom, living-room, kitchen, back-screened-porch, and a toilet-room. So in case we rent this house we have to use a large galvanized tub and heat some water and use the tub to take a bath in. Anyway, that's what Hon and I wanted, a place of our own even if we do not have furnitures. If we are able to rent, we will just buy things that we really needed like pots and pans and dishes and spoons and forks. I hope and pray that Hon and I will be hired Monday so we can earn some money. We went to bed with happy thoughts and happy hearts and our hearts full of love for each other. Do you know that my "monthly period" has not stop. I thought I would be pregnant by now, but I'm not.

186

Monday night, March 5, 1928

Ninang, Hon, and I were hired today. I was so glad that we were hired. Ninang and I cut spinach, we cut off the roots. Oh, first we pick out the bad leaves and the yellow then cut off the roots and put the spinach leaves on a wide moving-belt. We are paid 20 cents a crate for every crate we finish. Today I finish 10 crates only, so I made $2.00 exactly. I hope I can finish more than 10 crates tomorrow. The women are all pieceworkers, especially the spinach cutters. The women who have been working in the cannery every year works faster and so they make more money. Me, I was satisfy that I made $2.00 today. I am glad that I am working and that I made 2.00 today. As for Hon, he is working by the hour and he works 2 hours overtime. I waited for Hon, so we can eat supper together. I helped Ninang in the kitchen with the dishes after they have eaten supper. I told Ninong and Ninang Roxas I am going to wait for Hon, we will have supper together. Hon and I made plans, that as soon as we have enough money save we will rent the next door house and move in. I can hardly wait for that day to be here. Before I put this away, I ask my "floor-lady" today how long the cannery will be running. She told me for about 1 month or 6 weeks or the cannery will stay open until the end of April, it will depend on the spinach farmers, how much spinach they have. Oh, I nearly was not hired this morning because I am only fifteen years old, but Ninang Feliza know the floor-lady, so she told her that I am a married woman (just got married 2 months ago) and Ninang

Feliza told the floor-lady that I am a good worker and that I need the work badly. So the floor-lady hired me. I was so glad that she did. Oh, I hope we will work over a month.

Hon is still working at the cannery. Just the men are working, cleaning up, and as soon the clean-up-job is finished, we know that Hon will be out of work. Anyway, Hon and I saved a little bit to last for a few months for food and rent. The women, including myself, we work until yesterday, April 13, 1928. Anyway, this will give me a chance to clean up the house next door that Hon and I have rented. We told Ninong and Ninang that we can rent the empty house next-door. It was $10.00 a month. We will use the back-porch as our bathroom. We will have to cover the screen up whenever we take a bath—we have a big galvanized tub. Hon bought this when we got married so I can do my washing in it. So today I swept the floors first and I used hot water and soap on the kitchen floor and scrubbed the floor with our broom, then I clean the bedroom and parlor-room, using hot water and soap and scrubbed the floor with the broom, then I did the toilet-room and back porch. I clean the windows too. I rinse all the floors and swept out the soapy water thru the front door from the bedroom and the living-room. The kitchen I swept out the soapy water thru the kitchen-door. By doing this I was able to wash out the front porch too. We are having warm days now so I think it will take about 2 or 3 days for the floors to dry up. Since we can't buy a bedroom set, Hon told me he will make a bed-frame but we'll have to buy a mattress and so by next week we will be moving into the house next door. You know, I feel so happy inside now that we are going to be by ourselves. Ninong and Ninang Roxas were happy for us that we can be by ourselves now. They are the nicest people that we have ever met. They have helped us so very much. They would not accept the money that Hon wants to give them for the rent and for the food. Ninong told Hon that we save our money because you will need it when you find a house to move into. We thank them for being so good to us. So when Hon found out about the house for rent next door he went to the "owner" and paid a month's rent right away. The landlord gave the key to Hon right away. And so, today, Hon and I are anxious to be by ourselves. Oh, Hon and I already bought 3 pots, 1 frying pan, couple large plates, 3 bowls and spoons, forks, teaspoons, and 1 large pot to heat the water in.

188

Oakdale, California
Wednesday, April 18, 1928

Hon and I are now by ourselves, we moved into the house yesterday. We were so busy I did not have time to write in this book at all. Hon fixed our bed first thing, then he put sheets to cover one of the parlor-room window. It is a good thing there were shades, green shades, it rolls up or down when you pull the string that's on the right side of it in the bedroom in the parlor-room and 1 shade in the kitchen. We put 1 cot bed in the parlor to be used as sofa. We bought 3 chairs, they were cheap. We put 2 chairs in the kitchen. Oh, we have to buy 1 drop-leaf table too and Hon was also able to buy an old iron-wood stove for $5.00. It's small, but it's heavy. It looks like Ninang's stove only theirs is so much bigger. Our stove has an oven too. We do not have very much in anything but that does not matter. Right now, we have each other and we are in good health. We are very thankful to our Father in Heaven for what we have and now we are living by ourselves. I cook the rice yesterday and Hon cooked the "Olam." We enjoyed our simple lunch and our supper. Hon bought some fried fish. He call them "toyo" and he told me to fry some rice and we bought watercress and some groceries the other day. So really and truly, we are happy and now that we are by ourselves and our second day in "our house."

It's not really our house, we are just renting, but I pretend it's our house because we are by ourselves now and we are in it.

Saturday, April 21, 1928
Tatay and Manong Julian visited us today. We were very much surprise when we open the door to them. They were the last people I would like to see at this time. Tatay was not angry anymore, that's what he says. Anyway, he cursed me and Hon, saying that as long as he lives that Hon and I will have bad luck—we can't save money and all that kind of talk. Hon says he is, meaning Tatay, bluffing, but deep in my heart I know Tatay means everything he had said to us. Anyway Hon and I will always be together even if we are going to have hard luck. Tatay and Manong Julian, oh, Esperanza, her husband Jose and her 2 stepdaughters Sayong and Beatrice, and also Robert, the youngest came with Tatay and Manong Julian, to visit me and Hon. We were glad to have them visit us, we were glad to see them. About 2 o'clock they left early because they have a long ways to go home. Hon and I hug each other when we were alone in the house and we both say it is good to see them leave, because of Tatay. Anyway, Manong Julian told us that we do not have to worry about Tatay now, because we are legally married and there is nothing he can do but leave us alone. Manong Julian before they left he gave me $2.50 and he told us they are working in Salinas now, there are plenty of work there. I am glad for their sake that they are working. Hon says, "I am really getting hungry." I just had to make Chicken Sinigang—there was the back 1 thigh, 1 leg, and 1 wing of the chicken that took half hour to cook. We had left-over rice which I fried while the chicken was cooking. I sat the table. You know, since we moved in this house, Hon and I are so happy. I know I am. We are freer in our feelings. We don't have to hide to kiss each other, not like when we were staying with Ninong and Ninang Roxas. I feel ashamed if we kiss in front of them. Sometimes Hon and

I are caught in each other's arms kissing, I feel my face getting hot and feeling so ashamed; but now that we have a place living by ourselves, we do not have to be careful. I know one of these days I am going to get pregnant, for now we can start really saving money for our future and for the baby we are going to have someday.

190

Monday, April 23, 1928

Hon, Ninong Roxas, and his men went to pick cherries today. There will be at least 2 or 3 weeks of work, so I am going to be by myself most of the time now but I won't mind because I have things to do. I have the rooms to sweep every day and tomorrow I am going to town and buy some meat and vegetables and some washing soap so I can wash our clothes. When I do not have anything more to do in the house I have my crocheting to do. I feel so happy. Oh, I love to read, too. I just bought 2 magazines when I went to town to buy some groceries the other day. I passed the news stand and saw the "magazines" so I bought the Good-Housekeeping Magazine and True Story Magazine, and I bought white crochet thread and 1 crochet needle. I'm going to make a scarf for our vanity and our chest of drawer. I'll make my own pattern. I'll try and crochet about four scarfs. I have in mind to make a table cloth for our kitchen table.

Oakdale, California
Monday, May 14, 1928

Hon and Ninong finished with the cherry picking. They are staying home until Ninong finds another rancher with orchard of fruit trees. Oh, I met a friend today who is living with Hon's Cousin Leonardo. They are not married, just living together as husband and wife, and they rented the house to our left. And they came from Oakland, Emily did—that's my new friend's name. Emily, she's pretty and tall about 23 or 24 years old and she is Portuguese and she is a very nice person, but we shall see. I am hoping we become good friends. You know, since we came here, she is the first person that really become my friend. I like her and I told her so and she said, "I like you too," and she said, I'm going to call you "Angie"—pronounce An-gee. She says, "Angeles is too long for me." She went on to say, "I hope you don't mind being called 'Angie.'" I told her that I do not mind at all.

Oakdale, California
Monday, June 4, 1928

I'm working again in a apricot-dry-yard. Emily is working here too. Hon and Nardo are picking apricots with Ninong Roxas and his six other boys—I should say men. And they are picking by piecework, they get paid for every box they fill up. Oh, before we came out here, Emily and I, we worked for 2 days in the cannery then we were transferred here to the dry-yard. Anyway we like the work. We work outside but we are working under a roof. Emily and myself and quite a few other women, I am the youngest, are all working piecework. That means we are working by the box of apricots we cut in half which goes on a tray which when we filled up, the men pick up and put it out in the sun for the drying up. I don't know how long the fruits will last. I know I am going to work as long as they (the owners) keep us. Hon and I are both tired when we get home but we are happy because we are earning "money." We take a bath as soon as the water gets real hot. So while the water is getting hot I start cooking our supper too. So when we finished bathing, we are ready to eat. Hon talk to me mostly in his Native tongue which is Tagalog; but I answer him back in English because I cannot speak his dialect. I understand Tagalog, but I can't speak it. Someday I will learn to speak his dialect.

Oakdale, California
Friday night, June 29, 1928

Hon and I went with friends to go shad fishing by net last night. It was a moonlight night and I sat on the side of the bank of the river and just watch Hon pulling up the pole with the net on the other end with a fish or 2 in it. Our friends caught much fish too. It did not take long to catch a lot of shad. With in an hour and half Hon and the others have caught enough fish. When we got home, Hon put the fish in the tub and half filled with water so it will keep the fish scales moist like. Hon says it help to scale the fish much easier tomorrow. Hon and I had some doughnuts and coffee. Hon and I sometime have something to eat, just something small. Hon like to munch on something just before we go to bed, like tonight. After we both finished washing and cleaning ourselves up, we had something to eat. Hon usually develops an appetite, especially after hoisting the long-pole-fish-net for $1\frac{1}{2}$ hours. I think that was hard on the arms. It was a good thing Hon is a young man, he is only 25 years old. And Hon told me tonight we'll go shad fishing sometimes next month again. This time he says he will salt most of them (like the Chinese do) but he has to buy either a 3 or 4 gallon keg (made of wood) and Hon says we will have fish all the time. Anyway, I leave that to him, because he knows what to do with the fish.

Saturday, June 30, 1928

Hon and I went to Stockton today to buy rice. I think we will buy the 100 lbs. sack. It will last us a long time. And Hon wanted to buy Lichon and roast duck. Oh, also, some Bituka, cooked the Chinese way, it's good. There is not a Chinese store here in Oakdale, so Hon and I go to Stockton to buy rice and the other oriental food that we like to eat. Anyway, I enjoy the one-hour-ride to Stockton. Sometimes we go to Modesto, which is only 15 miles away, but we do not go there too often.

Oh, we have a chance to visit friends for a few hours. Hon does all the talking, he know them, I just keep quiet. If they ask me questions I answer and talk to them, but otherwise, I keep my mouth shut. Many times they would say to him, "Your wife does not talk much—she is a very quiet person," and Hon answer them, "Yes, she is a quiet person, she does not talk unless you talk to her." I kind of smile to myself when I hear them talk about me. I have found out that Hon is a hard-working guy. When he is out of work, he goes out and look for work and he always finds work. Ninang Roxas tells Hon and me that the cannery will open soon. The cannery will open for the "peach season," Ninang says. I pray that I will be hired again and I pray for Hon that he will be hired too. We all need to work because we must have money to live, money to buy groceries and to pay our house rent and save a few dollars if we can for the days to come, especially for wintertime.

Monday, July 9, 1928

Hon and I and Ninang and Ninong Roxas and the 3 men that's boarding with them, are working in the cannery again. Yes, the cannery opened today, for the peach season. I was hired for cutting and pitting peaches and it was piecework at 20¢ for each box of peaches that I have cut and pitted. For all peaches cut and pitted goes on the belt. I was slow at first, but by noontime I was able to work faster. I made $2.75 today. I hope to work a little or make more tomorrow. I came home with Ninang and Emily, while the menfolks stayed on to work until 6 o'clock. Emily, Ninang, and I each went to her home, parting with "See you tomorrow morning." As soon as I came in, I put the bucket of water on our wood stove and started the fire going. I also washed the pot of rice and put it on the stove and I started cooking the pork meat that I have prepared early this morning. I won't put in the vegetables until Hon comes home. As soon as the water gets hot I will take a bath so I can put another bucket of water on the stove for Hon. Hon came home at 6:30 and the first thing he did was to give me a big hug and kissed me long and I kissed him back. I feel oh so happy when he comes home from work. I feel comforted and safe. I put Hon's clean clothes on a chair while he was bathing. We ate supper as soon as he finished bathing. When we had finish eating supper I wash the dishes and dry them. We talk how lucky we are that we are both hired today. Hon fell asleep before I did. I hope I can go to sleep as fast as Hon did. I have to get up early tomorrow morning to fix breakfast, our lunch and get ready to go to work. You know we have to walk about a mile to work? Hon and I do not mind the walk, we are young, we can do it.

Saturday night, July 14, 1928

We worked all week and my hand and wrist were hurting, my wrist got swollen, because I learned to work fast—we cut the peaches in half (we must cut a clean half) and we pitted them and place them on the belt which is constantly moving. I work fast, it is the only way that I can make more money. I felt so good last Thursday. I made $4.00. That's pretty good—don't you think? That's what I have in mind to make $4.00 if I can keep it up every day. We shall see. They have been working 10 hours a day. It is good that Ninang and I come home 2 hours earlier, the cutters and pitters (all women), because I can cook supper and I can take a bath before Hon comes home.

Sunday night, 11 o'clock, July 15, 1928

Hon and I went shad fishing tonight but somehow tonight I kept telling Hon that we should go home early. And I kept looking upwards to where the road was as if I was expecting someone to come down on us. It was a scary feeling. This was the only time that I can remember that I keep telling Hon "let us go home early." And Hon answers me, "Just a few more shad and we'll go home." He kept his word. By 8 o'clock Hon caught enough, so we went home. I felt so relieve. As soon as we reached home, Hon put the shads in the tub we use for the shads and he covered the fishes with water so the scales stays soft. He went on talking telling me he will scale them tomorrow before he goes to work. Anyway, Hon says let's clean up and wash up before we go to bed. It was 9:30 at night, when I crawl in bed and Hon followed. Then in my sleep, I woke up and Hon did too. There was a loud banging on our front door and a loud voice saying, "Andoy! Andoy! Wake up, wake up, your Ninong Roxas had been shot!" Hon got out of bed and put on his clothes fast and opened the door and told our friend to come in and he told him, "I'll go back with you." Hon came back to our bedroom and told me to be quiet and not open the door to anyone. I am going to lock you in, I don't know how long I'll be there. He kissed me and hug me tight and said, "Try and go back to sleep, I will tell you all about it when I get back." I can only look at him. I don't know if he saw in my eyes how scared I was, without being told actually what had happened. I sensed something terrible has happen. I wanted to go with Hon but I know what he will say. I heard Hon turned the key in the lock. I was scared to be alone. I just got under the blankets. I tried to go to sleep but could not sleep, I was wide awake. Hon finally came home.

195

Monday, July 16, 1928

I was so glad to see Hon. It was 1 o'clock when Hon came home. I was so glad to see Hon, that I put my arms around his neck, when he bend down to kiss me, and pulled him down in bed with me, and I kissed him as if he had been gone a long time and I told him how scared I was when he was gone. Somehow my fears went and left me when Hon came home. Hon told me that Marcus _____ shot Ninong Roxas twice, the second shot killed Ninong. The first shot went thru the fleshy part of his stomach. Hon says if only Ninong had fallen right away, Hon thinks Marcus would not have shot Ninong again, but fate didn't want it that way. It was fated that Ninong had to die. It was a terrible tragedy. We both felt terrible and sad, we felt sorry for Ninang. Oh, she must be crying so now. Hon says she is with Ninong now. Ninang told Hon not to **196** worry about her, she will be alright. Hon was told that Marcus was asking about us and someone told him that we went fishing. Now, I think that was why I had a feeling of wanting to come home early. I think I told Hon that Marcus was going to kill us, too. Hon agreed with me. Anyway, Hon put my mind at ease and told me not to worry because he says that by this time he must be far away from here. Hon went on to say that he won't be foolish to stay around to get arrested, and I believe Hon. It was 2 o'clock before Hon fell asleep. I had to write these events down before I laid my head on Hon shoulder and snuggled closer to Hon.

Friday, July 20, 1928

Hon was told yesterday that Marcus went to the spot where Hon and the other people go shad fishing. He was really going to kill us. I thank God for giving me that feeling of wanting to go home early. I think he passed by the house, but since Hon and I went to sleep early—all lights were out—Marcus perhaps thought we were not home yet, so whoever drove the car he was in just drove on. I shiver when Hon told me, Marcus must have gone crazy. And we do not know why he shot and killed Ninong Roxas. Ninang Roxas is sad. I sure feel so sorry for her. Hon and I try to comfort her the best we know how, but we know too, that she would like to be by herself. Oh, Hon told me that the "Gran Oriente Filipino" are looking for Marcus. You see, Ninong Roxas is a "33" in that fraternity and he was "a worshipful master" of "Mayon Lodge #19." Some say that Marcus could not be found because he fled to Mexico. I hope that he will be caught, I wonder. I do not think he will come back to Oakdale. Speaking of

"Gran Oriente Filipino" Hon is an "applicant." That is why Pete Braga, Isidro Gonzales, Ricardo (I can't think of his last name) help Hon; these are the 3 men that accompanied Hon when on that very important night in our lives to interpret to Tatay that Hon and I love each other and that we want to get marry and that is why too that Ninong and Ninang Roxas helped us. It was very sad that Ninong was killed, he was such a good person. Hon and I will never forget him and Ninang Feliza too, they have been very good to us. They have made things possible for Hon and I to be together.

197

Thursday, July 26, 1928

Hon and I are working steady in the cannery this week and Ninang is working too. I am glad that she is. Keeping busy will help her some, keep her mind occupied. Hon and I will work until the peaches are over for this season. I think the peaches will last for another 2 or 3 weeks, I really hope so. We will be able to save some money for winter. Hon and I are very thankful that we are both alive and have each other. I shudder when I think of what might have happened.

Thursday night, August 2, 1928

Today is my birthday. I am 16 years old today. We both worked today but when we got home, Hon cooked the supper because it was my birthday. So, I took a bath while Hon was cooking supper. Hon fried some chicken wings and the rest he made "pochero" chicken cooked with tomato-sauce potatoes and peas. I washed the rice and set the pot of rice on the stove and Hon will take care of it while he is cooking the chicken. Hon is so good to cook our supper. And so when I finish my bath, Hon had to wait about 20 minutes before the water to get real hot to take his bath. Hon and I always take our baths first before we sit down to eat. We feel better. After we have our supper and I finish washing the dishes we sat down and talk. Here, I am sixteen years old today and as I look at Hon so handsome and I am so in love with him and I belong to him; I am truly happy that he is my husband, that we will be together for all the days to come.

Saturday, September 1, 1928

Hon and I like the movie we saw last night, it was very good. When we came out from the theatre last night, the night air was cool. It was really a nice night for walking and when you are in love, it makes that much more nicer and so much more romantic. Where there was no light Hon would stop and kiss me. I like that very much, and we continue walking home. It takes Hon and I about 15 or 20 minutes to reach home. It is truly wonderful when you walk with the one you love. Oh, when we come out of the theatre, we stop at the donut coffeeshop and Hon bought a dozen donuts. So when we reach home we warm up some donuts and I made some Postum, and we had donuts and Postum before we went to bed. I am content to just stay home and do my house-chores, crochet-read, and cook for Hon.

Friday, September 14, 1928

Ninang Feliza moved to San Francisco. She told Hon and me that she has some friends there. We hate to see her go, but there is nothing we can do. She has her life to live. She is as old as Hon, I think, and I know she will be alright. We will miss her. It is so sad what happen to Ninong and Ninang Roxas lives—now Ninang is a widow. I wonder if Hon and I will meet her again someday in the future. We wish her good health and good luck and wish that she will find happiness again, someday. And we thank her for all the wonderful things that Ninong Roxas did. He is gone now but Hon and I will always remember what they have done for us, and we will never forget them.

Diary

Sunday, September 16, 1928

Hon and I are by ourselves—Ninang Feliza moved away and now Emily have moved back to the city to Oakland where she came from. She did tell me she missed the "big city." I guess she can't live the hard times of a "campo-life." I am going to miss her. We had so much fun together, even if she is so much older than I am, and we have known each other just a short while.

Monday, September 24, 1928

Do you know that Hon and I have been married eight months and eight days and I am not in the family way yet. I wonder why? I am very young, maybe that's why. Anyway, when the time is right, I will get pregnant. So I will have to be patient, like Hon tells me, "Wait and see, you will get pregnant" and he would kiss me.

Hon is picking Thompson grapes (seedless). I wanted to work with him but the owner of the grape farm do not hire woman workers. So now I just stay home. I sew and I crochet a lot. I bought some stamped pillow-cases so I can embroider them and I am going to crochet the open ends. Whenever I get tired crocheting, I read. I have a white neighbor who lives 2 houses from us. She is a big woman and her name is Helen and I call her Mrs. Brown. She is a very nice person, very friendly. I like her. She has a dog who have some pups and they are cute. Hon and I admired them so she gave us one, a golden-curly-fur dog. He looks so cute. So Hon and I name him "Rex," and he is ten weeks old. Hon fixed him a box where he sleeps and we put a lot of papers on 1 side where he can do his, you know what, and other side we put an old blanket for his "bed" and a space to put his food and water. As soon as we have him long enough, we will teach him some tricks. We put his box near the wood box by the "iron-stove" that we have. I like my "iron-stove" and it has an oven and I bake biscuits in it. (Alonzo taught me how to make biscuits while we were still living with

Ninong and Ninang Roxas. I'm so glad he taught me how to make biscuits 'cause Hon and I love biscuits besides donuts.) Alonzo also taught me how to roast a chicken, and how to roast a big turkey, and Alonzo told me that the stuffing I make for the chicken is the same for the turkey, only I have to make a large amount for the turkey.

200

Friday, September 28, 1928

I am at home all the time. The only time I go out is when I have to buy some groceries. I walk to town when I do. When Hon is not working we go and buy our groceries together. I like that, another thing, I learn to buy meat that Hon like and too, Hon knows what to buy and since we got married I learned what he really likes and the things that he does not like. Yes, I learned his "ways" and I loved all what I learned about him. On some days Hon and I visits some friends. At one time Hon and I went with his friends to Turlock to play baseball. We stayed there all day. Hon played baseball practically all day. Hon enjoyed playing baseball. I met and made friends with the people that we came and visit and that Hon had met thru working with them. I enjoyed our visit with them, they are nice people. It was really nice meeting them and their familys.

Monday, October 1, 1928

Hon went to work today. After I swept the floor I did my embroidery. I am embroidering a pair of pillow-cases. Oh, I forgot to write down that I made some curtains for our bedroom and living-room, the rooms really look better with curtains. I made the curtain by hand. You know, Hon and I have been married 8 months and 3 weeks and I am still very happy with my life with him as he is with me. Rex, our dog, is good company. Sometimes I go out to visit Mrs. Brown. I usually just stay outside her house because of Rex and we talked for a while while Rex stay close to me. You know, she is a very large person, maybe weigh about 300 pounds maybe more, but she is a very nice person. She is the only one I visit and I talk to around here.

Saturday, October 6, 1928

Hon is not working today. He told me last night they have finished the work at Atwater and they have a new place picking grapes next Monday. Mr. Ellorin is his boss and he says they will be working at Escalon. So he stays home and rest today and tomorrow; so wonderful to have him home full day. So today, this morning at 10 o'clock we went walking to town and bought groceries. We bought meat, vegetables, coffee, milk, sugar, and bread, also some flour and baking powder so I can make some pancakes tomorrow for breakfast. We both like pancakes, they are so easy to make. Alonzo taught me how to make the batter. Hon and I enjoyed our grocery shopping together—I love it, just being together. You know, I do not miss my father. I should, but I do not, but I love my father, in a different way, because he is my father.

Friday, October 12, 1928

My monthly period did not come on the second of this month. It has always come on time before. It usually come the day before and never was late, but this month my monthly is late. So I think I am pregnant but I will wait until next month, I will know for sure if my monthly does not show up. Hon is busy working; Hon works every day if there is work and Hon tells me that winter will be upon us and work will be very scarce. And so when there is work he works.

Oakdale, California
Saturday, October 20, 1928

Hon has no work today. He told me that they have finish the work at river bank. They have a new place to work Monday. So today while I was washing clothes, Hon was busy cutting wood for our stove and he was storing them up in an open garage we have in the back yard. Hon is cutting wood whenever he can so we'll have a lot to pull us thru the winter. Hon goes by the river and collects wood. There are plenty of wood along the river banks, whenever he has the time to pick up some wood after work. Hon always looks after our needs. I do not have to tell him nothing, what to do and all that. I do have to walk to town by myself sometimes to buy a few groceries, when Hon is working. Otherwise, we go to town together to buy groceries, because two people can carry more groceries than 1 person.

Wednesday, October 31, 1928

Oh, I forgot to write you about the big salmon caught by hand. Hon and 2 of our friends helped Hon catch it in a shallow stream; I was very surprise to see the big fishes swimming up stream and I pointed them out to Hon. And Hon yelled out to his friends to come over where we were, he has something to show them. They were really surprise too. Hon recognized the big fish—they were salmon and he says they have to go upstream to lay their eggs and if they do not reach the ocean most of the salmon die. Yes, they try to swim back to the ocean Hon says, but most of them die. Being weak, I suppose after laying their eggs, the salmon just die afterwards, how pathetic. Each one of our friend have big fish to take home. I don't know how Hon found the place, but he told me that Ninong and his men and Hon used to work close by, when they pruned trees this past January. Anyway, we came home as soon as Hon and our friends caught a fish to bring home. We were all so glad about the fish they forgot about the wood they were supposed to gather for our stoves. Hon says we will get the wood later. Hon was really happy about the big fish. Hon scaled and cleaned the salmon. He made sinigang out of the head and we fried some of the stomach. It's a good thing Hon knows how to clean the big fish.

I watch Hon how he was cleaning the fish and how he was cutting and slicing them up. He salted them and put them in a keg, and you know what—we had fried fish and sinigang tonight. Oh, Hon gave our neighbor some fish, they thank Hon because they do not sell salmon here in Oakdale. You have to go to Stockton or to Modesto to buy fish.

Saturday, November 3, 1928

I am only sixteen but I know that Hon is my whole life. I am sure that Hon will take care of me. I know we are not rich, we are poor. We have no money in the bank, but we are happy. I love to keep house. Here is what I do when Hon goes to work. I fix the bed, we have a wooden bed that Hon made when we moved into this house and we bought a new mattress and made a table by the bed. I made a table cloth for it that matches the curtains on the windows which I sewed by hand. Hon gave me money to buy the material. Doing all this really kept me busy for a while, but I always do my house-cleaning first. Than I sit down to do my sewing, crocheting, or reading. And so my days are always like this and I am happy doing them, and than by 3 o'clock I start to cook the rice. We have an iron wood-stove. It did not take long for me to learn because for the few months we had lived with Ninong and Ninang Roxas, I learned from Ninang Roxas how to cook on it. And by the time Hon gets home, I have the hot water ready for his bath. My day is complete when Hon comes home from work.

Saturday, November 17, 1928

Hon went to work today with Mr. Nick Flores. Hon do not know what they are going to do today. You know what, starting the first part of November I was feeling bad every morning, I felt like vomiting—and I do and did. I just want to lie down and sleep it off. By noontime, I feel better, the bad feeling I had in the morning was gone. So, I swept the floor and straighten up whatever there was to do. I just don't like getting sick in the morning, but there is nothing I can do about it. I just do my housework and I try to finish them as soon as I can, so I can lie down and try to sleep it off.

204

This is Mom's last entry. She said she felt too sick in the mornings to write anything in her diary. But when her morning sickness stopped after three months, she said she just didn't feel like writing in her diary again. I was born on July 14, 1929.

—Editor

Memoir

I was born February 27, 1903, in the District of Tondo in the city of Manila, Philippine Islands. I was baptize in Tondo Catholic Church and given the name of Alejandro. My mother's full name is Folgencia Ponce and my father is Gabino Raymundo. I don't exactly know my mother's parents, which I'll explain later. My mother and parents and all kin are all from Bulacan Province.

My father was born in the Province of Rizal, so my grandfather, whose name is Juan and whose kin are all from Rizal Province. My grandmother, I was told, was from Cavite Province and her name is Juana Salvador y Corpus. I'll try to remember my childhood days up to until I was 18 years old, the time I left for the United States of America. It was January 21st, 1922, when I left Manila aboard the United States Hoosier State.

As a kid I live with my grandparents of my father's side, together with my auntie, the only sister of my father, her husband, and their children. The first I can remember as a small boy, I can't go out and play with the other kids from the neighborhood, and I can't go far from the home where we live. If I do so, I sure get a severe spunking from my grandmother, and I always have to do all chore in the house like washing the dishes, mopping the floor, cleaning the yard, and carrying water from the public faucet which is several blocks away from the house. I have to fill all the water jar which was about six of them each holding about 25 gallons each. I have to do all this while all my cousins, children of my auntie, are playing outside and are free to roam wherever they please, and if I fail to do my chore, I surely have good spunking from my grandmother or my auntie.

My father and mother separate while I was a very small boy. I can't remember any of those days. I was told that I had two sisters, the oldest died when she was a baby, then I was born, and after me my younger sister was born but also died when she was a little baby. So I am all by myself, but I don't remember those happening. I was too young to know. After I grow older and could understand, our oldest neighbor and friend of the family, not my parents, told me the story of my father and mother, how they separate, and that once in a while my mother would come around the neighborhood, just to see me and how I am getting along, but I can't remember that I had seen my mother or talk to me at all because our neighbor will tell my grandma or my auntie that (Manciang), that's the nick name of my mother, that she is around the neighborhood, and that right away my grandfather would take me for a walk until she leave the neighborhood.

As I grow older, I realize the reason why as a small boy they won't let me play with the other kids in the neighborhood, or I can't even go out of our yard. If I do I get a good beating. I believe it is because they are afraid that my mother might see me around and take me away with her. So you see, I never had known or see my mother until I was 18 years old, which I'll tell later.

Then when I was about 13 years old, one day I was walking home from school, a Ford automobile with a government license pull up by me and the driver called me Andoy. Well, I don't know him, but he get out of the car and come to me. He said, "I'm your uncle, the young brother of your mother. You see, you don't know me, but every time I have chance to come around here, I always look you up without your grandparents knowing it. Well, you are growing up now and it is about time to get acquainted, but don't tell your grandparents that we met, they wouldn't like the idea." You see, my uncle was driving for some government official, so he go around a lots and from there on we met now and then to say hello.

When I get to the age of seven, I was allowed to play with neighbor kids but can't go far away, just around the block but from home. Then I got a few fun. That was the time I start school. First my grandmother took me to the Spanish school. You see my grandmother speak

Spanish fluently. She had a high schooling in Spanish, so she want me to go through Spanish school too, but in Spanish school it was very strict and cruel. Once you make a little mistake, they punish you like a criminal. They would kneel you with your bare knee on the floor with mongo beans spread around or have your arms spread like a cross and stay that way for hours. I can't stand it so I told my grandmother I don't want to go to Spanish school, I want to go to English school. You see, in Spanish school you have to pay at least 5.00 pesos a month, and being we are very poor my grandmother agree for me to go to English school that public school is free, nothing to buy but pencil and paper. Books are also free. But unfortunatly, I can't go beyond the first year in high school. Being we are so poor and my grandfather is too old to work steady, I have to quit school and have to find work, which was not so easy in those days.

I remember my first work. It was school vacation time and I was around 14 years old. I work in Manila Railroad as a painter. I paint the signal sign along the rail all the way along the city limit and I got 80 centavos an hour eight hours a day which in those days was very good for my age, and that I could help my grandparents a bit. I got paid once a week and would get only 1 peso allowance and the rest go to my grandmother to buy food and clothing. I was in that job for three months and went to school when vacation was over. But half way through the semester in the first year in high school, I have to quit and go to work permanently. By that time my granduncle, the younger brother of my grandmother, his name was Pablo Salvador, everybody call him Don Pablo, but I call him Lolo Momoy. He is opening a bazaar store of his own. You see, he was a well to do man. He want me to work for him in the store, and pay 30 pesos a month which was very cheap, but my grandmother wants me to work for him, he need my help. So I go ahead and work for him from 8 o'clock in the morning to 9 o'clock in the evening. It was long hours, but I stay on the job. I figure I will learn something in salesmanship. My work in the morning was to go out to collect from those people who owe money in the store and most of them work for the government, and in the afternoon and evening, I stay in the store as salesman. I stay in this job until the day I left for the United States of America. I was 18 years old then.

When I was eight years old I was having fun with the neighborhood kids, but I always get spunking from coming home late, and not doing my chore, I got the spunking either from my grandmother or my auntie, but I take it as it come to me, that is life. You see, my auntie have two sons, and a daughter. The oldest boy was about two years younger than I am. And you know, kids always fight, and when we do my auntie always side to her son, right or wrong. I always get the spunking. Well, I guess it is nature, you always side with your own, right or wrong, and I still remember some fun as a kid we did have.

In Tondo, quite a few people raising fighting chicken, and it is their habit in the evening to take their fighting rooster out and gather around the street under the light where they talk and exchange experience how to raise fighting chicken. Sometimes a few of them would let their rooster fight, just like sparing (practice) and we kids use to gather around and watch the rooster fight.

One evening as usual this people are gather around sitting in circle petting their rooster while we kids, about six or seven of us, is standing outside the circle watching. Among the group there was an old man, oh, he's about 70 years old and toothless, sitting among the group in the circle. This old man always chew nganga (bitternut leaves with lime mix together). Well, he cannot chew it as it come, so he got a bamboo pipe about 12 inches long and about 1 and 1½ inches wide, and he got a long chisel knife very sharp at the end. He would put the nut and leaves inside the pipe, and would crush it with the chisel knife, and when it is crushed, he would tap the pipe on his palm, put it in his mouth and chew it.

Well, this evening as usual, he was very talkative telling which rooster is good, which rooster should be a winner. Well, two of the rooster owner decide to let their rooster practice, let them fight without knife, so they step in the middle of the circle and let their rooster loose. One was white and the other was red in color. While the rooster were circling around poised to fight, this old man with the bamboo pipe pulled the chisel out of the pipe, point it to one of the rooster, and shouted, "Sa pula ako, sa pula, sa pula," meaning, "I am for the red, for the red, for the red," at the same time he was holding his pipe high by his side. One of the kid who was standing behind the old man, I notice he drop something inside the bamboo pipe. I was not far from this kid, so I saw it but the old man didn't notice it. He was too busy watching the fighting chicken and keep shouting and cheering the red rooster. After a few moment the fellows pick up their rooster and the practice was over. So the old man resume his business, put his chisel in the bamboo pipe, and start crushing the nut and leaves while talking and laughing with the groups. While he was talking he tap his bamboo pipe in his palm, while he was saying, "I tell you that red is very good, I'll bet for that red any time, that red is good," and at the same time he put his nganga in his mouth and he says, "That red . . . phew, phew," he says, "sa lintic sa lintic" (meaning, "The hell, the hell . . .") and he start spiting his chew out. The fellows were surprise, and ask, "What happen old man, what's wrong?" "Sa lintic," he says, "Sa lintic. Some body put hot chile pepper in my nganga. Sa lintic." By that time we were already away from the old man. We were afraid he might start swinging with that sharp chisel and, instead, he stood up and start walking for home still mumbling, "Sa lintic, phew, sa lintic," and when he is gone the fellows start laughing, some rolling on the ground, laughing like mad.

This is one of all the fun we were having in those days. Here is another one. In those days the Moro they are very popular. It use to be the story of Prince and Princess, the Christian Prince and the Princess against the Moro Royalties. They were shown in the local theatre and the actor and actress are pickup among the young woman and young man from the locale resident. This show was always sponsored by the Pampanga people and about 305 of the resident of our district are Pampanganian people, so that show was very popular in our district especially when the actor and actress were among the local resident. They always rehearse their act in the backyard of the group of nipa houses, which was very common in Tondo and those backyard mostly are good size, enough room for their act and quite a few people use to watch the rehearsal and that's where we kids gather around and watch, usually in the evening.

One evening one of the rehearsal was in progress in one of that backyard of those group of nipa houses. You see, these houses are about six feet high on bamboo pole and no fence around it, so we kids, if we want to watch this practice, we just go through under the house to the backyard, and there they are shaking and dancing and doing their action like nobody's business. (You see, most of them kids in those day if they are playing around they have only camiseta, no pants, no drawers, the lower half of the body is naked). The rehearsal continue about the life of the prince and the princess. So come the last act, they put a artificial rock on the middle of the yard and here come the princess walking slowly as if she is walking under the moonlite and a little while, here come the prince too and come toward the princess and express his love to her. The princess answered, "I cannot love you. You are a prince, yeah, but you have no ability at all. You have no power. Nothing at all." And the prince says, "I have no power? Well, watch this." He draw his sword and says, "Sa bisa itang encanto, maging silla itang bato," meaning, "The strength of my power this rock become chair," and sure enough, the rock split open, and come out a beautiful chair and the prince ask the princess to sit down on the chair. Soon as the princess was seated, here come a little kid from under the house, his lower half was naked. He was just a spectator like us. He was carrying a little paper bag, he walk right in the midle of the yard, and everybody was watching him then. He drop the paper bag on the ground and say, "Sa bisa itang encanto itang tackla manging puto," meaning, "The strength of my power this shit become bread." Soon as the prince heard this, he start chasing us with his sword. Believe me, did we move. We sure ran so fast we were hitting our head on the bamboo posts, but keep on running for dear life and everybody around there are all laughing like anything.

I still remember as a kid, I was thinking, sometimes wondering, on things that was happening. For example, when I was a kid I was not allowed to look or talk to my own mother if she happen to be around. The old folks never tell me the reason why, and I have no way of knowing. Well, that is the old generation way, and I hope that it all change now.

As a kid I still can remember the eruption of Taal Volcano. It was in 1911. I was 8 years old. It was about 11:00 in the evening. I was standing at the door of our house and I was watching the sky. It was bright red, and the ground was shaking, and the ashes are all over Manila as much as 200 feet high in the air. Boy, it was frightening. And I still remember it was in 1916 when almost half of the District of Tondo burn down. We are lucky our place was not on the way of the fire. You see, in those days the houses in Tondo were mostly nipa houses, and when a fire start, boy, the flame really goes wild. I mean wild. No way of stopping it. The fire lasted about 24 hours and I also remember in the same year, 1916, it was around Fourth of July. One evening a hurricane come without much warning, and that wind really blow and those big acacia trees in Moriones Park are all uprooted and blown down, but the surprise, those nipa houses only few were knock down. They only sway and tremble but stay standing up, but some of roof of those nipa houses are blown away, but the big surprise was the next morning. I was at Moriones Beach. There was a four-masted Maru liner laying in the 20 feet of water. They claim that it miss the light house and sail right to the beach. It took them almost a month before they could pull it out in the deep.

And I also remember a very sad news about my father. It was December 1915. I was 12 years old, when my grandmother received a letter from the Province of Palawan. I can't remember the name of the town. The letter says that your son, Gabino Raymundo, passes away December 15, 1915. And my grandmother told me that my father pass away. I just cried and was very sad of the news. You see, my father and I had not been together very much. He was always traveling from island to island. The death of my father lost my hope to be raised by my own parents and I was left under the care of grandparents and auntie on the side of my father, and I was always hoping that someday when I grow older that I will meet and got to know my own mother if she is still alive. And being not satisfied how I was treated by my auntie, the sister of my father, I began thinking of running away from home, but I don't know where to go, so I thought that if I grow a little older, I'll try if I can have a chance to go to America.

You see, in the Philippine, the dream of most of the young man is to go to America. You see, some of those who had been to America and come back to the Philippine, they are always telling us tall stories about the United States 'cause every evening when we gather around in the barber shop they are there. Boy, they are really telling those stories about how nice those girls are, how easy to earn money, and we travel from place to place in a car, and so we kids, while we are listening, we are getting anxious to go to America and find that kind of life here in the United States and, boy, I don't know, when I was back home when I was a little kid, I have different kind of dreams, different kind of thoughts, and all of that.

Between the age of nine to 11 years old, I think it was the time I had most fun as a kid. You see, at that age I was allowed to play outside provided I finish all my chore at home after school. After I filled all the water jar with water, then I would take off. Often I would take my sling shot, go across the street out in the open in about 50 acres of vacant land where there are lots of tree, guava tree, cheresa tree, coconut tree, and many others, and when the fruits are ripening, there are lots of different kind of birds, mostly Maya, the small lark, and that was what I was hunting for, and they are good to eat when cook and there were lots of wild dove too. You see, I was a good sling shot. I seldom miss. I used a small size of peble rock about the size of a marble which were lots scattered around. I make my own sling shot out of rubber band, and a fork guava branch the size of a pen. Sometimes I would climb the guava tree to pick some ripe fruit, but the owner would chase me out. You see, he didn't mind the fruits taken, but he didn't want the broken branches in the tree. It is alright if you have a long stick and knock the fruit down, but sometime there is no long stick around, so I take a chance and climb, and that's when I'm driven out. Sometimes the owner would ask me to climb the coconut tree and knock some fruits down and I love to do it. I climb the coconut tree like a monkey.

Sometimes late in the afternoon a few of us kid would gather to go to the river to learn how to swim. You see this river, called Canal de la Rayna, it begins in Pasig River, it crosses the District of Binondo and across the District of Tondo, and flow into Manila Bay. We live between Morionese Street and Ricafort Street and the street we live on was Elena Street, just one block long from Morionese to Ricafort and just a few blocks from the river, Canal de la Rayna. On Morionese Street, there was a low concrete bridge about 15 feet high across the river and it was here where we do our swimming. I learn how to swim by myself. You see, in those days there was no swimming instructor, no swimming pool around. Boys and girls go to the river or the beach and learn to swim by themself. The beach is at the end of Morionese Street about a mile from where we live and sometimes we go at the beach and do our swimming there, and we learn how to swim. We go on top the bridge, climb the railing and jump into the river. Lots of fun!

Around our neighborhood there were a few people that own water buffalo (carabao). They use this buffalo to pull two wheel wooden cart. They would park around the railroad depot and when the freight train come in loaded with sacks of rice from the mill, the buyer of these rice would hire these buffalo cart to transport their rice to the warehouse. Hardly any truck in those days. So these people with buffalo and cart make their living loading those rice. Believe it or not, those carabao are strong animal. Those cart have two long wooden bar, at the end is a yoke. A carabao go between the two bar and put the yoke on top of the neck. That's all. No spring on those cart, just a wooden bed about 6' by 10' right on top of the wooden wheel, no spring and they load this cart from 25 to 40 of 100 lbs sack of rice, and those carabao pull that cart single handed from three to five miles away to the warehouse. Those animal are really strong.

Toward evening these people come home on their cart, unhitch the carabao, and feed them in the manger. Then we kids, sometimes three or four of us, will ask the owner if they want us to bring the carabao to the river and let them swim. If the owner say yes, which they usually do, then we would take the carabao out, jump on top of it which is hard to do without help, then we take the carabao one for each kid, we go down the river, and let the carabao go down to the water down the gentle slope. The carabao love water so much and love to swim around. We let them swim around with us still on top, we let them swim for about one hour, then we let them lay down in the shallow water, and we kids keep swimming around, and after a while we take the carabao home and the owner would give each of us five centavos, and we are very happy to earn that money.

In the evening when there is moonlite, we have a game of hide and seek. Boys and girls together play this game. One will be the seeker, and stay with the leader, then we all would take off going under those nipa house, which I already explain, about 6' high and no fence around and there are chicken roosting under those houses in chicken nests, and sometimes we would pick some of the eggs, give it to the leader, and if we have enough, he would boil them and divide among the kids. If the seeker catch one he or she will bring the captive back to the leader and he or she will be the seeker on next round. Oh yes, I remember this happen to me.

As usual, one evening we were playing this game hide & seek. I had no place to hide, so I went to hide under our own house. You see, we got a few chicken and some laying eggs, and the nest are under the house on top the rafter which are held by two cross bamboos. Well, while I was hiding I decide to get some of our eggs because we had a few in those nest. Well, my folks are upstairs talking stories and were laughing. So slowly I climb up the cross bamboo post to the nest. Well, before I climb I put my camiseta bottom inside my salawal (drawer) so I can put the eggs inside my camiseta. So I took about a dozen eggs and put them inside my camiseta, and I start to climb down, but unfortunately I step on some chicken droping on the bamboo post, which had quite a few. I slip and fell down on the ground stomach first and the chicken were disturb and start clacking flying and running about and making lots of noise and for myself I cannot get up soon enough and get away. Before I could move, some of my folks are there already with a lantern, and saw me siting on the ground. My auntie saw me holding my stomach, She pulled my hand and touch my stomach and she felt wet and slippery and she scream, "Nabiyak ang tian, lunaton ang bituka" (meaning, my stomach is cut and the intestine came out). Everybody get excited and they pulled my camiseta up, but instead of intestine, they saw eggs shell fall down. At that instance I jump and run out. I hide out and my cousins can't find me. By midnite, I walk slowly toward home. I go slowly inside to go to my bed but sure enough they are waiting for me. Did I got it? Boy and how, and from then on I never touch those eggs in the nest again.

Sometimes after school in the afternoon, a bunch of us kids would go to the beach each carrying a gunny sack. If the tide is low, the water on the beach is shallow for about half mile out up to the first sandbar. There are lot of those clams with corrugated shells. We call them Halaang Lalake (male clam). Oftentime we could gather ⅓ to ½ sack each kid, and they are good to eat, just plain boil with a piece of ginger. If there's not much clam, we hunt for some crab in the shallow water. You can see them walking on the bottom, and when you get close they bury themself in the sand, and we could pick them up easily. Those crab are different than we have here in America. They have pointed needle on both end of their shell long wise and have longer arm and pincher and they are good to eat especially the female.

During the rainy season from the month of May to July, when there is no school on Saturday and Sunday, a few of us kids would go to Balintawak to gather some ripe fruits. You see, Balintawak is a little barrio (community) in the Province of Rizal, about 4 miles outside of Manila City Limit. This was the town where Andres Bonifacio (the father of the Philippine revolutionary) first organize the Philippine Katipunan, who carry the first Philippine flag, red, white, and blue with 3 initial letter K.K.K. meaning, Kagalangaland Kapatirang, Katipunan. So in this town they erected his full size statue, with this inscription at bottom of the statue.

"Andres Bonifacio ama ng Himakaikan, Puno ng Kagalangalang Kapatirang, Katipunan" (meaning, "Andres Bonifacio father of the revolutionary, and leader of most respected Brotherhood of Katipunan"). To go to Balintawak we will take the short cut. We would cut across the cementery of Paang Bundek (Foot of the Mountain). This is the largest cementery in the city of Manila. When we get to Balintawak we pay the land owner five centavos each of us kids and we can pick all the fruits we can carry. We don't pick the fruits one by one, we just cut the branch where there's lots of fruits in it and carry it, branch and all. We pick santol, guava, macopa, and many more kind of fruit to take home, and we sure are loaded, shouldering those branches with fruits of different kind. One day we came home kind of late, it was already getting dark. There were four of us, so we talk together going to the short cut, but there was still a short cut we know because we know that cementery very well. Taking a more short cut we have to scale an 8 foot stone wall that divide the Catholic cementery and Cemeterio del Norte (North Cemetery). When we get close to the wall it was really pitch dark. On the other side of the wall, the Catholic side, there was a pasture along the wall. A boy was sitting on top his carabao grazing, but we don't know that he was there. Farther down we climb the wall and walk on top which was about 3 feet wide, carrying the branches of fruits on our shoulder. We were going toward the end of the wall which was close to the main road to the city limit. When we were getting to the end of the wall, we suddenly hear a pitch voice start singing. We look around and we saw somebody sitting on top a big object. All the fruits we were carrying go flying all over the place. We jump out of the wall and took off toward the road. The faster we run the more we hear that big footstep gaining on us. Boy, we really gave all what we got until we get to the main road where there are street light. We really can't go anymore so we slump on the ground under the street light and sure enough following us was the boy on the carabao, and when he get to us, he stop the carabao, and drop to the ground breathless. After a while we gain our breath, the boy asked what happen. Well, I said, well, we are walking on top the wall for a short cut, when suddenly we hear this voice singing and we saw somebody sitting on top a big rock, so we know it is multo (a ghost) so we took off. Heck, that's me singing he says but I saw some kind of an animal jump from the top of the wall and I got

scared, so I took off with my carabao. You see, my carabao was grazing on the pasture. You see I graze him there every evening. Well,
that's it. We go home without fruits and very tired.

I was about 15 year old when us kids form a vocal band (musiko de
voca). We are compose of several kids and some adults join us too. You
see this group orchestra, but all by vocal, no instrument. Most we sing
duet and quarter, and accompanied as bass, drum, and guitar, all by
vocal, and I would say we were good. You see, I know lots of popular
song and music, so I was elected as the principal. 2 or 3 nites a week
we are always invited to play in party, which was always quite a few in
our district. If somebody pass away in a family, they will have what we
call padasal for 8 nites. These will have Rosary in the house of the
deceased and the neighbors around mostly are there. On the 9th nite
that will be the end of Padasal and they will throw a party—no dancing, but lots of singing and after we were invited to that occasion, sometimes they would invite another group of musico de voca from another
district, and we will have competition of vocal music and singing, and
most of the time we come out the winner. You see, in our bunch we
have a few regular musician so we have the advantage.

And by that time I got interested in ball game too, like basketball,
indoor baseball (softball), volleyball, and I was also in the regular baseball team of the school and also in the regular softball team in the
school I was attending. You see, the Tondo Intermediate School have
got a big playground with light, so there we play most every nite of basketball and you know they call me the bear, because I was a good guard,
they call me "oso." In those day in Manila basketball was really a rough
game. We wrestle, we nip, and we punch without being call foul. We
have funny rule of basketball in those days. So if you play basketball in
those days you prepare yourself for anything. Almost every nite about
8:00 we kids gather in the Tondo Intermediate play ground, the lights
are all on and we will split 5 in a team and we would play basketball
until 11 o'clock at nite. It was lots of fun in those days.

After a freshman in high school, I had to drop out because my grandfather can't support and send me to school at the same time, so I had to
quit school. It so happen that year my granduncle, the younger brother
of my grandmother on my father's side, open up a store, a bazaar, that
carry almost everything from nails to shoes, hats, and shirts, and also
phonograph records. That is why I learn to know many popular Amer-

216

ican songs. The name of the store was El Exito Bazar. My work there was sales-clerk but in the morning up to 2 o'clock in the afternoon, I go out to collect from those who owe money to the store, and believe me it is hard collecting money. Quite a few had so much alibi and won't pay. My pay was not much 30.00 pesos a month and I had to work until 9 o'clock in the evening. But I stick to it to gain experience.

You see, they told me my father was a good salesman. What I remember that he was a jack of all trade. He can do almost anything from barber, carpenter, to bank teller, almost anything. To me he was a great man, only he didn't live long enough to teach me much of what he know. You see, when I was with him I remember, he didn't buy toys for me. He build them himself or carve them out of wood.

I stay with my granduncle in the store for about 3 years. I was 17 years old when things happen that change my life entirely. Like I says before, I never know my mother. I was raised by my grandparents of my father side, and as I was growing they didn't give me a chance to meet my mother or talk to me about her. They really hate my mother for the reason they only know. So then I don't know how my mother look like. I only know her first name. Our neighbors have told me. So this is how it stand until I become 18 years old.

One day while I was walking on Rosario Street in Binondo on the way to my morning collection, my Uncle Godencia, the brother of my mother, stop on the curve in a Ford car he was driving. You see he's a driver for the Philippine government transporting city official to their distination. He called me and after a few greeting he ask me, "Don't you want to see your mother, Andoy?" "Sure I do very much, Uncle," I says. Well, next Sunday, he says, I should go over to his house. He told me how to find his place. "When you get to the end of the Avenida Rizal toward Paang Bundok, there is a railroad track, the main railroad track. Turn to the right and follow the track for about 100 yards and on the left hand side you will come to a line of several houses. My house is second from the last of the row. Be sure and be there. You mother will be waiting." And I says, "OK, Uncle." So the next Sunday at about 10 o'clock in the morning, I went to the Avenida Rizal and when I get to the railroad track, I followed the direction of my uncle. About half way, I notice a woman and 3 children walking ahead of me. After a while, I notice they are standing looking around as they have a problem and when I get closer, sure enough they had a problem. They can't jump a wide concrete drain which cross the railroad. I notice the woman was pregnant, but she is a beautiful woman and the 3 children, the biggest was a boy, about 10 or 11 years old and about 10 or 9 years old is the girl. The youngest was a boy about 5 years old. When I get close enough, I ask the woman if I can help and she says please the children are afraid to cross the drain ditch. You see, the ditch is deep about 10 feet deep, so I help them one by one by guiding them on the trestle of the rail, and the last one was the woman.

After they thank me, and I was on my way, but I miss the house and I keep walking until I came to a distance where there is no more house to see. When I look back I noticed the woman and the children are standing on the side of the track watching me. I walk a little farther more, when there's no more house to be seen, so I turn back and I notice that the woman and the children are gone. As I was walking back and get in front of the second house, I heard my uncle called out, "Andoy, over here this is my house." So I turn and go to the house. It was a small nipa house typical of the poor family. When I go upstair, there in the living room sitting is this woman whom I just help, with those children by her side. Then my uncle said, "Andoy, here is your mother and your half brothers and sister." I held my mother and kiss her, there was crying around because of happiness that we met. I was introduced to my grandmother and to my uncle's wife and his children.

So that was how I met my mother whom I never know & see since I was 2 year old. So from time to time I come to see my mother, but I never told it to my relative on my father's side. I believe my mother was 3 or 4 months pregnant, I never see my sister, because I am here in the United States when she was born and her name is Rosalina. So I have 3 half brothers and 2 half sisters. They are Pandador, Elisa, Avelardo, and Rosalina Baltazar. Funny, I forget the first name of my stepfather. Well, it had been so long.

The way I met my mother was unusual but I wouldn't recognize her if I met her some other place, and she wouldn't recognize me too. I thank God that my Uncle Godencio took all the trouble so we could meet and know each other. Well, my mother live far from my uncle's place. She lives in the District of Sampaloc, and every time I have a chance I go to my mother to see her and the kids and my stepfather. It was the year 1921 when all this happen. I was 18 years old then.

I remember I told my mother one day that I like to go to the United States of America if I could have a chance. A few months after that I remember it was after Xmas I went to see my mother as usual, and when she saw me, she said, "Andoy, I remember you told me once you like to go to United States of America if you have a chance. Well, you have a chance now. There is a seaman strike on the Pacific Mail and a friend of the family name Paras, he is an agent to the seaman employee, and you can go and see him. He is supplying men to replace the striker in the Pacific Mail Boat. Tell him I am your mother and I send you over."

So I went next day and I took with me a friend of mine name Felicisimo Miletar. And we are accepted. And the boat we are suppose to work in was in Hong Kong named USS Wenachi later named USS President Lincoln. We have to take a boat in Manila as passenger to Hong Kong and from there we will take our boat, where we are assigned to work. This was my first ride in a steamer ship this size, and was it rough, boy! We left Manila January 21, 1922, at 5:30 P.M. and while we sail out of Manila Bay, we could see the City of Manila. As it was getting dark we could see the full lighted Manila. I feel so lonesome and get home sick right there, but on the other hand I was happy, because I will see America, which is the dream of most of the Pilipino youth. The next day we enter the port of Hong Kong. We can see from there are lots of people on the water front. We are not allowed to go ashore. Instead, we are transfer right away to the boat we are assigned in, Pacific Mail SS Wenatche. I was assign in the bar hall as a waiter. This was the first time I did this kind of work. I was having good tips from my service.

We pass Yokohama then Honolulu. We didn't stay long in those ports, just a few hours, just enough to ride around and back to the ship. Next port was San Francisco, our distination. It took us 23 days trip from Manila to Frisco. There in Frisco we are told we can get off and stay in Frisco, and they will get replacement for us. So we get our pay and get a room, in town, in Colombus Avenue, next to Kearny. We were 8 in our group, all Tagalog except Felicisimo, which is Visayan, but he live long enough in Tondo, so he can talk good Tagalog. We applied for Alaska salmon season work for $250.00 for the season which will take us six month. And after we sign the contract for the Alaska salmon, we were given meal by the cannery contractor, and about 3 weeks, we were taken by boat to Astoria, Oregon, and there we got our boat which will take us to Alaska. It was an old schooner boat name San Nicolas, and boy what a trip we had!

It took us 32 days for the trip from Astoria, Oregon, to Nusgak, Alaska. For 30 days we were out in the Pacific Ocean without seeing any mark of land. In Alaska, we were there 2 weeks before the salmon season start, and when we start working in the cannary, it was fun, and I had seen salmon I had never seen before. Those King salmon are really big. They come up to about 75 lb size. Well, we work about 2 months in the cannary, we go back to Astoria with the same boat, but the trip was quicker because the wind favor us all the way back. In Astoria, we were paid, and from there I was thinking which way I'd go. Go to Seattle, Portland, or Frisco. Well, our gang of 8 had a meeting and we decide to go back to Frisco.

So I stayed in Frisco for a year. I worked in San Francisco Hospital in the employee's dinning room for a year, then I met Nardo from a trip around the world. He work in the oil tanker. After a month we were together I quit my work in Frisco. It was in the month of August 1922, we decided to go in the country and work in the farm. So we went to Knight Landing in Woodland to work topping sugar beets there, and boy it is a hard work. Stooping whole day, holding the beet in your hand and cut the top with leaves with a big knife. It was the first work I ever did in the farm. The work finish about October. It was piecework. From there we went to Stockton to look for another work.

This is something I can't forget. The nite we were leaving the camp in Woodland the truck driver of the truck that haul our sugar beets offer us a ride. He was on his way to Sacramento. We were glad it save half of the fee to Stockton. Well, the driver don't have enough room in the cab, so I volunteer to ride in the back of the truck. It was an open truck no top and I was wearing only a thin shirt. At first I love it, but when we hit the hiway and speed up to the speed limit, and the nite was a little chilly, boy did I suffer, I was stiff cold, I thought I can't make it. When we get into Sacramento I was stiff and can't talk. Nardo put a heavy coat on me and start laughing, but it was no fun. Boy, believe me. So we thank the driver and walk down town looking for hotel room. The first hotel we approach, we ask for a room. The landlady said, no I have no room, but I have girl, and Nardo says, you give us room and you supply the girl. No room, she says. I supply the girl and you pay for it. So we turn around laughing like hell and I ask Nardo, is this the style here in America, Oh yes, he said, you got the room and you got all the girl you want, and I said, Oh, boy. By the way, I wonder if he is still alive. You see, in 1936 he live with us in Delano, and he kind of lost his mind, I don't know why, so I sign to have him sent back to Philippine Islands through the Government Reparation Act. That way he can't come back anymore, and I never heard from him, so I don't know what happen to him.

Well, back in 1923 in Stockton, we went to asparagus cutting. It was piecework. So much per 100 lb. We were 13 in the gang, 12 cutter and 1 sled boy. I was the sled boy, and the season start March and finish at the end of May. As I says, topping sugar beets was a very hard work, stooping whole day cutting the top of the beet, but that was only play compare with cutting asparagus. In asparagus work you wake up 3:00 in the morning, have breakfast, and be out in the field by 4:00 in the morning. You start walking thru the rows stoop and cut the grass [nickname for asparagus] about 6 inches below the ground, walk, stoop, cut, walk, stoop, cut, and so on. You do this from 4:00 A.M. to 3:00 or 4:00 P.M. every day, 7 days a week, rain or shine for 3 months. It is really hard work but I did it season after season for several year. I don't mind it because I was young and only 20 years old. I never done this work in Manila. There I never done even a shovel of dirt but here in America, I had to do it. It was the only chance I have, because I have no professional training. Well, from then on I stick in the farm work, and I kind of get use to it.

In 1927, I thought I'm going home but I realize, going back home is not so good, so I decide to stay and I stop working the farm and I look for work in town, in Stockton. That was in 1926. I found a work in Stockton Box Co. I don't remember the pay, but I was making enough to get by. Soon in 1927 I quit that work, and I went in partnership with Remigio Antentico selling men suits. We used to travel from farm camp to camp where there were lots of Pilipino working in the farm, and we really make good business from these Pilipinos. They love good clothes, so they buy suit left and right. I was in this business when I meet Angie in San Ramon. She was about 16. In those days I was known among the Pilipino circle in Stockton, because in every Pilipino Festival in Stockton like Rizal day or installation of Pilipino fraternal order like Gran Oriente Filipino and Dimasalang I would recite a patriotic poem, call Tula, which I wrote them myself, and it was very popular then, and they call me Makata. In those days everything is going alright with me, and I always dress good going around.

It was summer in 1927, one day me and Remigio just come back from a trip selling suits around the Pilipino camp. Soon as we arrived in Stockton, I went to the pool hall of Cesar where I hang around a bit. Guess who I met there? It was Angeles, and she told me she, her father and brother move to Stockton from San Ramon. They will live in Stockton, and she is looking for work, and I say good I'll see you quite a bit then. So for me in Stockton life go like this, I go lucky way. I saw quite a bit of Angeles then, she work as a table girl in the Japanese pool hall on Market St. It was December 1927, it was December 30th, there was a Rizal Day celebration in Stockton City Hall. I was to crown the Rizal Queen Glazeria, and I perform my part very good. After I crown the queen I recite a patriotic poem about Rizal the Martyr, which I wrote myself. After that, there was dancing until midnite. Angeles and her friend Mary Ihapon were there too. After a while I ask Angeles for a dance, and we dance and the music was "Always." I ask if she know the name of that music. Well, I kind like her and I said I mean the word of that music toward you and I was surprise when she answered me too. So from there on we become sweetheart. So from then on every nite I go to the pool hall where she work and stay there for an hour or so.

It was about in December of 1927, I ask Angie to marry me and she say yes, so I said I'll go and see your father about us getting married. So, one evening after her work at the pool hall I went to her house, and I took with me Pete Braga, Isidro Gonzales. Pete Braga is a Visayan and he can talk well to her father in Visayan. So we were sitting around and with us was Mrs. Isabel Sapanta, the owner of the house, and I and Pete and Gonzales and Angie. We were talking and finally Pete ask her father to sit with us so we can explain our purpose. And he say "no." I don't want to talk to that Tagalog, walang batason, I don't want him for my daughter. So that's it. He don't want me, he want Bastian who was about 45 years old, because he give him money and promise to buy a car if Angie marry him. Angie was sixteen years old then, and I was 23.

Well, I continue to go to the pool hall to see Angie every nite, and we were getting serious. So one nite in January 1928 I ask Angie if she would like to run away with me she say yes and so I talk to Luis Roxas who live in Oakdale, but always come to Stockton 2 or 3 times a week. You see, I was an applicant for membership in the Filipino Masonic organization, call Gran Oriente Filipino and they have a lodge in Stockton, Mayon Lodge #19, and there I was applying too, and Luis Roxas was a member of this organization, and was in a high degree 32°, so we become good friend; and I explain to him my situation with Angeles, and her father don't want Tagalog to marry his daughter, and he agree to help me run away with Angie, so we made the plan. It was going to be Sunday. So that Sunday we were ready. It was noontime and Angie and her father and brother went to the restaurant at El Dorado and Market St. to eat lunch. While they were sitting waiting to be serve Angie excuse herself to go out and right there Luis was waiting with his car on the curve. Angie jump in it and they took off, and pick me up on Hunter St, by the park, and we were off on our way to Oakdale. We live with Lou in his house, and next day we went to Modesto to apply for marriage license. We waited seven days. We went back to Modesto to pick up the license, then we went back to Oakdale and we get married by the justice of the peace. I tell you when I get married I got only $3.50 in my pocket and Angie got $35.00, that's all what we start with and boy was it rough.

223

I work around Oakdale in the orchard field. And after winter that year, I went for cutting asparagus again and I go with Ellorin. After asparagus we went back to Oakdale, and Angie was about to have a baby. It was in the month of July 1929 and I have to take Angie to Modesto County Hospital, because she was having pain and I left her there. Then it was July 14. I was working in a peach cannery and that afternoon, I got a call from the hospital and notify me that Angie gave birth to a baby girl. Well, I was happy to hear that and after 20 days I took Angie and the baby home. Then about the month of October 1929 we went to Terminus Island. I got the work of making celery crates. It was piecework for 4¢ a crate, and I can make about 250 to 300 crates a day, and it was very good money then. See, I was good crate nailer by hand, I can nail fast.

After the crate nailing season, about February 1930 I went share crop farming celery, for Morrer & Son. My partners were the Deados. Well, I don't make anything in the venture. From there I went again farming for sugar beet for Spreckel. It was 1931. Oh, by the way by August 1930, I join the Gran Oriente Filipino, I was initiated in Mayon Lodge #19 in Stockton, and I am still a member of this lodge up to now. I was elected master of this lodge 3 times. By the way, about this sugar beets farming we were 5 partners. The head of us was Enrique Braga. Anyway nothing happen, and we don't make anything at the end. This was the year 1931. My son was born.

It was after the beet season and we move in Ripon and live in Luis Albas house. He has a big house, and he gave me one room for free rent. I tell you that year was the toughest, and up to now I was wondering how we live then.

It was December 30th when Angie complain of pain so I went to borrow a car from a friend, and load Angie and start for Stockton hospital. It was in the afternoon, and on the road I got a flat tire. Boy, did I go like hell to change that tire. We arrive at the hospital at 4:00 P.M. and I got word from the hospital about 5:30 that afternoon that I have a baby boy. The year my son was born was December 30th 1931, which is the Filipino National holiday, the death of Filipino martyr Dr. Jose Rizal. And that year 1931 was a depression time, and boy was it tough. In those days farm work was 10¢ an hour, yet can't find any work around even in town. I still live in Albas house, my father-in-law and brother-in-law live with us there too.

I would go to Stockton in a borrowed car, and my brother in the Lodge knows my situation, and those who have money would buy me a sack of rice and a bottle of soyo and that would last me over a month. Sometimes I go where we farm sugar beets, there are lot of willow trees where lots of tree mushroom grow and I gather lots of that. Well, rice and fried mushroom that's all we eat 3 times a day. Sometimes I wonder how we survived. Well, from there in Ripon, we moved from 1 place to another. We move back in Stockton. Work there was very few and apart, so we moved to Delano to work in grape season. That's around 1932. From there we moved to Sherman Island in 1937 to asparagus season, after the season we moved back to Stockton. Work in Stockton was again hard to find, and so we moved to Salinas. There we stay in Salinas until after the war. In Salinas, I first work for Premier Produce as irrigator, after about 3 years, I moved to work for Stolich & Co as tractor driver. In the evening I go to diesel mechanic school, and in about a year and a half I finish the course. Our instructor in the school, Morris Robert, happened to be the chief mechanic for Stolich repair shop, and he told me since I am working for Stolich as tractor driver, I can work in the repair shop if there is no tractor driving in the field. I accepted so I drive tractor in summer and when all the tractor work is done, I go to the shop, to overhaul tractor and repair whatever is to be done and I'd work in the shop thru winter and part of spring until the tractor work start again in the field, so I was part tractor driver and part tractor mechanic. I start to work for Stolich in 1942 and quit Stolich in 1949 to go to Watsonville for share cropper farming straw-berry. Well, I don't make any in that strawberry venture so I move to Saratoga near San Jose, again in strawberry share cropper. This time I was a little lucky, I made a little money, and I bought a new 1953 Kaiser car. But the following year 1954 was not so good, and again the fol-lowing year the worst, the weather ruin most of my berries, and the berries was cheap and the freezer went on strike, so that was the end. I come out in debt. So I plow all my berries, and plant vegetables to pay my debt. So by 1959 I quit farming entirely. I got a job in a box company in San Jose. The pay is not much but it is a steady job. After 2 years on the job, the boss Babe give me the foreman job. The job don't pay much, but I like it, and it is my job up to now. Anyway Babe, my boss passed away in 1976, and I was left to run the box business, because his son Joe don't know very much about boxes, so I stay to help him out. So this is about all, anyway I forget about farming now. And I am better off now then when I was farming or working in the Ranch.

The "Memoir" was typed exactly as my father taped it to retain his accent, his voice. My father passed away at the age of 78 on March 13, 1981.

Filipino American History in Hawai'i:
A Young Visayan Woman's Perspective

JONATHAN Y. OKAMURA

Angeles Monrayo's *Tomorrow's Memories* is a significant contribution to
our understanding and appreciation of Filipino American history in
Hawai'i, particularly because it provides a contemporary female account
of their life and labor prior to World War II. Such a voice is generally
absent from the works predominantly by or about Filipino men during
the period of their plantation labor recruitment (1906–1946). The book
also is important insofar as it constitutes a Visayan view of the Filipino
community in contrast to the primarily Ilokano perspectives that tend
to dominate our knowledge of Filipino labor migration and their plantation and other employment in Hawai'i, especially those based on the
experiences of single, young male Ilokanos who constituted the largest
group in the Filipino community.

Tomorrow's Memories tells a very touching, innocently honest, and
occasionally sad story of an immigrant Filipino girl growing up
quickly in both Hawai'i and California while separated at times from
both her mother and her father. The only other major personal
account of Filipinos in Hawai'i is Ines Cayaban's autobiography, *A
Goodly Heritage*, that was published in 1981, fifty years after she had
arrived in Honolulu from the Philippines, and thus does not provide
a contemporary description. *Nana* Ines, as she was fondly known in
the Filipino American community, was a public health nurse and thus
came from a much more privileged class background than that of
Angeles. She also was Ilokano rather than Visayan, as was the latter.
Ruben R. Alcantara's *Sakada: Filipino Adaptation in Hawaii*, also

published in 1981 (the seventy-fifth anniversary of Filipino immigration to Hawaiʻi), includes oral history accounts of immigration and plantation life and labor from former plantation workers (primarily Ilokano) and hence like Ines Cayaban's book is not a contemporary work. Thus, *Tomorrow's Memories* is a significant book in providing us with information particularly on the daily life activities of Filipinos as they experienced them, especially in Honolulu, about which there are only general and limited descriptions such as Roman R. Cariaga's article on "Filipinos in Honolulu" (1935). Since a comprehensive history of Filipino Americans in Hawaiʻi has yet to be written and is acutely needed, works such as *Tomorrow's Memories* can be appreciated as a contribution toward the writing of that history.

228

Despite the very short period of three and a half years of her life in Hawaiʻi encompassed by the book and the very young age of Angeles during those years (eleven and a half to nearly fifteen), she was a very perceptive and thoughtful observer of family and community events among Filipinos at the time. Given the limited and irregular formal education she received (until the fifth grade in Hawaiʻi) and her not being a native speaker of English, her writing ability is all the more remarkable. It is clear from Angeles's diary entries about going to school and her often repeated gratitude to her father for allowing her to attend school that she was a very bright student who had a great desire and enthusiasm for learning. Unfortunately, her limited education was a common experience of many second-generation Filipino Americans in Hawaiʻi in the 1920s, especially at the high school level.[1]

Tomorrow's Memories covers a relatively brief period of Angeles's life in Hawaiʻi, from January 1924 to July 1927, when she and her father boarded a steamship to San Francisco to join her older brother, Julian. This was a significant historical period during which the Filipino population was increasing substantially in both Hawaiʻi and California. In the five years of her life encompassed by the book, she and her family were directly involved in some of the major social, economic, and political processes affecting Filipinos in Hawaiʻi and the continental United States, such as the 1924 strike by Filipino plantation laborers, their subsequent movement to Honolulu, the severe social and economic problems they encountered as a racialized minority, their migration from Hawaiʻi to the West Coast, and their repatriation back to the Philippines. Angeles's descriptions of her life and the Filipino community in the 1920s are also significant because most of the social science research and publications by and about Filipinos written during their labor migration period concern especially the 1930s.

In the discussion below, I highlight the contributions that *Tomorrow's Memories* makes to our knowledge of the history of Filipino Americans in Hawai'i and provide a social and historical context for fully understanding some of the more significant observations and comments made by Ms. Raymundo. Focusing on the 1920s and 1930s, I discuss the development of the Visayan community in Honolulu, the 1924 Strike and its leader Pablo Manlapit, the scarcity of Filipino women and the social practices that resulted, the limited employment available to Filipinos, the extremely harsh racist stereotyping of them, and their movement to California and back to the Philippines.

The Visayan Community

Angeles states that her family immigrated to Hawai'i in 1912 from Romblon Province, that consists of three main islands in the northern Visayas region of the Philippines. The Monrayo family apparently spoke Ilonggo, the language spoken on Negros island, rather than Cebuano, the dominant Visayan language spoken in Hawai'i since immigrants from Cebu were the largest group among Visayans. Filipino labor recruitment to Hawai'i had begun in 1906, just six years prior to the arrival of the Monrayos, so that in 1910 there were only 2,361 Filipinos in Hawai'i. In comparison to other Visayan and Ilokano provinces, a very small number of Filipinos immigrated from Romblon through the Hawaiian Sugar Planters' Association (HSPA); for example, only forty-nine came between 1916 and 1928 (Teodoro 1981: 18). Visayans, particularly Cebuanos and Boholanos, were the first and largest group of Filipino labor migrants arriving annually until 1923, when Ilokanos emerged as the major immigrating group.

Angeles and her family were part of the 5,234 Filipinos who arrived in 1912, a significantly large number of arrivals that would not be exceeded for another ten years (Dorita 1954: 131). The immigration of her entire family, rather than just her father, was more typical of Visayans than Ilokanos, who came predominantly as unattached young men. As a result, there was a greater proportion of women and children among Visayan immigrants than among Ilokanos who, if married, often left their wives and children behind because of the great difficulty in supporting a family on plantation wages intended for a single person.

The eviction of striking Filipino plantation laborers during the 1920 and 1924 strikes contributed to the emergence of a Visayan and larger Filipino community in Honolulu. A survey conducted by the Inter-Church Federation of Honolulu (1936) demonstrated the greater presence of families among Visayans compared to Ilokanos and especially Tagalogs who were not recruited in significant numbers to Hawaiʻi. Visayans (65 percent) constituted nearly two-thirds of the respondents in the married sample of the survey, while there were much smaller proportions of Ilokanos (16 percent) and Tagalogs (14 percent). In contrast, of the sample of unattached men, Ilokanos (81 percent) were the great majority of respondents, with far lesser numbers of Visayans (14 percent) and Tagalogs (4 percent). The total sample of 1,359 adults in the study reflected the substantial Visayan presence in Honolulu at the time insofar as they were the largest group (45 percent) compared to Ilokanos (41 percent) and Tagalogs (10 percent).

Given their significant presence, Visayans formed residential enclaves in working-class areas of Honolulu where they were, as Angeles comments, "like one big family, everyone knows each other." This tendency of Visayans to associate with one another in the city and on the plantation very likely explains how she learned to speak Cebuano even though her parents spoke Ilonggo. Besides Hall and River streets, where Angeles lived, another Visayan enclave in the late 1920s that demonstrates their community cohesion was in the Iwilei district at the intersection of Kalani Street and Waiakamilo Boulevard adjacent to the Libby, McNeil, and Libby pineapple cannery (Okamura 1983: 100). Beginning in 1928, the residents of this area, who were from the town of Carcar, Cebu, used to organize an annual fiesta in November in honor of their provincial patron saint, Santa Catalina, in keeping with Philippine tradition.

The 1924 Strike and Pablo Manlapit

In 1920 there were only 2,113 Filipinos in Honolulu (Lind 1980: 57). This urban community began to emerge especially during the strike of Filipino and Japanese laborers that year when both groups were evicted from plantation housing by the management since as strikers they were no longer considered employees and therefore not entitled to "free" housing. The HSPA followed the same strike-breaking tactic of evicting striking workers during the 1924 strike, which is why the Monrayo family went to the strike camp on Middle Street in the working-class Kalihi area of Honolulu.[2] Although it had begun on April 1 at O'ahu Sugar Company in Waipahu where he worked in the mill, Mr. Monrayo joined the strike in May in solidarity with the 500 Filipino striking laborers at that plantation.[3] At the Middle Street strike camp, workers and their families lived in an abandoned jelly factory, the "one big house" to which Angeles refers, between Rose and Notley streets that housed up to 462 occupants during the strike (Reinecke 1996: 39). In contrast to her comments about how much "fun" she had playing with the other girls in the strike camp, conditions were so crowded and unsanitary that the Board of Health eventually closed down all of the camps for lack of sanitation facilities.

231

Labor historian John E. Reinecke (1996) has referred to the 1924 strike as the "Filipino Piecemeal Sugar Strike" because many plantations were struck only partially, with the most militant workers going on strike first and then later trying to encourage or intimidate the others to join them. The strike also was piecemeal in that it proceeded in an uncoordinated manner, with some laborers returning to work and others and their plantations going on strike as late as January 1925. The strike slowly spread to include thirty-four of the forty-nine plantations on the four major islands of Hawai'i over the course of nearly a year and involved at most 12,000 laborers, or about 60 percent of the Filipino plantation workforce, who were on strike for widely varying periods of time. Due to the divide and control tactics of the HSPA, only Filipinos participated in this strike, as they alone would again in 1937, and not until the 1946 strike did all ethnic groups join together in "one big union," the International Longshoremen's and Warehousemen's Union (ILWU), against the HSPA. Reinecke (1996: 1) is highly critical of the 1924 strike, going so far as to state: "No other major strike was so haphazardly planned or conducted or failed so completely." However, another noted historian of Hawai'i labor, Edward D. Beechert (1985: 224), contends in his *Working in Hawaii* that "the behavior of the Filipino worker in this [1924 strike] and other labor actions suggested that a high premium was placed on dignity and respect," which may account for the lengthy duration of the strike.

Among the demands made by the Filipino strikers were an increase in the minimum daily wage from $1.00 to $2.00 (a demand they would continue to seek ten years later), equal pay for men and women who performed the same kind of work, an eight-hour work day instead of ten hours in the field and twelve in the mill, time and a half pay for overtime work, and recognition of the principle of collective bargaining and the right of workers to organize themselves for their mutual protection and benefit. Many of these demands would not be granted until after the 1946 strike, but they indicate the progressive nature of the goals of Filipino plantation laborers.

In one of the very first entries in her diary, Angeles refers to Pablo Manlapit as the leader of the High Wages Movement, the Filipino labor union in the 1924 strike. Manlapit arrived in Hawai'i as one of the earliest HSPA recruits in 1910 from Batangas province in southern Luzon and worked on a plantation on the Big Island of Hawai'i. He lost his job in 1913 for participating in a strike, and two years later he moved to Honolulu, where he worked as an interpreter and janitor for an attorney in downtown Honolulu. With the encouragement and mentoring of this attorney, Manlapit became a licensed attorney in 1919, becoming in his own words, "the First Filipino lawyer to practice law in Hawaii" (cited in Kerkvliet 1991: 154).

Manlapit led the Filipino Labor Union in the 1920 strike in which both Filipino and Japanese plantation workers participated, although separately.[4] Like Japanese labor union leaders in the 1920 strike, Manlapit was harassed by the police and the HSPA during the 1924 strike. He and another High Wages Movement leader, Cecilio Basan, were indicted and convicted of conspiracy to commit subornation of perjury, very likely on the basis of perjured testimony against them, in a case involving the death of a striking laborer's child. They both received sentences of two to ten years at hard labor in O'ahu Prison. About a year after the conspiracy trial, Angeles comments that she did not hear "anything more about the Pablo Manlapit Strike," which is precisely why the HSPA sought to have him imprisoned.

After serving more than two and a half years, Manlapit was released on parole on the condition that he leave Hawai'i for the U.S. continent, which he did for California, leaving behind his wife and four children. In California he again became involved in the labor struggles of Filipino farmworkers and spoke out against their exploitation; Manlapit thus played a major role in the labor movement of Filipino agricultural workers in both Hawai'i and California. As a result, he was placed under government surveillance and was described in a federal intelligence report in 1932 as "probably the most able, the most intelligent, and the most dangerous radical Filipino in the world" because of his suspected ties with the Community Party. Manlapit returned to Hawai'i in 1932, bringing along Manuel Fagel, another Filipino labor leader, and resumed his labor organizing activities in rallies at A'ala Park near downtown Honolulu and on the neighbor islands. Manlapit would again be hounded by the authorities and the HSPA because of his efforts on behalf of Filipino workers. In 1934 he was arrested and convicted of overcharging a Filipino U.S. Army veteran for assistance in obtaining a loan and chose to return to the Philippines instead of going to prison. Our full appreciation of Manlapit's contribution to the labor movement in Hawai'i, and not just for Filipino workers, had come with the publication in 2002 of Melinda Tria Kerkvliet's biography, *Unbending Cane: Pablo Manlapit, a Filipino Labor Leader in Hawai'i*. Manlapit was the first of a number of Filipino labor leaders in Hawai'i, including Carl Damaso, Tony Rania, and Eddie Lapa (see Alegado 1996: 31), and both those leaders and Filipino workers have made labor organizing one of the major contributions of Filipinos to Hawai'i's working people.

233

The 1924 strike is especially known for the "Hanapepe Massacre" on the island of Kaua'i, in which sixteen Filipino plantation laborers and four policemen were killed in a brief exchange of gunfire on September 9 (Reinecke 1996: 75–84). This confrontation developed after striking Visayan workers had beaten and detained two Ilokano youths who along with some other Ilokanos had declined to join the strike. During the strike Ilokanos were being imported by the HSPA as strikebreakers, and this very likely contributed to the animosity between the two groups. The Hanapepe violence provided the immediate context for the conspiracy trial of Manlapit and Basan that began less than a week later, and to no great surprise they were found guilty after the jury had deliberated for only half an hour.

Scarcity of Women

Even as a preteenager, Angeles describes how she was the object of much attention from older men and later received a marriage proposal at the age of fourteen from such a man. She relates how at weekend dances at the strike camp she and her friend earned as much as $9 a night dancing with the men, who paid them ten cents for a three-minute dance in an improvised version of the taxi dances that Filipino men in both Hawai'i and California frequented.[5] The privileged status held by Filipinas, even very young ones like Angeles, was due to the highly unbalanced sex ratio among Filipinos in Hawai'i. In 1920 among Filipinos twenty to thirty-nine years old, there were nearly seven males to every female. The major reason for this gender imbalance was the far greater number of men sent by the HSPA to Hawai'i (110,000) compared to women (9,400) and children (7,000) during the period of plantation labor recruitment (Dorita 1954: 131). Cariaga's (1974: 22) description of the good fortune of a family with daughters could have applied to Angeles's family:

234

> The family with an eligible daughter or two is on its way to prosperity in Hawaii. Presents of all kinds from hopeful suitors pour in: everything from grocery supplies to automobiles, and of course jewelry and personal gifts for the girl. Money is loaned and favors and requests cheerfully carried out by the suitors.

These behaviors, including wanting to marry young teenagers, should not be considered as evidence of the sexual deviance of Filipino men but should be understood as expressions of their keen desire for family life under historical conditions not of their making in which it was extremely difficult for them to marry.

The disproportionate ratio between the sexes perhaps was a factor in Angeles's mother leaving her husband for another man (Delphin)[6] since Filipinas, if willing, could have their choice of suitors. As noted by Cariaga (1935: 42), perhaps in exaggeration, "plantation women are so few that they have a decided advantage in choosing husbands. If the first is outshone by another, the wife seldom hesitates to take advantage of the better opportunity."

There were far more serious consequences of the greater number of Filipino men than women. Cariaga (1974: 98) maintained that the "great majority" of crimes for which Filipinos were sent to prison resulted directly or indirectly from the gender imbalance. The latter also contributed to a practice called *coboy coboy* (from "cowboy") or wife abduction, in which a woman would be kidnapped and raped by unattached men on a plantation. While an infrequent occurrence,[7] the fear of *coboy coboy* contributed further to the disproportion between the sexes, as married men sent their wives back to the Philippines or decided against bringing them when they immigrated to Hawai'i.

Employment Subordination

Angeles indicates that her father was employed in a number of different jobs in Hawai'i, and this was typical of Filipino men in the pre–World War II period, who often moved from the plantation to the city and back again in search of work, especially during the Depression years of the 1930s. After first working at Ewa Plantation on O'ahu for several years after their arrival, Mr. Monrayo worked at Schofield Barracks, a U.S. military base, and was employed as a mill worker at O'ahu Sugar Company in Waipahu when the 1924 strike began. After the family had moved to the strike camp in Honolulu, he worked at the Hawaii Pineapple Cannery and at the nearby docks as a stevedore, two jobs that were very common among Filipino men in the city. Cannery workers constituted the largest group of Filipinos employed in Honolulu, but the canning season was at its peak only during the summer months, after which most of the employees were laid off. Mr. Monrayo's last job before leaving for California was as a pineapple field worker in Kahuku on the north shore of O'ahu.

All of Mr. Monrayo's occupations were generally low-paying and somewhat unstable laboring jobs and thus were indicative of the economic subordination and exploitation of Filipino labor before World War II. Angeles relates that her father was illiterate, and this was a common characteristic of plantation labor recruits, since the great majority of them were from rural areas of the Philippines. It should not be surprising then that in 1930, 90 percent of employed Filipino males were laborers, and 80 percent of them worked on the plantations. The situation was far worse among Filipino women since in the same year less than 8 percent of them were employed (Cariaga 1974: 39). There is considerable validity in Cariaga's (1936: 46) observation that "the Filipinos . . . have come too late to participate in the founding of the economic basis of the Territory [of Hawai'i]." Following annexation by the United States in 1898, the economy of Hawai'i underwent a substantial expansion during the first two decades of the new century that created considerable jobs in the manufacturing, transportation, and wholesale and retail trade industries and in clerical services, while the number of agricultural jobs remained the same. The earlier recruited immigrant groups such as Chinese and Japanese took advantage of these economic opportunities since the former already had left the plantations, while the latter had been in the process of doing so since the turn of the century. However, the onset of the Depression prevented Filipinos from embarking on a similar process of socioeconomic mobility by leaving the plantations, diversifying and improving their occupational profile, and developing a significant urban population. Filipinos were forced to remain on the plantations during the 1930s due to the lack of alternative employment opportunities, and this restriction retarded their upward social mobility.

While they were living at Ewa Plantation, Angeles recalls the removal of human waste from their toilet box every morning by a "Japanese man" and comments that "No Filipino man would do this kind of work." She adds that when the Filipino boys had a fight with the Japanese boys, the former would sing a derisive rhyme to them that included Hawaiian words: "You know what your father used to do some years ago. Filipinos *kukae* (defecate), Japanese *hapai* (carry)." The rhyme actually reverses the general social and occupational roles and statuses of Filipinos and Japanese on the plantations. As the last major group recruited by the HSPA, Filipinos received the least desirable work, the lowest pay, and the worst housing, and were severely restricted from skilled and supervisory positions.

In his well-known novel, *All I Asking for is My Body*, about growing up in a plantation community on Maui in the 1930s, Milton Murayama (1988: 96) also employs the metaphor of human waste to convey in graphically powerful terms the rigid racial hierarchy and its enforcement on the plantation:

> It rained so continually a damp smell of the outhouse hung over Pig Pen Avenue. The camp, I realized then, was planned and built around its sewage system. . . . Shit too was organized according to the plantation pyramid. Mr. Nelson [the plantation manager] was top shit on the highest slope, then there were the Portuguese, Spanish, and *nisei* [Japanese American] *lunas* with their indoor toilets which flushed into the same ditches, then Japanese Camp, and Filipino Camp.

In other words, shit flowed down literally and metaphorically on Filipinos since they were at the very bottom of the plantation hierarchy in jobs, housing, and community life. Even as a bodily waste product, feces were used to demonstrate power and control over Filipino (and Japanese) bodies and to maintain them in their subordinate positions on the plantation.

237

Stereotyping and Racism

The racial structure that located Filipinos at the lowest end of the plantation status scale was supported by demeaning representations of and attitudes toward them prevalent in the wider society. During the pre–World War II period, Filipinos were subject to extremely negative stereotyping that began shortly after their arrival in Hawai'i when the Honolulu Police Department used the derogatory terms "poke knife" and "Bayao" to refer to Filipinos (Cariaga 1935: 40). The first term referred to the supposed tendency of Filipinos to use knives while engaged in fights, and the latter term, which means brother-in-law in all three major Philippine languages, was appropriated by the police and other non-Filipinos after hearing Filipinos address each other by that kinship term.

Even seemingly learned academics at the University of Hawai'i engaged in the racist stereotyping of Filipinos without bothering to interview or otherwise conduct any systematic research with them. In a book coauthored by Stanley Porteus and Marjorie Babcock, *Temperament and Race* (1926), Filipinos were characterized as being "at an adolescent stage of development," "impulsive, suggestible, unstable and undependable," and having a "pathological distrust" based on the responses of twenty-five "judges," all of whom were white and sixteen of whom were plantation managers. All that these supposed knowledgeable persons on Filipino psychology and behavior did was to repeat demeaning stereotypes prevalent in Hawai'i at the time concerning Filipinos. Nonetheless, Porteus and Babcock concluded in clearly racist terms,

> With a curriculum whose content should be practical and fitted to Filipino intellectual status something might be done to lessen the period of their social maladjustment. . . . It is our opinion that no matter what labels of citizenship we may put on these people they

remain Filipinos, and it will take much more than a knowledge of the three "Rs" to make them Americans.

This view of the unassimilability of Filipinos due to their race was very typical of the 1920s, and their presumed inability to assimilate was taken as evidence of Filipino racial inferiority.

238   Other prevalent stereotypes of Filipinos prior to World War II depicted them as sexual threats, prone to violence, criminally inclined, and primitive in behavior. One extreme result of this demonization of particularly young Filipino men is that Filipinos constituted a majority of those executed (twenty-four of forty-two persons) in Hawai'i between 1900 and 1957, when capital punishment was abolished by the territorial legislature soon after the Democrats gained control for the first time in 1954 from the Haole-dominated Republican Party. At their peak in 1930, Filipinos were 17 percent of Hawaii's population, yet they comprised 57 percent of the persons executed during the period concerned. Only one white person was ever executed (Hormann 1953: 4). Clearly, Filipinos were inequitably subject to the death penalty that was an especially severe manifestation of the racism against them.

Angeles notes that her father had her mother and the latter's lover Delphin arrested, and they both were sent to prison, although she does not mention for what crime. Her mother's incarceration was very unusual in the Filipino community since Filipinas were not commonly imprisoned, one reason being that they were not very numerous in Hawai'i. In 1934 only fifty-one immigrant Filipinas were arrested on O'ahu, and very likely a minority were actually imprisoned (Cariaga 1974: 97). Due to their majority young male population, the involvement of Filipinos in criminal activity was a common stereotype during the pre–World War II era. Romanzo Adams (1925: 35–36), the leading sociologist in Hawai'i in the 1920s and 1930s, accounted for what he termed the "bad showing" of Filipinos with regard to conviction and incarceration as due to their being primarily between eighteen and thirty-five years of age and to most of them not having wives in Hawai'i since "trouble frequently arises between two Filipino men on account of a woman." He provided statistics on the average annual number of convictions in all courts of the Territory of Hawai'i between 1915 and 1924 for males eighteen years and older that indicate a higher rate among Filipinos compared to all races for gambling, murder, burglary, and "offenses against chastity," a slightly higher rate for manslaughter and robbery, and a lower rate for drunkenness (Adams et al. 1925: 36–37).

Writing a decade later in the mid-1930s, Cariaga (1974: 96) observed, possibly in exaggeration:

> For some time many, and for the last decade a majority of the pris- **239**
> oners in the Territorial prison have been Filipinos. A visit there
> reveals brown cooks, brown barbers, brown musicians everywhere
> from recreational yard to death cells, brown faces; and mingled
> among them a modest number of yellows and a rare "pale-face."

A widespread stereotypic perception was that Filipinos were involved especially in sex crimes. However, data for O'ahu in 1934 indicate that the most prevalent crimes for which Filipinos were arrested were gambling, (nonaggravated) assault, disorderly conduct, drunkenness, and burglary (Cariaga 1974: 97). Cariaga (1974: 98) argued that the "special forms" of crime among Filipinos resulted from the economic and social situation faced by such a young male-dominated group, particularly unemployment during the Depression years. Statistics on arrests (not convictions) for sex offenses in 1934 on O'ahu indicate a lower rate per 1,000 males for Filipinos (4.9) compared to other groups such as Puerto Ricans (18.3, highest rate) and Hawaiians (7.7), and the Filipino rate was only slightly higher than that of Portuguese (3.7) and Koreans (3.2) (Cariaga 1974: 99). Cariaga (1974: 98) cited Adams as contending that the Filipino crime rate was "rather low" in relation to their total population and taking into consideration that they were a recently arrived immigrant minority.

Cariaga (1974: 100) provided a likely explanation for the prevalence of the view of Filipinos as criminally inclined by noting the role of the media in disseminating that stereotype:

> Newspapers have tended to play up their misbehavior, so that the
> public has been constantly made conscious of the Filipino as pro-
> viding a bad element in the community. Whenever a serious crime
> is committed by a Filipino his nationality is designated—"Juan de
> la Cruz, a Filipino is charged, etc." whereas a case involving a
> Spaniard, a Portuguese or a Puerto Rican (nationalities whose names
> are often the same as Filipino names) does not mention his race.

As I have written elsewhere, "Filipinos were very much essential-ized and marginalized as the archtypical racialized other to a far greater extent than were other groups in Hawai'i during the 1930s," and as a result they suffered severe social and economic consequences such that many of them decided to leave (Okamura 1996: 42).

240

Movement to California and the Philippines

When Angeles's brother and later herself and her father migrated to California in 1927, they were part of a larger movement of Filipinos from Hawai'i to the West Coast. Between 1924 and 1929 nearly 12,000 Filipinos, predominantly men, made such a move because of the higher wages being paid and, as Angeles comments, there was "plenty of work there." One reason for this migration from Hawai'i was the eviction of striking laborers from the plantations, and some of them might have found themselves "blackballed" from being hired at other plantations after having gone on strike. Another factor was the failure of the 1924 strike to increase wages and improve harsh working con-ditions on the plantations. The HSPA began importing Ilokanos in substantial numbers in the early 1920s so that there was a considerable increase of more than 6,000 Filipino plantation workers between 1920 and 1924, and this abundance of labor served to keep wages low. The 1924 Immigration Act brought an end to Japanese immigration to the United States and contributed to the much increased demand for Fil-ipino labor in both Hawai'i and the U.S. continent.

Angeles relates that her mother and the latter's lover Delphin along with their children were able to return to the Philippines with free pas-sage. They were part of a considerably larger movement than that to the West Coast. About 30,500 Filipinos returned to the Philippines from Hawai'i between 1907 and 1929, especially in the last five years of the 1920s (Teodoro 1981: 17). More than two-thirds of these returnees were not surprisingly men since they were the great majority of immi-grants, but the group also included more than 4,000 children, some of whom like Angeles's half siblings had been born in Hawai'i as Ameri-can citizens. Unfortunately, by leaving these returnees also contributed to the smaller second generation of Filipino Americans in Hawai'i that was a significant factor in limiting their socioeconomic mobility over time. While some of these original balikbayans (return migrants) may well have returned with savings from their hard labor in the plantation fields and had earned their free passage home by meeting the terms of their three-year labor agreement,[8] most probably returned with their dreams of financial riches unfulfilled because of the great difficulty in supporting themselves on the low wages paid to Filipinos, both on and off the plantations. This movement back to the Philippines increased substantially during the Depression years to nearly 31,000 between 1930 and 1935, when the HSPA took responsibility for repatriating thousands of Filipinos, many of whom were among the unemployed in Honolulu (Cariaga 1974: 4). During the year and a half preceding June 1933, the HSPA reported that it had returned 9,200 Filipinos back to their homeland, which was a major factor in the decrease of nearly 17,000 Filipino workers on the plantations between 1932 and 1942.

241

Significant Sites

Comment can be made about the different places mentioned by Angeles, especially in Honolulu, since some of them still exist more than seventy-five years later and are significant locales for the Filipino American community. The Monrayo family residence on Hall Street, where they lived for nearly two years between 1925 and 1927, was in the poor, densely populated district adjacent to downtown Honolulu colorfully known as "Hell's Half Acre"; however, the street, which connected Beretania and Kukui streets, no longer exists. As evident from Angeles's reference to watching sumo matches from the second-story balcony of their tenement, Hell's Half Acre had a substantial Japanese immigrant population in the 1920s and was described by University of Hawai'i sociologist Andrew Lind (1930: 208) as part "of the slum where vice and crime are particularly rampant." The Filipino American community in Honolulu was primarily located around the nearby intersection of King and Liliha streets until the arrival of post-1965 immigrants into the adjacent Kalihi area. In 1950 a majority of the total Filipino American population in the city was concentrated within less than a half-mile radius of the intersection of those two streets (Lind 1980: 67).

The tenement building on River Street in downtown Honolulu where Angeles lived with other Visayan families was demolished and replaced with the John R. Gilliland Sr. Building in 1958, a two-story structure currently occupied by various small commercial establishments that still has the same street number (1335). At the opposite end of River Street in Chinatown are several Filipino American businesses, including the oldest Filipino restaurant in Honolulu, Mabuhay Café, and tailor shops and travel agencies, and opposite these establishments across Nuʻuanu Stream is a statue of Jose Rizal, the Philippine national hero. Aʻala Park, which Angeles used to walk through on her way to the public library, is also situated just across Nuʻuanu Stream. The park was the site of regular Sunday afternoon labor rallies during the 1924 strike that were attended occasionally by a reported several thousand Filipinos who went to hear speeches by strike leaders such as Manlapit and George W. Wright, president of the AFL Central Labor Council of Honolulu and a Manlapit ally. Until the 1980s many Filipino "old-timers" spent their days socializing with one another in the park since many of them lived in nearby Chinatown in inexpensive rental housing where they also frequented the Cebu Pool Hall.

The Catholic church, Our Lady of Peace Cathedral, in downtown Honolulu that Angeles used to attend has had a substantial Filipino American congregation since at least the 1950s. The Palama Theatre on King Street where she regularly watched Saturday matinees was later renamed the Zamboanga Theatre but stopped showing movies decades ago. About fifty yards down King Street is Kaiulani School, where Angeles attended elementary school. The pineapple canneries along Dillingham Boulevard in the nearby Iwilei district where she and her friends unsuccessfully sought summer employment closed operations in the early 1990s and until then provided employment to many post-1965 Filipino immigrants.

I very much look forward to assigning *Tomorrow's Memories* in my Filipinos in Hawaiʻi course in ethnic studies at the University of Hawaiʻi and to taking my students on a tour of the sites in Honolulu mentioned by Angeles that were part of her personal life that she has kindly shared with us.

Notes

1. About three-fourths (76.4 percent) of six- to thirteen-year-olds among Filipinos were enrolled in school in 1920, which was the lowest percentage for all ethnic/racial groups, and this figure declined drastically to 17.6 percent among sixteen- and seventeen-year-olds (Adams et al. 1925: 31).

2. Other strike camps in Honolulu were in Iwilei, on Libby Street, on Kukui Street, and in "Watertown," which is now the site of the Honolulu International Airport (Reinecke 1996: 39).

3. The strike began on February 1 at plantations at Kahuku, Waialua, and Waipahu on the island of Oʻahu.

4. It is just not the case that the 1920 strike was the "first major interethnic working class struggle in Hawaii," as claimed by Ron Takaki in his *Pau Hana* (1983: 174), because of the lack of coordination between the Filipino and Japanese labor unions. For a different interpretation of the strike, see Ruben R. Alcantara's "The 1920 Hawaii Plantation Strike: Ethnicity and Class in Hawaii Labor Organizing" (1987).

5. Nine dollars was a considerable sum of money during that time when it is understood that Filipino plantation laborers were being paid a minimum wage of a dollar a day and were seeking two dollars a day during the 1924 strike.

6. Reinecke (1996: 44) mentions a "Delphine Fernandez" with the same name (although slightly different spelling) as Angeles's mother's lover, who was a prosecution witness against labor leader Cecilio Basan in his trial for malicious burning of a cane field during the strike. This Delphine also was provided with free return passage to the Philippines in November 1924, very likely in exchange for his testimony against Basan. I am not certain if he is the same person as the mother's lover, but she also returned to the Philippines in 1925 with free passage, although it is not mentioned who paid for it.

7. Alcantara (1981: 50) cites the Welfare Director's reports at Waialua Plantation in the 1930s that indicate an average of only two incidents of *coboy coboy* per year.

8. Beginning in 1915, the HSPA provided free return transportation to the Philippines to laborers who had worked 720 days in three consecutive years.

References

Adams, Romanzo C., T. M. Livesay, and E. H. Van Winkle. 1925. *The Peoples of Hawaii: A Statistical Study*. Honolulu: Institute of Pacific Relations.

Alcantara, Ruben R. 1981. *Sakada: Filipino Adaptation in Hawaii*. Washington, D.C.: University Press of America.

————. 1987. "The 1920 Hawaii Plantation Strike: Ethnicity and Class in Hawaii Labor Organizing." In E. Quito (ed.), *Festschrift in Honor of Dr. Marcelino Foronda, Jr.* Manila: De La Salle University Press, pp. 182–206.

Alegado, Dean T. 1996. "Carl Damaso: A Champion of Hawaii's Working People." In J. Y. Okamura (ed.), *Filipino American History, Identity and Community in Hawai'i. Social Process in Hawaii,* vol. 37, pp. 26–35.

Beechert, Edward D. 1985. *Working in Hawai'i: A Labor History.* Honolulu: University of Hawai'i Press.

Cariaga, Roman R. 1935. "Filipinos in Honolulu." *Social Science,* vol. 10, pp. 39–46.

————. 1936. "Some Filipino Traits Transplanted." *Social Process in Hawaii,* vol. 2, pp. 20–23.

————. 1974 (1936). *The Filipinos in Hawaii: A Survey of Their Economic and Social Conditions.* San Francisco: R and E Research Associates. MA thesis (Anthropology), University of Hawai'i.

Cayaban, Ines V. 1981. *A Goodly Heritage.* Hong Kong: Gulliver Books.

Dorita, Sister Mary. 1954. "Filipino Immigration to Hawaii." MA thesis (History), University of Hawai'i.

Hormann, Bernhard L. 1953. "The Significance of the Wilder or Majors-Palakiko Case, A Study in Public Opinion." *Social Process in Hawaii,* vol. 17, pp. 1–13.

Inter-Church Federation of Honolulu. 1936. *Filipino Life in Honolulu.* Honolulu: The Federation.

Kerkvliet, Melinda T. 1991. "Pablo Manlapit's Fight for Justice." In J. Y. Okamura, A. R. Agbayani, and M. T. Kerkvliet (eds.), *The Filipino American Experience in Hawai'i. Social Process in Hawaii,* vol. 33, pp. 153–68.

————. 2002. *Unbending Cane: Pablo Manlapit, a Filipino Labor Leader in Hawai'i.* Honolulu: University of Hawai'i Press.

Lind, Andrew W. 1930. "The Ghetto and the Slum." *Social Forces,* vol. 9, pp. 206–16.

————. 1980. *The Peoples of Hawaii.* Honolulu: University of Hawai'i Press.

Murayama, Milton. 1988. *All I Asking for is My Body.* Honolulu: University of Hawai'i Press.

Okamura, Jonathan Y. 1983. "Immigrant Filipino Ethnicity in Honolulu, Hawaii." Unpublished Ph.D. dissertation (Anthropology), University of London.

————. 1996. "Writing the Filipino Diaspora in Hawai'i." In J. Y. Okamura (ed.), *Filipino American History, Identity and Community in Hawai'i. Social Process in Hawaii*, vol. 37, pp. 36–56.

Porteus, Stanley D., and Marjorie E. Babcock. 1926. *Temperament and Race*. Boston: Richard B. Badger.

Reinecke, John E. 1996. *The Filipino Piecemeal Sugar Strike of 1924–1925*. Honolulu: University of Hawai'i Press.

Takaki, Ron. 1983. *Pau Hana: Plantation Life and Labor in Hawaii*. Honolulu: University of Hawai'i Press.

Teodoro, Luis V. 1981. *Out of This Struggle: The Filipinos in Hawaii*. Honolulu: University of Hawai'i Press.

Writing Angeles Monrayo
into the Pages of Pinay History

DAWN BOHULANO MABALON

I became familiar with the life of Angeles Monrayo Raymundo through what my colleague and friend Emily Porcincula Lawsin likes to call the "coconut wire"—our connections in the Filipina/o American community. I read Angeles's diaries when they appeared in the journals published by the Santa Clara Valley Chapter of the Filipino American National Historical Society in 1991.[1] Riz called me in 1998, and I became closely connected with Angeles's life. Riz had heard about my research on Filipinas/os in Stockton, California, and offered her resources; she told me that the Raymundo family trips to Stockton's Little Manila in the 1930s and 1940s always included a visit to the Lafayette Lunch Counter, the restaurant owned by Pablo "Mang Ambo" Mabalon, my late *lolo* (grandfather). Pablo Mabalon and Riz's father, Alejandro (known as "Ray" in the diaries), had been close friends and lodge brothers in Gran Oriente, the Filipino frater- nity. I was excited and touched to learn about our families' close bonds. Riz sent her mother's complete diaries to me, and plans were made for an interview with Angeles.

I was excited when Angeles's daughter Riz decided to publish the entire volume. Riz wrote that she decided to self-publish the diaries, because her mother was getting on in years; she wanted to make sure that she could see it all in print before it was "too late." With assistance from her daughter and a friend, Riz typed it all, word-for-word, and added photographs, recipes, and her father's autobiography, and took it to her local print shop. Her mother, who had become partially blind, was pleased. Less than a year later, in 2000, Angeles passed away. Sadly, school, work, and geography prevented me from meeting Angeles in person before she passed away. This book is a testament to Angeles's and Riz's perseverance.

Angeles's diary is a precious gift to all of us who are students of Filipina/o American history and culture because it provides such a wealth of information about gender roles, work, family, culture, and community life. The wonderful diaries, photos, recipes, and memories that Angeles left behind help us to understand what it was like to be a young Pinay in Hawai'i and California during the 1920s.[2] Angeles records in faithful detail her life and the experiences of the people in her tightly knit world of Filipina/o immigrants and their families in Hawai'i and California, creating a valuable and rare perspective on early Filipina/o American community formation.[3] Throughout her diary, we get a sense of the rhythm of her life and the lives of other Filipinas in America.

In the pages of her diary, Angeles is insightful, intelligent, observant, and articulate. She writes with the raw and honest voice of a young girl juggling the pressures and tensions of her life: family issues, work, sexuality, and love. In the four years that the diary spans, Angeles grows from a young girl to a newly married sixteen-year-old shouldered with the responsibilities of running a household. In her diaries, we learn about her dreams, desires, and tragedies as well as her joys as we follow her journeys from Honolulu to *campo* life in San Ramon to city life in Stockton's Little Manila. Her days are full of hard work, but her diary entries also reveal the fun, excitement, laughter, and happiness she experiences.

Angeles was one of only a handful of Filipinas in the United States and Hawai'i, and few Filipinas of her generation left such a detailed record of their lives. Her diaries offer a window to the past through which we can understand the daily lives of Filipinas in Hawai'i and the West Coast during the decades before World War II. For these reasons, the Angeles Monrayo Raymundo diaries are invaluable documents in Filipina/o American history. Her diaries challenge much of what we know about early Filipina/o American life, which has been drawn largely from narratives written by men. The "Manong" (older male) experience is best known as told through the semi-autobiographical accounts of Filipino life in Carlos Bulosan's *America*

Is In the Heart (1943), Manuel Buaken's *I Have Lived with the American People* (1948), and Bienvenido Santos's *Scent of Apples* (1955).[4]

The Filipina immigrant population was miniscule in comparison to the number of male immigrants arriving in Hawai'i and the United States before World War II, and most historical accounts of pre–World War II Filipino American communities ignore or obscure women's roles.[5] In general, little research on Filipina American women has been published.[6] Although Pinay histories are integral to understanding early Filipina/o American experiences, women have been largely absent from the historical narrative of the Filipina/o American experience prior to World War II.[7] Consequently, little is known about the critical roles Pinays played in their communities in the pre–World War II period. Courtship, marriage, family, labor, and gender roles and relationships remain unexplored realms of the Filipina/o American experience in the early twentieth century.[8] This is precisely why Angeles's diary is so important to our understanding of the everyday lives of Pinays.

249

The immigrant and second-generation experience was often a harrowing one for Pinays like Angeles in the pre–World War II era. Pinays played multiple roles: women were breadwinners, wage laborers, homemakers, mothers, consumers, culture-bearers and -producers, community organizers, and family gatekeepers. These women endured racism, sexism, class exploitation, and the hardship of life in a community in which they were so few. They negotiated and transformed gender roles and expectations, forged their own women's networks as well as community institutions, were essential to the social and economic survival of the Filipina/o American family, and produced, maintained, and transmitted Filipina/o and Filipina/o American culture. The Pinays' power and status in family and community grew because women were so scarce; the sex ratio imbalance strengthened their position in their families, in their marriages, and in their communities. Despite the obstacles they faced, they were not victims; in fact, Angeles's diary gives us concrete evidence that they faced their challenges and lived their lives with humor, courage, strength, and dignity.

In this essay, we provide a background and context for understanding the world that Angeles creates in such detail. How typical was Angeles's life when compared with other Filipinas' experiences? What hardships did they encounter? How were they able to keep their families intact, and create and pass on Filipina/o cultural traditions? How did they cope with the hostile, racist environment of the 1920s and 1930s, and what survival strategies did they develop?

The Gendered Journey to America

Although they had fought valiantly against Spanish colonizers beginning in 1896, Filipinas/os would have a long wait for freedom. The Treaty of Paris in 1898 ended the Spanish-American War and ceded the Philippines to the United States for $20 million. Armed resistance followed, and the Philippine-American War lasted until 1902 (and even until 1910 in some areas). American colonial rule began in earnest in 1901. As part of a colonization policy President McKinley called "benevolent assimilation," a nationwide public school system (modeled after the American one) was established, in which English would be the medium of instruction. The curriculum focused on American history, culture, and values.[9]

The pervasive influence of American education, Western lifestyles, dreams of success and wealth, coupled with the extreme poverty of rural life exacerbated by American capitalism, all combined to push more than 100,000 mostly young Filipinos to Hawai'i and the U.S. mainland by 1946. Filipinos were classified as "nationals" (an ambiguous identity between citizen and alien), and there were no restrictions on immigration until the Tydings–McDuffie Act was enacted in 1934, which promised the Philippines independence in ten years but limited immigration to fifty Filipinos per year.[10] The Hawaiian Sugar Planters Association (HSPA) enticed more than 126,831 Filipinas/os to Hawai'i between 1909 and 1946. Angeles's family, like many other rural Ilokano and Visayan families, were among these immigrants, who were called *sakadas*. Later, they joined several thousand other families and went to the United States; Angeles, her father, and her brother were part of the 16 percent who left Hawai'i and moved to California and the West Coast during this time period.

More than 31,000 Filipinos landed in the ports of San Francisco and Los Angeles from 1920 to 1929, and less than 10 percent were women. Throughout Angeles's diary, she writes that she must say good-bye to close friends whose families are seeking better luck in the States. Mary Ehapon (her "Igsoo," or godsister, in Visayan) and her parents leave Hawai'i in 1926. Her friend Esperanza and her husband and children depart for America the next year. Angeles, Mary, and Esperanza were among a miniscule number of women traveling to the United States.[11] The 1930 Census counted 2,500 women out of a total of 42,500 Filipinos in the United States.[12] Filipinas were outnumbered by 10 to one in Hawai'i, 14 to one in California, 33 to one in Washington, and 47 to one in New York, and comprised only 7 percent of the Filipinas/os on the U.S. mainland. As a result, the sex ratio imbalance in the Filipina/o community prior to World War II was extreme. Of the 100,000 Filipina/o immigrants in Hawai'i and the U.S. mainland in 1946, less than 20,000 were Filipinas.[13] In 1928, when Angeles arrived in heavily Filipina/o Stockton, California, she upped the female population to seven.

While Chinese and Japanese women were restricted from entering the United States, Filipinas encountered no restrictive immigration legislation in the 1920s.[14] Family economics, labor recruitment strategies, and gender role ideologies that emphasized domesticity had a significant impact on the numbers of female immigrants.[15] Religious and cultural beliefs rooted in Roman Catholicism and Spanish colonial influences, and the ideologies of the Cult of True Womanhood brought over by American educators mandated that a woman's place was in the home, and movement outside of the home required a chaperone in most cases.[16]

Labor recruitment strategies and the labor conditions faced by the *sakadas* also contributed to the sex ratio imbalance.[17] Most poor Filipino immigrants left wives and children in the Philippines because most believed they would eventually return, and it simply cost too much to transport and maintain a wife and children. In order to send just one son to the United States, some families were forced to sell or mortgage their land (which led to increasing land loss and farm tenancy). Male recruits to Hawai'i wanted to make quick money and return home rich to their families after their contracts expired in two to three years. Women who came to Hawai'i through the HSPA recruitment program had to be the spouse or dependent of a male plantation worker. Although the HSPA attempted to correct the sex ratio imbalance by offering an incentive of 20 pesos to recruiters who could bring entire families to Hawai'i, most planters demanded a docile, dutiful, hardworking, and permanent labor force for the grueling sugar harvest. Single male workers were cheaper to import and house in dormitory-style buildings.[18]

Despite these cultural beliefs and economic barriers to immigration, women continued to immigrate, albeit in small numbers. Those several thousand women who came to Hawai'i and the United States sought education, employment, broadened life opportunities, and adventure. Many families in rural provinces in the Ilocos and Visayan regions who were experiencing poverty and farm tenancy also saw America as a golden land of opportunity. Some female immigrants—like Angeles—arrived with their families as babies or young children, or at the behest of their husbands. Angeles Monrayo's family left Romblon, in the Visayas, and arrived in the Territory of Hawai'i in 1912. Whether they were alone or accompanied by family members or husbands, thousands of Filipinas like Angeles's mother challenged gender role expectations and left sheltered and restricted lives in the Philippines to take their chances on life in Hawai'i and America. [19]

Those Filipinas who immigrated to the United States were largely young (most were under twenty-two) and single, and most hailed from the rural areas of the Ilocos and Visayan regions of the Philippines. Only a few women came from Tagalog-speaking regions. Neither the starving poor nor the elite, some immigrant Filipinas tended to come from the provincial middle class.[20] Most, like Angeles Monrayo, came from rural families with little economic means. Less than half—about 40 percent—of Filipinas coming to America before World War II were married and came with their husbands.[21] Filipinas who came to Hawai'i and the United States in the 1910s and 1920s were coming from a society undergoing radical changes in gender roles and expectations. Changing perceptions of women's roles in the Philippines, the extreme sex ratio imbalance, the lack of elders who would uphold traditional views, the entry of Filipinas into the wage labor market, and the influence of American ideas about women's roles created a situation in which immigrant Filipinas (such as Valeriana Monrayo) and their American-born and/or-raised daughters (such as Angeles) could subvert and transform constructs of gender and femininity in their immigrant communities.

Spanish colonial culture enforced, via religious education, gender role ideologies that idealized docility, modesty, and purity.[22] The model of nineteenth-century Filipina womanhood was the devout and demure Maria Clara, the heroine of Jose Rizal's nationalist novel *Noli me Tangere*. Gender ideologies shifted again after American occupation and colonization. American gender ideologies of the late nineteenth and early twentieth centuries which promoted domesticity and the increasing numbers of women entering waged work challenged long-held Hispanic ideologies about women's roles. In the American colonial period before World War II, the role and status of Filipinas in the Philippines changed dramatically, especially in urban areas like Manila, where middle-class women were entering the public sphere and attending college in large numbers, like women in the United States.[23] Educational and occupational opportunities began to broaden for middle-class Filipinas when the American colonial government implemented co-ed public education throughout the islands and encouraged college education for elite women. Some of the first Filipina immigrants to the United States were a handful of *pensionadas* (government-supported students), who attended American universities.

253

The American colonial educational system imported reinforced racial, gender, and colonial hierarchies, and new ideas about gender roles. The archetype of the "New Woman"—educated, single, athletic, and independent—became a new model of womanhood for middle-class Filipinas. Men of the elite classes complained that women were becoming too American.[24] "Shall this new Filipina, the unconscious vicim of Modernity, be allowed to lose her characteristic simplicity?" an *ilustrado* (educated elite Filipino) wrote in the early colonial period. "Women . . . are already walking about alone, a little handbag under the arm, just like true bold little American missus."[25] In 1930, *Graphic* magazine in the Philippines ran an article entitled "Who Needs Maria Claras anyway? They belong to the Past."[26]

The American colonial public school curriculum emphasized domestic science and home economics courses for girls. Filipinas attending public schools in the colonial period had to learn the "household arts" of sewing, cooking, gardening, and lacemaking.[27] Although some women began to attend college, marriage and family remained the primary goals for all women, regardless of class.[28] Working-class immigrant Filipinas, like Angeles's mother Valeriana Motia Monrayo, had few options. Although educational and employment opportunities and a broader role in community and government transformed middle-class Filipino women's lives, little changed in the sexual division of labor in the home or in the general expectations that all women's lives would revolve around the home, especially those of poor and working-class women. In rural areas, education for poor women beyond basic literacy and domestic science was not a priority.[29]

254   With immigration to the United States, Filipinas/os were forced to reexamine and redefine ideas about womanhood and manhood brought from the Philippines. Furthermore, racism and sexism had a lasting impact on the ways women and men negotiated gender roles and relationships. Filipinos attempted to reconstruct and assert their manhood in a society that often humiliated them through racist and sexist legislation.[30] The small number of Filipinas and the conditions in which Filipino men and women lived in Hawai'i and Stockton shifted the balance of power toward women within Filipina/o families and communities. Pinays had to negotiate their changing perceptions of womanhood and femininity with the static and restrictive constructions idealized by Filipino men. Traditional ideas about Filipina womanhood brought from the Philippines clashed with the everyday realities faced by Filipina/o immigrants, creating conflicts between idealized and romanticized notions of Filipina womanhood and the stark realities of Filipina life in Hawai'i and the United States.

Family and Kinship, Love and Marriage

Three themes resonate in Angeles's diaries in regards to family, friends, and love: the flexible boundaries of "family" in Filipina/o American communities; the patriarchy and power relations in her parents' marriage, her immediate family, and her own marriage; and the courtship and love rituals in the male-dominated Filipina/o communities of Hawai'i and California. In her diaries, Angeles identifies her immediate blood family: Enarciso, her Tatay (father); Manong Julian, her older brother; her Nanay (mother); and several half brothers and sisters.[31] Through the course of the diaries, we meet many people with whom the Monrayos form strong bonds of kinship and love. We also learn early on that Angeles's family life has been riddled with conflict: her parents are separated, and she lives with her father and brother. In the Filipina/o American family, gender roles and patriarchy were constantly challenged.

The Family and Kinship Network

For Filipina/o immigrants, home and family were havens from oppressive work environments. A flexible sense of family and a large kinship network helped immigrants cope with harsh conditions. For example, Filipinos streamed into Stockton for job opportunities as well as to be closer to family and townmates already settled there.[32] Angeles, like many other Filipinas, relied on many other young girls and women for friendship and support; these women became part of her family network. Girlfriends like Mary Ehapon, Esperanza, and Rose become like her sisters. She found a second mother in her Ninang Feliza Roxas, who served as her marriage sponsor (sponsors in Filipina/o weddings served the same role as godparents, and therefore were also called "Ninangs" or "Ninongs").

Filipinas/os in the United States drew on the power of an extended family and kinship network to help them cope with immigration and settlement experiences. Distant relations and townmates could become one's only family members in America. When a Filipina/o arrived in Hawai'i or the United States, he or she searched first for blood relatives, then townmates and province mates, and others from the same region. Sharing origins from the same town, province, or region made strangers into intimate kin. In Hawai'i, Tatay must leave Angeles and Manong Julian for long periods at a time, entrusting their welfare to friends. In Stockton, the Monrayos and the Ehapons all share one large room in a residential hotel in Little Manila, a very common arrangement among poor immigrant families. In fact, anti-Filipino exclusionists cited the propensity for several Filipinas/os to crowd into small apartments as an argument for exclusion.[33]

Power and Patriarchy

For Angeles, family was both haven and a source of conflict.[34] A common theme in Filipina/o American history, and in Angeles's diaries, is the shifting power dynamic between Filipina/o men and women. Filipinas took advantage of this shift by asserting themselves as valuable partners to their husbands and essential to their family's economic survival. In the absence of his wife, Enarciso Monrayo (Tatay) must take on the full responsibilities of being the family caretaker, rather than just its patriarch. Filipino immigrants like Enarciso

255

Monrayo were fighting a losing battle over control of their wives and daughters, who could defy patriarchal control through elopement, desertion, and divorce. Valeriana Monrayo's extramarital affair, divorce, and remarriage is a prime example of how patriarchal control could be challenged. Enarciso Monrayo's attempts to control his wife and daughter prove futile: Valeriana refuses to leave her lover, and Angeles elopes.

Angeles's diaries contain numerous references to her parents' marriage and its violent end. The shifting balance of power between men and women gave Filipinas more leverage in dealing with their husbands. Filipinas like Valeriana Monrayo in Hawai'i and the United States soon realized that one did not have to stay in an unhappy marriage (divorce was, and remains, illegal in the Philippines), and taking a lover was not uncommon. The scarcity of Pinays led to the *coboy-coboy* (literally, "cowboy") phenomenon, in which Filipinos "stole" other men's wives.[35] However, Angeles's diaries tell us that some Filipinas took lovers and left their husbands on their own accord.[36]

Enarciso Monrayo is defiantly opposed to her marriage to Ray; Angeles defies him and they elope, which enrages her father. Many Filipino immigrant parents wanted their daughters to marry older men with stability, particularly those who were labor contractors or who had well-paying jobs, and several second-generation Filipina/o American couples in the Stockton area eloped when their parents refused to bless their unions.[37] For Angeles, Tatay prefers a Visayan man with a strong work ethic, such as Sebastian Gravera, a chef at a local Stockton hotel. Ray is a Tagalog from Tondo, near Manila (his urban origins were immediately suspect to rural Visayans), and he works as a traveling suit salesman.[38] This is lazy work, Tatay believes. Riz Raymundo remembers that it was decades before her grandfather Enarciso could forgive her father.

Angeles's diaries give us further evidence that Filipinas in the United States were challenging patriarchal control and constrictive gender roles within the family. New attitudes about women's roles and abilities, and the rising status of Filipinas in their communities, gave Filipinas an opportunity to make changes in their lives, marking paths radically different from their mothers' and grandmothers'. The scarcity of Filipinas made them highly valued within their families and communities and gave them great power to make their own choices about love and marriage.

Courtship and Marriage

"Gosh, I am only 12 years old—and already someone is telling me about love," Angeles writes on March 9, 1925. Too many suitors and too few women made courtship and dating a painful process for lonely bachelors. Filipino men—barred by law in most states from marrying white women—competed fiercely for Pinays. Because of their scarcity in Hawai'i and the United States, Filipinas were highly valued commodities. Angeles's diary brings us firsthand accounts of the tricky courtship rituals between Filipina/o men and women in the United States, which were complicated by the extreme sex ratio imbalance. All Filipinas—young and older, married and single—experienced the effects of the sex ratio imbalance on Filipina/o courtship rituals. At the time that Angeles wrote her diaries, most Filipina/o immigrants were in their twenties and thirties, and anticipated marriage and family building. Pinays were like "gold" and "diamonds," according to Camila Labor Carido, who arrived in Little Manila as a nineteen-year-old in 1929.[39] From the age of eleven to her elopement, when her diary ends, Angeles refuses marriage proposals and resists the love letters and physical advances of persistent Filipinos. Angeles is surprised by all the attention she receives; after all, she thinks of herself as an average girl.

In America, complicated courtship rituals from the Philippines became fairly obsolete. In the Philippines, courtship and marriage rituals were strictly monitored by parents and family members, as marriage meant the union of the two families. In many provinces in the 1920s, courtship was a complex and protracted process that involved negotiations between families for dowry. A suitor would customarily bring his parents and a respected, articulate elder to serve as the spokesperson to his prospective bride's home.[40] But the Filipina/o American community was largely devoid of elders who could exercise such social control. Without elders or his parents to represent him when he asked for Angeles's hand in marriage, Ray brings three trusted and respected friends—Visayans Pete Braga and Isidro Gonzales and Ricardo Trumbullo, a fellow Tagalog, who serve as his spokespersons and interpreters.

257

Filipinos like Ray went to great lengths to marry Filipinas, spending large amounts of money on gifts and meals to win the hearts of their prospective brides and their families. Angeles often took advantage of the situation and allowed her suitors to treat her and her family to frequent meals in Little Manila's numerous restaurants. Suitors who could have only been making several dollars a day plied her with expensive gifts like gold watches, evening gowns, and lingerie. Writing during the 1930s, *pensionado* Trinidad Rojo complained that Pinays seemed to be more "fickle" than girls in the Islands, because "a pretty Filipino girl has several times more admirers than if she were in the Islands."[41]

Because of the scarcity of unmarried Pinays, some men pursued and harassed women who did not show interest. In the worst scenarios, they reacted negatively and violently to rejection, or insisted on physical intimacy. Angeles has such negative experiences with Filipino men that she fears them. In a mostly male labor camp in San Ramon, she asks her brother for a pair of pants, which she pulls on under her dress to wear to bed. She needs such clothes, she implies, to protect against harassment. Other Filipinas in the community were similarly harassed by insistent suitors, and competition for women could turn ugly. In the summer of 1929, *The Three Stars* newspaper reported that a love-crazed Filipino man stabbed another Pinoy who was admiring his wife.[42] In Vallejo later that year, a thirty-six-year-old Filipino man killed a fourteen-year-old girl and then himself when she refused his advances.[43] Intense jealousies over women fueled fistfights and stabbings among Filipinos.

Despite being disillusioned by and afraid of men, Angeles continues to pursue dreams of romance, love, and marriage.[44] Ray is everything she is not: he is Tagalog, city-bred, glamorous, a suit salesman. He is someone "I could fall in love with," she writes. She decides impulsively to elope with him. Readers may react with surprise upon reading that Angeles and Ray elope when she is 15 and Ray is 25, but it was not uncommon for Pinays during that time period to marry and bear children in their teens.[45] In fact, Angeles's diary tells us that many Filipinas married and bore children when they were very young, particularly in Hawai'i. She is also careful to avoid premarital sex, as it seems that many of her peers—some as young as thirteen and fourteen—became pregnant.

Angeles's diary reveals the private struggles of Filipina/o men and women to create and maintain families before World War II. As there were few elders to mediate courtship, the gender imbalance shifted the dynamics between men and women. No longer were women confined to complicated courtship rituals; they could choose to marry whomever they wanted, even if it meant defying their families. Their entry into wage labor would further complicate and transform gender role definitions.

259

Pinay Labors: Redefining the Meanings of "Work"

Angeles's diary reminds us that Filipinas—like most women of color and immigrant women of her time period—worked a double day. Angeles performed waged labor to ensure her family's survival, but she was also responsible for all domestic labor. Expected to do both work within the home as well as to contribute to the survival of the family through waged labor, Filipinas and their daughters never stopped working. The entrance of Filipinas into the labor market during this period in the Philippines and in the United States is an indicator of the tensions between the gender ideologies propagated in the Philippines in regard to women's roles and the conditions under which Filipinas lived in the United States.[46]

The wages that Angeles contributed to her family both in Hawai'i and in California ensured their survival, particularly when her father and brother could not find work. As we learn from Angeles's diaries, Filipinas bore the primary responsibility for the domestic sphere, continuing patterns brought from the Philippines. But in order to survive in Hawai'i and the United States, all members of the family had to work outside of the home. Pinays and Pinoys in the 1920s who dreamed of picking up money on the streets in America, instead found themselves picking fruits and vegetables. Striking it rich in America became only a remote possibility. Even before the stock market crash of 1929 and the Great Depression, depressed farm prices made work difficult to find, even in the lush San Joaquin Valley; Tatay and Manong Julian do not find work for many months after they arrive in Stockton.

Filipina immigrants, like their male counterparts, found few jobs outside of the service sector and agriculture, especially during the 1930s. Angeles and Igsoo joined many other Filipinas performing wage labor in canneries, in the agricultural fields, and in service-sector jobs in the food industry as waitresses, cooks, and servants, or in domestic service.[47] Pinays, even those with college educations, worked on the delta island farms and cooked for the field crews, served as domestic helpers, waited tables, or worked in the pool halls in Little Manila. These Pinays, like Angeles and Igsoo, probably handed their wages over to their parents, forming an economic partnership that was key to survival. Women's historians have called this "the family wage economy," in which all members of the family pooled their income.[48] Because her wages were essential to the family's subsistence, Angeles gained a great deal of respect within her family.[49]

260

At a young age, Angeles feels responsible for her family's welfare, and her labor becomes indispensable to her family's survival. Whenever she makes any money (dancing with the Pinoys in Hawai'i, or sewing for 4-H leader Mrs. Patterson), she immediately gives her money to Tatay. When the Ehapon and Monrayo families arrive in Stockton, only the girls can find work. Pinay pool hall girls were magnets for Pinoys, so Angeles has no problem securing a job. Ultimately, they become the family breadwinners, and their families depend solely on their incomes for rent and food.

Although Angeles repeatedly expresses her desire to continue her education in the United States, the economic survival of her family and lack of good job opportunities for Filipinas dash her ambitions. After she arrives in California, she never mentions education again in her diaries. It may have become clear to Angeles that there were few job opportunities for educated Filipinas. Even the most educated and professional Filipina/o immigrants were forced to work in the fields, or in restaurants and hotels as janitors, busboys, and dishwashers until after World War II, when Filipinas/os were able to gain citizenship and as racist attitudes toward Filipinas/os were less blatant.[50]

Angeles's life changes again when she marries Ray, moves an hour away to rural Oakdale, near Modesto, and becomes a farmworker's wife. For the Pinays working on the farms, the day began long before the sun rose. Angeles does not complain, but the working conditions in the fields and canneries in the San Joaquin Valley during the 1920s, 1930s, and 1940s were horrific. Families living in the *campo* (agricultural camp) endured polluted water, substandard housing, and wages of 10 to 40 cents an hour. Some slept in windowless shacks on the dirt. Angeles and Ray are so poor when they start out in Oakdale that she is happy to earn only a few dollars a day. Angeles finds little time and motivation to write in her diary when she becomes pregnant, and abandons the diary entirely as she raises her children. Angeles probably had little spare time, since the lives of Filipina mothers centered around constant cooking, cleaning, ironing, laundry, and sewing. We learn later on from Riz that the Raymundo family struggled to survive the Great Depression. The family moved from camp to camp to work, sometimes scavenging mushrooms and wild greens to survive.

261

For Pinays like Angeles and Igsoo, the sex ratio imbalance and their wage-earning power strengthened their position within the home.[51] This was in contrast to the experiences of other racial-ethnic women, particularly immigrant Chinese, Japanese, and Mexican women during this same time period.[52] Although Filipinas may have enjoyed power in the home relative to other racial-ethnic women, particularly other Asian American women, this "power" did not spare them from unceasing work and longer workdays. In fact, the decision-making power held by Pinays *increased* their workload. According to Elizabeth Uy Eviota, the dominance of Filipino women in the domestic realm is really "men's ability to shed their responsibility for housework and child care."[53] In Hawai'i, Angeles was working in the home even as a tiny girl, assisting in childcare and housework when she lives with her mother and her stepfather and responsible for the housework when she returns to live with her Tatay and Manong Julian. When she and her father and brother move to the urban environment of Stockton's Little Manila, Angeles is freed from having to cook and clean, as the family eats at restaurants most of the time. However, her responsibilities and burdens grow when she marries, and it is her responsibility to cook and clean.

In addition to wage labor and reproductive labor, many immigrant and second-generation Filipinas were responsible for organizing the family's finances and budget.[54] This responsibility led Filipinas to seek out ways to find extra money with which to bolster the family's meager earnings. Although domesticity was idealized for middle-class and elite women in the colonial, pre–World War II Philippines, working-class and rural women were engaged in trade, weaving, manufacturing, domestic service, and side businesses in significant numbers.[55] Some Pinays used their expertise at running side businesses and opened their own stores and businesses. Filipinas in Hawai'i and in the United States often sold treats and snacks, such as *maruya* (banana fritters) and *lumpia* (spring rolls) to supplement their families' incomes. When she realizes that she can help contribute to the family wage, Angeles takes on extra laundry. This practice is similar to what young women and girls in the Philippines did during World War II, when American soldiers set up camps near their homes.[56] In fact, women were some of the more successful Filipino immigrant entrepreneurs in Stockton.[57]

Filipinas' roles in the family economy were transformed in the immigration and settlement experience. While colonial-era Philippine gender roles idealized domesticity for middle-class and elite women, Filipina/o immigrants were largely working-class. Filipina labor within the home and outside of the home became crucial to the survival of Filipina/o American families. The Monrayo and Raymundo families could not have survived without Angeles's wages and her housework. Angeles's diary forces us to reconsider the concept of "labor" in Filipina/o American history to include women's work on the farms, in stores and pool halls, in canneries, and at home.

Becoming "Filipina/o" in America: Building Community, Sustaining Ethnicity, and Creating Culture

Angeles's life—so typical of many Visayan and other Filipina/o immigrants—is characterized by constant movement: from Hall Street to River Street and back again in Honolulu, from Oahu to the glittering San Francisco pier, from the sleepy, rural Harlan Ranch in San Ramon to the bustling city life of Little Manila in downtown Stockton. From the 1920s to the 1960s, thousands of Filipinas/os like Angeles and her family were drawn to Stockton, one of California's most important urban centers in the 1920s. By World War II, the city was home to the largest Filipina/o community outside of the Philippines. Stockton, located 80 miles east of San Francisco, sat at the crossroads of a West Coast Filipina/o labor migration flow that began in the early 1920s and continued until the 1960s, when California farmers grew to rely on Mexican immigrant labor. Filipina/o migrants carved an annual path from Alaskan canneries to southern California's Imperial Valley, and thousands stopped and settled in Stockton, dubbed the "Manila of California."

Agricultural work was plentiful in the Stockton and San Joaquin County area for Filipina/o laborers because the area provided work year-round.[58] After exclusion laws decimated the numbers of Asian immigrant laborers, and as Asian workers began demanding higher wages and leasing or owning their own farmland, California growers turned to Filipino and Mexican laborers, continuing a pattern of exploitation.[59] Filipinos were in high demand in the San Joaquin Delta asparagus industry, as growers believed that their short stature made them ideal to do stoop labor on wet soil.[60] Filipinos could also find work in the surrounding areas. Angeles's brother, Manong Julian, finds work in Salinas, and later brings the family to Harlan Ranch, in San Ramon, in Contra Costa County.[61]

Unwelcome in most of the city, Stockton's Filipinas/os transformed a six-block section of the downtown ghetto into a vibrant enclave they called Little Manila, bordered by Center Street on the west, Market Street on the north, San Joaquin Street on the east, and Sonora Street on the south.[62] The intersection of El Dorado and Lafayette streets in downtown Stockton was the heart of Little Manila. As soon as the Monrayos arrive in Stockton, Angeles writes that Tatay and Manong Julian go to "El Dorado Streets" (sic) to make friends. Anywhere from 4,000 to 10,000 Filipinos lived in Stockton and in Little Manila during its heyday in the decades before World War II. During the asparagus season, which ran from late February to June, the Filipino population would double.[63] This enormous Filipina/o presence created a need for goods and services: low-rent rooming houses, cheap hotels, restaurants (Angeles makes frequent references to eating at chop suey diners and Filipina/o restaurants), barbershops, tailor shops, gambling dens, pool halls, and shoe shine stands.

When the Monrayos move to Stockton in 1928, the city's Filipina/o population was mushrooming, and Filipina/o entrepreneurs opened businesses to serve their compatriots. Tatay plays pool at Caesar's pool hall at 223 S. El Dorado Street. The Raymundo family might have patronized Filipino photographer John Y. Billones at his studio at 249 S. El Dorado, located next door to the Mayon Restaurant, where Angeles and her father and brother share many meals of *adobo* and *dinuguan*. Filipinos bought the latest McIntosh suits from Placido and Juliana Lazaro's Los Filipinos Tailoring shop at 110 E. Lafayette Street, next door to the Stockton Filipino Community Center. Other businesses and institutions located in Little Manila at the time that Angeles lived there include the California Filipino Farmers Association, the Engkabo and Espanola billiard halls, the Legionarios del Trabajo fraternity, the Filipino Information Bureau, the Samahang Filipino Mission, the Caballeros de Dimas-Alang, and the Mapa and Acepcion barbers, located within the Japanese-owned pool hall on Market Street where Angeles worked.[64]

The Little Manila area, especially El Dorado Street, was densely populated by Filipina/o immigrants who had nowhere else to go; they were barred from much of the city's northern areas. Constant police surveillance ensured that Filipinos weren't allowed north of Main Street, where white Stockton began.[65] It is surprising that Angeles's diary does not mention one incident of obvious racism, especially since many remember Stockton police as especially brutal to Filipinas/os, and Stockton hotels boasted signs that read "Positively No Filipinos Allowed." Only four years before Angeles's arrival in Stockton, the Klu Klux Klan attracted over 1,000 people to a rally at the Civic Auditorium.[66] Perhaps the tightly knit world that Angeles paints for us—one that was almost exclusively Pinay and Pinoy—insulated her from the most blatant discrimination. Filipinas/os turned to each other for clothing, shelter, food, employment, and leisure, creating their own social world in the 1920s and 1930s.

Becoming Filipina/o in America

Angeles's diary provides evidence that Filipina/o immigrants did not immediately view themselves as *Filipinas/os;* rather, they identified primarily with others from their town, province, and region. Angeles's world is composed almost entirely of other first- and second-generation Visayans in Hawai'i and in Stockton. Visayans and Ilokanos socialized with those who spoke the same or similar languages; Tagalog did not become the national language of the Philippines until after World War II, and most immigrants from peasant and rural backgrounds had only a perfunctory command of English, like Angeles's father Enarciso. But there were language differences even *among* Visayans. Angeles's family probably spoke Hiligaynon, the main language spoken throughout the western Visayas; they may have also spoken Aklanon or Capiceño, the dialects spoken by residents of the provinces of Aklan and Capiz on Panay Island near Romblon. Angeles's diary gives us ample evidence of the ways that language barriers prevented Filipinas/os from creating relationships across regional lines. Antagonism and stereotyping certainly existed among Visayans, Tagalogs, and Ilokanos; Angeles writes several times that her father hates Tagalogs, but she doesn't understand why. Filipinas/os raised in the United States, like Angeles, became multilingual and bridged differences among regional groups. Angeles learns to speak Cebuano, the Visayan dialect spoken by Mary Ehapon and her family.

Filipina/o community organizations like Gran Oriente were also a vehicle for Ilokanos, Visayans, and Tagalogs to *become* Filipina/o American. These groups offered mutual aid benefits, a surrogate family, a support system in times of sadness and joy, and a sense of cohesion, belonging, and unity. They also served as sites within which Filipina/o American cultural traditions were created.[67] Community organizations held dances, parades, and gatherings to celebrate American and Filipino holidays such as Rizal Day, Fourth of July, and Christmas.[68] The night before they elope, Ray crowns the queen of the Rizal Day celebration in Stockton. Despite the popularity of queen contests in Filipina/o American social life, Angeles found the queen contest circuit boring. Angeles writes on December 20, 1925, "I do not know why they are making so much of this doing, called Rizal celebration. . . . Anyway, I am not too interested in their doings."

Some of the largest and most powerful organizations in the Filipina/o American community were the fraternal associations Gran Oriente, Legionarios del Trabajo, Caballeros de Dimas Alang, and the Filipino Federation of America. These were mutual-aid organizations rooted in the ideals of the Katipunan and loosely based on Masonic rituals, with the exception of Gran Oriente, which was Masonic.[69] The lodges offered benefits such as burials, life insurance for surviving family members, medical care, and general assistance. These organizations boasted thousands of members (both male and female, from all regional groups) by the 1930s. Angeles's diaries tell us about Ray's involvement in the Stockton-based Mayon Lodge of Gran Oriente. Ray's lodge brothers become his family and spokespersons when he requests Angeles's hand in marriage. Gran Oriente is based in San Francisco and is one of four major fraternal groups brought over from the Philippines and established in the United States and Hawai'i in the 1920s.[70] All of the lodges remain active today.

Although they were excluded from Gran Oriente (the other fraternities accepted women members), Filipinas, like Chinese immigrant women in San Francisco in the early part of the century, sought to create their own organizations for self-improvement and community service.[71] However, Angeles does not mention her involvement in any of them, and her attendance at church seems confined to her years in Hawai'i. Perhaps this is because some Catholic churches in California were indifferent to the needs of Filipino immigrants.[72]

Sustaining Ethnicity, Creating Culture

Filipina/o immigrants and their families created distinctly Filipina/o American cultural traditions. Filipinas/os, with a long history of colonialism and occupation, are accustomed to cultural blending, transformation, and rearticulation.[73] The process by which immigrants and their children "select and create cultural forms" is called "cultural coalescence."[74] Filipina/o American food and Filipina/o American youth culture, both prominent themes in the diaries, offer readers colorful examples of the ways that Filipina/o Americans created new cultural identities.

More than just sustenance, food is a celebration of ethnicity, group identity, and shared history; as such, it is a powerful vehicle for both cultural maintenance and cultural synthesis.[75] Angeles's diary is rich with references to her favorite foods and the meals she cooks for her family and husband. Angeles loves both Filipino and American food. In Hawai'i, she yearns for a stove so she can bake the cakes she tastes with her 4-H group. The Americanization efforts of the 4-H women did not make rice and fish distasteful for young Pinays; rather, they simply added ham sandwiches and cakes to the wide array of foods (Filipina/o, Chinese, Japanese, Korean, and Portuguese) which were available to them in Hawai'i. Filipinas like Angeles, who were cooking for work crews and their own families in Hawai'i and on the mainland, created *Filipina/o American* cuisine by cooking with local ingredients using Ilokano, Visayan, and Tagalog methods and seasonings. The ease with which they blended their indigenous foodways with American ingredients and methods is further evidence of how Filipinas/os negotiated their multiple identities.

Angeles's experiences with movies, music, dancing, clothes, and makeup in Hawai'i and the United States demonstrate the different ways young Pinays were negotiating parental boundaries, American mass culture, and ethnic identity. At every possible opportunity, Angeles, Ray, and her family and friends go to movies (the 1920s was the decade that the movie-house became a pleasure palace for people of all classes). She wears her hair short in the sleek bob popularized by flappers in the teens and 1920s, and she likes to dress in the latest fashions. Along with other American women in the 1920s, Angeles begins to wear lipstick and other cosmetics.[76] Angeles, like many other American women, turned to popular American women's magazines, *Good Housekeeping* and *True Story*. When her father buys her a Victrola in Hawai'i, she writes, "Mary and I will be dancing like crazy when we have the time for it." Angeles and her friends love to sing and dance to both Filipino traditional songs and American pop songs. Throughout the 1920s, Angeles is consuming American pop culture passionately: she is dancing the Charleston, reading *Good Housekeeping*, and watching movies almost weekly. These diversions were necessary to endure the hardships of life in America.

Writing Angeles into the Pages of Pinay History

Women like Angeles were central to the development of a vibrant cultural and community life that sustained Filipinas/os in times of hardship and sacrifice. But traditional accounts of Filipina/o American communities during the 1920s and 1930s describe a bachelor community that was womanless and transient, bent only on gambling and taxi-hall dancing. Angeles's diary offers a different perspective, one in which Pinays are central to the building of the early Filipina/o American community. These early Pinays paved the way for more Filipina/o women, children, and families to immigrate, settle, and create communities in America in the postwar era.

Despite the many challenges they faced, Pinays developed a special place for themselves within the ethnic community as the centers of kinship networks, as wage earners and businesswomen, as community leaders and organizers, and as retainers and producers of Filipina/o and Filipina/o American culture. Moreover, women like Angeles challenged and transformed traditional gender roles in regards to the family, work, and the community. These women laid a strong foundation of women's leadership in the Filipina/o community for the war brides, for their second-generation daughters, for their third-generation granddaughters, and for the women who would arrive after 1965.

By the 1960s, the gender-skewed environment of Angeles's girlhood had changed forever. The 1945 War Brides Act brought large numbers of Filipina women and children to the United States, tripling the size of the Filipino population on the West Coast between 1945 and 1965. In 1965, the Immigration and Naturalization Act eliminated race-based quotas, set a system of immigration preferences, and increased immigration from the Philippines to 20,000 per year. In 2002, Filipinas constituted the majority of the emigrants leaving the Philippines to work and settle around the world, and Filipina/o Americans are the nation's second largest Asian American ethnic group. It would be interesting to know what Angeles would think of all of this change.

In mid-November 1928, Angeles's diaries tell us that morning sickness prevented her from writing more frequently. On November 17, 1928, she writes her last entry: "I was feeling bad every morning." Many years later, she would tell her daughter Rizaline that she just did not feel like writing in it any longer, even after the morning sickness passed. Angeles's diary ends in late 1928, a critical juncture in Filipina/o American history. In less than a year, the United States would be mired in the Great Depression, and thousands of Filipinas/os would not find work. Anti-Filipino sentiment would gather such momentum that Filipinas/os could not walk the streets of Stockton and other California cities without fear for their safety. In a few short months, anti-Filipino riots in Watsonville would claim the life of farmworker Fermin Tobera. In five years, the U.S. Congress would grant Philippine independence but curtail Filipina/o immigration to fifty per year. In a decade, Filipinas/os in the Philippines, the United States, and Hawai'i would be forever transformed by war.

Angeles's diary offers us a portrait of a time before these tumultuous changes. In January 1924, Filipino strikers in Hawai'i are demanding a living wage. Angeles Monrayo is an eleven-year-old Visayan girl living at a strike camp on Middle Street in Honolulu. She is concerned with finding new friends, starting her own laundry business, and dancing to earn extra money.

It is January 1924, and young Angeles starts a diary.

Notes

I would like to thank Emily Porcincula Lawsin, Rizaline Raymundo, Professor Joan May T. Cordova, Professor Allyson Tintiangco-Cubales, Drs. Fred and Dorothy Cordova, and the anonymous reviewers for their assistance, critiques, and suggestions. The materials and resources at the National Pinoy Archives of the Filipino American National Historical Society in Seattle and the Filipino American Reading Room at the San Francisco Public Library were essential to this essay, and I am grateful for the kind assistance I received in San Francisco and Seattle. Finally, I am grateful for the assistance of my father, Ernesto Tirona Mabalon, who translated Hiligaynon phrases and shared his recollections of the Raymundo family with me.

1. Angeles Monrayo Raymundo, "Excerpts from the Diary of Angeles Monrayo Raymundo, 1924," *Lost Generation: Filipino Journal* 1 (1991): 31–41; and Angeles Monrayo Raymundo, "Diary Excerpts of Angeles Monrayo Raymundo, 1927," *Generation Insights, Reflected Memories: Filipino Journal* 2, no. 2 (1992): 3–13. Published by the Santa Clara Valley Chapter of the Filipino American National Historical Society.

2. The terms "Pinay" and "Filipina" are used interchangeably in this essay. "Pinay" refers specifically to a Filipina in the United States, whether or not she is immigrant or American-born. "Filipina" refers specifically to any woman of Filipina/o descent. For a discussion of the first time "Pinay" and "Pinoy" appear in print, see Emily Porcincula Lawsin, "Pensionados, Paisanos, and Pinoys: An Analysis of the *Filipino Student Bulletin*, 1945–1965," *Filipino American National Historical Society Journal* 4 (1996): 33–33P.

3. I use the terms "Filipina/o" to identify anyone of Filipina/o descent and "Filipina/o American" for those of Filipina/o descent born or living in the United States. However, it must be noted that identification through region was and continues to be a primary source of identification for many Filipinas/os; for example, many immigrants considered themselves primarily Ilokano, Visayan, or Tagalog, and a Filipina/o American ethnic identity emerges from the collective experience of these immigrants. Throughout this essay, we use "Filipina/o" to refer to both men and women, "Filipino" when referring to men, and "Filipina" when referring to women. We avoid using the masculine as the generic

as is the common practice with Spanish terms such as *Filipino*. Because women's voices have been obscured in much of the literature on Filipina/o Americans, I avoid embodying sexism in our terminology. Women scholars writing Filipina/o American history have responded to the historical neglect of Pinays in the pre–World War II period by avoiding the use of "Filipino," which, as Dorothy Fujita Rony writes, "serves to reinforce the historical absence of women." See Fujita Rony's dissertation "You Got to Move Like Hell: Trans-Pacific Colonialism and Filipina/o Seattle, 1919–1941" (Ph.D. diss., Yale University, 1996), vii. Other scholars who use the term "Filipina/o" include Teresa Amott and Julie Matthaei in their book *Race, Gender and Work: A Multicultural Economic History of Women in the United States* (Boston: South End Press, 1996), Allyson Tintiangco Cubales in her essay "Pinayism," *maganda* magazine, University of California, Berkeley, 1997, and historian and educator Joan May Timtiman Cordova.

4. Manuel Buaken, *I Have Lived with the American People* (Caldwell, Idaho: The Caxton Printers, 1948); Carlos Bulosan, *America is in the Heart* (Seattle: University of Washington Press, reprint 1973); and Bienvenido N. Santos, *Scent of Apples: A Collection of Stories* (Seattle: University of Washington Press, reprint 1979).

5. Even key texts on Filipina/o experiences in the United States before World War II (Buaken's *I Have Lived with the American People* and Bulosan's *America is in the Heart*) have neglected the presence of Filipino women in the United States. The two most widely read texts on the Asian American experience are Ronald Takaki's *Strangers from a Different Shore* (Boston: Little, Brown & Co., 1989) and Sucheng Chan's *Asian Americans: An Interpretive History* (Boston: Twayne Publishers, 1991). These works focus mainly on the bachelor society created by male Filipino immigrants in the 1920s and 1930s. The portrait which Bulosan paints of pre–World War II Filipina/o life does not include women's experiences, and makes little mention of Filipina presence in the United States.

6. For a good comparison, see Ines Viernes Cayaban's book, *A Goodly Heritage* (Wanchai, Hong Kong: Gulliver Books, 1981), an autobiography of a Filipina nurse who immigrated to Hawai'i in 1931 and became heavily involved in that community. Rizaline Raymundo and the Santa Clara Valley Chapter of the Filipino American National Historical Society also published "The Frances Trimillos Interview" in

Lost Generation: Filipino Journal 1, no. 1 (1991): 47–51, in which
Trimillos, who came to the United States in 1937, tells of her life in
San Jose, California. Other Filipinas' oral histories are included in col-
lections such as Fred Cordova, *Filipinos: Forgotten Asian Americans, A
Pictorial Essay, 1763-circa-1963* (Dubuque, Iowa: Kendall/Hunt
Publishing, 1983); Caridad Concepcion Vallangca, *The Second Wave:
Pinay & Pinoy, 1945–1960* (San Francisco: Strawberry Hill Press,
1987); Joan May T. Cordova and Alexis S. Canillo, eds., *Voices: A
Filipino-American Oral History* (Stockton, Calif.: Filipino Oral History
Project, Inc., 1984); and Yen Le Espiritu, ed., *Filipino American Lives*
(Philadelphia: Temple University Press, 1995). For other writings on
Filipina women, see, for example, Dorothy Cordova, "Voices from the
Past: Why They Came," and Barbara M. Posadas, "Mestiza Girlhood:
Interracial Families in Chicago's Filipino American Community since
1925," in *Making Waves: An Anthology of Writings By and About Asian
American Women,* ed. Asian Women United of California (Boston:
Beacon Press, 1989), 42–49, 273–82; Belinda A. Aquino, "The History
of Pilipino Women in Hawai'i," *Bridge: An Asian American Perspective*
(Spring 1979): 17–21; Paul Ong and Tania Azores, "The Migration and
Incorporation of Filipino Nurses," in *The New Asian Immigration in Los
Angeles and Global Restructuring* (Philadelphia: Temple University Press,
1994), 164–95; Grace Chang, "The Global Trade in Filipina
Workers,"in *Dragon Ladies: Asian American Feminists Breathe Fire,* ed.
Sonia Shah (Boston: South End Press, 1997), 132–52; Christine T.
Lipat, Trinity A. Ordona, Cianna Pamintuan Stewart, and Mary Ann
Ubaldo, "Tomboy, Dyke, Lezzie, and Bi: Filipina Lesbian and Bisexual
Women Speak Out" in *Filipino Americans: Transformation & Identity,*
ed. Maria P. P. Root (Thousand Oaks, Calif.: Sage Publications, 1997),
230–46; Jovina Navarro, "Immigration of Pilipino Women to America,"
in *Lahing Pilipino: Pilipino American Anthology;* Susan Evangelista,
"The Pinay as Migrant: Filipina Immigration to the United States in
the 1930s," *Balai Reader,* and *Filipina: Hawaii's Filipino Women,* ed.
Pepi Nieva (Honolulu: Filipino Association of University Women,
1994).

7. See Benicio T. Catapusan, "Filipino Social Adjustment in the
United States" (Ph.D. diss., University of Southern California, 1940);
Honorante Mariano, "Filipino Immigrants in the United States"
(Ph.D. diss., University of Oregon, 1933); and Antonio Pido, *The*

271

Pilipinos in America: Macro/Micro Dimensions of Immigration and Integration (New York: Center for Migration Studies, 1986). For an overview of Filipina/o American experience from 1763 to 1963, see Fred Cordova, *Filipinos*.

8. Through exploring the gender imbalance and the role of Pinays in community development, the groundbreaking work of Dorothy Cordova, Jovina Navarro, and Susan Evangelista has begun to subvert this male-dominated historical narrative. Their work has shed light on the integral role of women in Filipino American history, while focusing more generally on the gendered dimensions of Filipina/o immigrant experiences. See Dorothy Cordova, "Why They Came," Jovina Navarro, "Immigration of Pilipino Women to America," and Susan Evangelista, "The Pinay as Migrant: Filipina Immigration to the United States in the 1930s."

9. For discussions of the American conquest of the Philippines, see Stuart Creighton Miller, *Benevolent Assimilation: The American Conquest of the Philippines, 1899–1903* (New Haven: Yale University Press, 1982); Stanley Karnow, *In Our Image: America's Empire in the Philippines* (New York: Ballantine Books, 1989); Luzviminda Francisco, "The First Viet Nam: The Philippine American War, 1899–1902," in *Letters in Exile*, ed. Jesse Quinsaat (Los Angeles: University of California, Asian American Studies Center, 1976), 2; and Willard B. Gatewood, *Smoked Yankees and the Struggle for Empire: Letters from Negro Soldiers, 1898–1902* (Urbana: University of Illinois Press, 1971).

10. The 1934 Tydings–McDuffie Act promised the Philippines independence in ten years, appeasing Filipinas/os and Filipina/o Americans who were pushing for the independence of the Philippines. However, the act reclassified Filipinas/os as "aliens" and restricted immigration—which had been unrestricted up to that point—to fifty per year. With the onset of World War II, the Philippines did not become officially independent until twelve years later, in 1946.

11. Women were less than 7 percent of the entire early Filipina/o immigrant population. Steffi San Buenaventura, "Filipino Immigration to the United States," in *Asian American Encyclopedia*, ed. Franklin Ng (New York: Marshall Cavendish, 1995), 445–46.

12. Fifteenth Census of the United States, 1930.

13. Linda Revilla, "Filipino American Women," in *Asian*

American Encyclopedia, ed. Franklin Ng (New York: Marshall Cavendish, 1995), 425.

14. The 1882 Chinese Exclusion Act barred all Chinese laborers, and the 1924 Immigration Act restricted the entry of all Asians except Filipinas/os. The 1875 Page Law targeted Chinese women suspected of being prostitutes, and the 1920 Ladies' Agreement stopped the entry of Japanese women who were entering the United States as picture brides.

273

15. Historian Carol Hemminger's suggestion that Filipinas were "too scared to leave" is a slightly exaggerated analysis of Filipina/o immigration. See Carol Hemminger, "Little Manila: The Filipino in Stockton Prior to World War II," Part II, *Pacific Historian* (Spring 1980): 208.

16. As Jovina Navarro has noted, if Filipinas could not travel to another locality without a chaperone, what more for a foreign land? See Jovina Navarro, "Immigration of Pilipino Women to America."

17. For a discussion of the impact of labor recruitment strategies and exclusion laws on Asian women's immigration, see Yen Le Espiritu, *Asian American Women and Men: Labor, Laws and Love* (Thousand Oaks, Calif.: Sage Publications, 1997), 17–21.

18. For discussions on the Hawaiian Sugar Planters Association (HSPA) recruitment strategies, see Mary Dorita Clifford, "The Hawaiian Sugar Planters Association and Filipino Exclusion," in *The Filipino Exclusion Movement, 1927–1935* (Quezon City, Philippines: Institute of Asian Studies, Occasional Papers No. 1, 1967) reprinted in *Letters in Exile*, ed. Jesse Quinsaat (UCLA Asian American Studies Center, 1976), 75, and Patria P. Ramos, "Filipino Women in Hawai'i: Where We Were, Where We Are Now," in *Filipina: Hawaii's Filipino Women*, ed. Pepi Nieva (Honolulu: Filipino Association of University Women, 1994), 21–25.

19. As Dorothy Cordova has noted, Filipinas came to the United States for a variety of reasons. Like Filipino men, they too sought education, employment, broadened opportunities, and adventure. Those who did immigrate were unconventional women, Evangelista has suggested. These women, who bucked gender role expectations and a sheltered and restricted life in the Philippines, were probably even hardier than the men who left the Philippines. See Dorothy Cordova, "Why They Came," and Evangelista, "The Pinay as Migrant."

20. Evangelista, unpaginated.

21. State of California Department of Industrial Relations, *Facts about Filipino Immigration,* Special Bulletin No. 3 (San Francisco: State Building, 1930), 32.

22. *Filipina,* 7.

23. Elizabeth Uy Eviota. *The Political Economy of Gender: Women and the Sexual Division of Labor in the Philippines* (London: Zed Books, Ltd., 1992), 73.

24. For a discussion of the New Woman, see Sara M. Evans, *Born for Liberty: History of Women in America* (New York: Free Press, 1989), 147–52.

25. From Lewis E. Gleek, Jr., *American Institutions in the Philippines (1898–1941)* (Manila: Historical Conservation Society, 1976), as quoted in Elizabeth Uy Eviota, *The Political Economy of Gender,* 73.

26. Eviota, *The Political Economy of Gender,* 73.

27. Camila Labor Carido, interview by Dawn Bohulano Mabalon, July 13, 2002, Stockton, videotape recording. For a discussion of women's public education in the Philippines during the American colonial period, see Dean C. Worcester, *Philippines: Past and Present* (New York: Macmillan, 1930), 403, and Catherine Ceniza Choy, *Empire of Care: Nursing and Migration in Filipino American History* (Duke University Press, forthcoming Spring 2003).

28. Eviota, *The Political Economy of Gender,* 75.

29. Camila Labor Carido, interview by Dawn Bohulano Mabalon, February 1996, tape recording. Camila Labor Carido remembers the heavy emphasis her teachers placed on darning, gardening, sewing, lacemaking, and other "household arts" in her domestic science courses at her public elementary school in Hinundayan, Leyte, in the 1920s.

30. Filipinos in the United States endured multiple attacks on their manhood. Anti-miscegenation laws barred them from marrying white women, and they were harassed for pursuing relationships with non-Filipinas. As aliens ineligible for citizenship, they could not own land, vote, or immigrate to the United States in large numbers. Educated professionals were subject to extreme occupational downgrading, and all Filipinos suffered extreme police harassment and mob violence, including lynching. Several scholars of Filipina/o American history have explored issues relating to attacks on and

274

attempts at reconstruction of Filipino American manhood. See Arleen de Vera, "The Tapia-Saiki Incident: Interethnic Conflict and Filipino Responses to the Anti-Filipino Exclusion Movement," in *Over the Edge: Remapping the American West,* ed. Valerie Matsumoto and Blake Allmendinger (Berkeley: University of California Press, 1999), and Linda N. España-Maram, "Brown 'Hordes' in McIntosh Suits: Filipinos, Taxi Dance Halls, and Performing the Immigrant Body in Los Angeles, 1930s–1940s," in *Generations of Youth: Youth Cultures and History in Twentieth Century America,* ed. Joe Austin and Michael Nevin Willard (New York: New York University Press, 1998). Mexican American families underwent similar transformations. For example, the work of George Sanchez on early Mexican American families in Los Angeles shows how gender systems and family structure shifted as immigrants adapted to and resisted the dominant society's norms. See George Sanchez, *Becoming Mexican American: Ethnicity, Culture and Identity in Chicano Los Angeles, 1900–1945* (New York: Oxford University Press, 1993), 149.

275

31. "Manong" is used by Visayans and Ilokanos as a term of respect for any older male, including brothers and older male relatives.

32. James Sobredo, "Filipinos in Stockton and Daly City," unpublished paper presented at the Association for Asian American Studies Conference, Seattle, Wash., April 17, 1997.

33. Stockton-based Dr. M. A. Rader, a former Methodist missionary in the Philippines and Filipino advocate, told missionary Albert Palmer that the Filipino's top three problems are exploitation, gambling, and overcrowding. Albert Palmer, *Orientals in American Life* (New York: Friendship Press, republished by R & E Research Associates, San Francisco, 1972), 84–85.

34. Vicki Ruiz reminds us that we need to be critical of the gender politics of work and family to address questions of power and patriarchy. See Vicki Ruiz, *From Out of the Shadows: Mexican Women in Twentieth-Century America* (New York: Oxford University Press, 1998), 15.

35. For a brief account, see "In the Old Days They Stole Wives Not Money: The Story of Kauai's Grand Old Lady Mrs. Josefina Cortezan," in *Filipinos in Hawaii: The First 75 Years 1906–1981,* ed. Juan C. Dionisio (Honolulu: Filipino News Specialty Publications, 1981), 100. See also Patria P. Ramos, "Filipino Women," 24–25.

36. The numerous stories emerging from oral histories Dawn Bohulano Mabalon conducted in her dissertation research regarding the desertion of husbands and subsequent remarriage by Filipina wives in Hawai'i and the United States challenge us to rethink the *coboy-coboy* phenomenon and whether or not "wife stealing"—the abduction of Filipinas from plantations—was always the cause for divorce and remarriage. Several individuals recalled that some Filipinas participated freely in affairs and sometimes left their husbands to remarry. Placing the blame on other Filipinos for their wives' extramarital affairs and divorces casts Filipinas as victims, stripping them of agency.

37. Jerry Paular, interview by Dawn Bohulano Mabalon, July 2001, Sacramento, California, tape recording.

38. For a discussion on Filipina/o male youth culture in Los Angeles and the Pinoy demand for a flashy McIntosh suit, see Linda N. España-Maram, "Brown 'Hordes' in McIntosh Suits: Filipinos, Taxi Dance Halls, and Performing the Immigrant Body in Los Angeles, 1930s-1940s."

39. Camila Labor Carido, interview by Dawn Bohulano Mabalon, January 1996, Stockton, California, tape recording.

40. For traditional Filipina/o courtship rituals, see Belen T. G. Medina, *The Filipino Family: A Text with Selected Readings* (Manila: University of the Philippines Press, 1991), 65–67.

41. Trinidad Rojo, "Social Maladjustment Among Filipinos," *Sociology and Social Research* 21, no. 5 (May–June 1932): 446.

42. *The Three Stars,* June 1929.

43. *The Three Stars,* November 15, 1929.

44. The concept of companionate marriage—that husbands and wives could provide each other with romantic love, sexual pleasure, and companionship—was a relatively new one, popularized through American movies and mass culture in the 1910s and 1920s. See Sara M. Evans, *Born for Liberty*, 178–79.

45. When she wanted to wait until she was nineteen to get married in the 1930s, Filipina immigrant Paula Dizon Daclan's circle of girlfriends teased her, telling her she would be an old maid. "We had about five in our group of girls," she said. "Some of them 14 and 15 years old and they get married already. They had children." Paula Dizon Daclan, interview by Dawn Bohulano Mabalon, Stockton, California, January 1997, videotape recording.

46. For a general discussion of the impact of American coloniza-tion on Filpinas, work, and gender roles, see Eviota, *The Political Economy of Gender.*

47. 15th Census of the United States, Table 14, Filipino Gainful Workers 10 years old and Over, by Occupation, by Age and Sex.

48. See Evelyn Nakano Glenn, *Issei, Nisei, War Bride: Three Generations of Japanese American Women in Domestic Service* (Philadelphia: Temple University Press, 1986), 207–8, and Valerie Matsumoto, *Farming the Home Place: A Japanese American Community in California, 1919–1982* (Ithaca and London: Cornell University Press, 1993).

49. As Glenn has suggested, racial-ethnic women's wage labor has profound implications for the family system. Their work is no longer under the control of their husbands and their contributions gain visi-bility. Glenn, *Issei, Nisei, War Bride,* 15.

50. Second-generation Filipino American Jerry Paular recalled that a family friend, a Filipino immigrant with a Ph.D., worked as a dishwasher in Los Angeles during the 1930s and 1940s. This scholar was the sociologist Dr. Benicio T. Catapusan, a USC graduate and author of several notable articles on early Filipino American life. Jerry Paular, interview by Dawn Bohulano Mabalon, July 2001, videotape recording. Hawai'i-born Stockton resident Flora (Arca) Mata, a UCLA graduate, could not find work as a teacher in the Stockton area and was forced to go to the Philippines at the eve of World War II to find a teaching position. Interview by Dawn Bohulano Mabalon and Joan May T. Cordova, June 2002, videotape recording. Stories of occupational downgrading of educated Filipinas/os in the United States from the turn of the century to the present abound.

51. Fred Cordova writes, "Pinay mothers . . . decided where the children went to school, what to eat, what to wear, where to live, when to go to church, whether the family could afford to buy things, or whether the children should go to college." *Filipinos,* 147.

52. See Yung, *Unbound Feet,* and Glenn, *Issei, Nisei, War Bride.*

53. Eviota, *The Political Economy of Gender,* 152.

54. This was a responsibility which Filipinas bore, as some histo-rians have suggested, since before the advent of Spanish colonialism. See Fred Cordova, *Filipinos,* 148.

55. Eviota, *The Political Economy of Gender,* 65.

56. See Emily Porcincula Lawsin, "Beyond 'Hanggang Pier Only': Filipino American War Brides of Seattle, 1945–1965," *Filipino American National Historical Society Journal* 4 (1996): 50–50G.

57. Early Pinay businesswomen included Margarita Balucas, who owned a pool hall and the Lafayette Lunch Counter (a popular restaurant she would later sell to Dawn's grandfather in 1931); Juliana Lazaro, who ran the Los Filipinos Tailoring and Clothing Shop at 352 El Dorado Street with her husband from 1929 to the 1940s; and Mrs. D.L.M. Marcuelo, who was the business manager of the Depression-era Filipina/o newspaper *The Three Stars*. Mrs. Menda, who owned the pool hall, was probably a Japanese American woman. See also Fred Cordova, *Filipinos*, 109.

58. Lillian Galedo, Laurena Cabanero, and Brian Tom, "Roadblocks to Community Building: A Case Study of the Stockton Filipino Center Project" (Working Publication # 4, Asian American Research Project, University of California, Davis, 1970), 8.

59. Antonio J. A. Pido, *The Pilipinos in America: Macro/Micro Dimensions of Immigration and Integration* (New York: Center for Migration Studies, 1986), 63.

60. Hemminger, "Little Manila," 24.

61. The Harlan Ranch, where Angeles and her family work and live through 1927, is near what is now the city of San Ramon in Contra Costa County in northern California. The "big house," called El Nido, which Angeles writes was "spooky" and uninhabited, is now the El Nido Museum. The Harlans migrated west to California in the mid-nineteenth century and became successful California farmers and ranchers. Joel Harlan bought the land in 1856, becoming one of Contra Costa County's earliest white settlers. The Harlan family also owned a farm in Fresno. The Harlan family history is available at http://www.harlanfamily.org/trek.htm.

62. The West End Redevelopment Project and the Crosstown Freeway Project razed most of Little Manila and Chinatown in 1964 and 1968, respectively, and a fast-food restaurant and a gas station project claimed another block in 1999. Most Filipina/o Americans had abandoned Little Manila after the first demolitions and the community-owned Filipino Plaza was built nearby, featuring low-income senior housing and retail space. Only four of the original buildings of Little Manila remain standing near the intersection of Lafayette and

El Dorado streets. In October 2000, the Stockton city council declared the Little Manila area a city historic site. Banji Menda's Pool Hall, at 31 E. Market Street, where Angeles worked as a pool hall girl, is now a bank parking lot across the street from the police station.

63. Donald Walker, "Race Relations and Specialty Crops: San Joaquin County Horticulture, 1900–1925" (Ph.D. diss, California State University, Sacramento, 1992), 270.

64. All locations of Filipina/o businesses are taken from the Polk City Directories for Stockton, California, 1925–1930.

65. Galedo et al., "Roadblocks to Community Building," 10.

66. Glenn Alvin Kennedy, *It Happened in Stockton* (Stockton: Kenco Reproduction, 1967), 216.

67. For a discussion of contemporary sites of ethnicity and identity, see Rick Bonus, *Locating Filipino Americans: Ethnicity & the Cultural Politics of Space* (Philadelphia: Temple University Press, 2000).

68. Rizal Day, celebrated every December 30, commemorates the death of the Philippine national hero, Jose Rizal.

69. Sucheng Chan writes that the proliferation of fraternal-style organizations among Filipinas/os reflects American cultural influence. In fact, freemasonry existed in the Philippines for more than a century prior to American colonization. National hero Dr. Jose P. Rizal was an active Mason, and the revolutionary activities of the Katipunan were based on secret Masonic rituals and recruiting practices. The guiding principles of most of these Filipino and Filipino American groups are inspired by the nationalist values of the Philippine revolution. See Chan, *Asian Americans* 75, and Mario P. Ave, "Characteristics of Filipino Social Organizations in L.A." (Thesis, University of Southern California, 1956), 13–32. The Legionarios del Trabajo, organized in the Philippines in 1919 and in the United States in 1924, was an offshoot of the strike against the Manila Electric Company. See Renato Constantino, *The Philippines: A Past Revisited*, vol. 1 (Manila: 1975), 365.

70. For a discussion of these fraternities, see Steffi San Buenaventura, "Filipino Folk Spirituality and Immigration: From Mutual Aid to Religion," *Amerasia Journal* 1, no. 22 (1996): 2.

71. Yung, *Unbound Feet*, 92–105.

72. Fred Cordova, *Filipinos*, 171. Roman Catholic parishes practiced a "benign condescension" toward Filipino immigrants, according

to Cordova. In areas like Los Angeles, Filipinos who were ostracized from the Catholic cathedral began to form their own spaces of worship, like the Filipino Christian Church, founded in the early 1930s. In Stockton, Filipinas/os congregated at the Lighthouse Mission and formed their own Protestant churches, such as Trinity Presbyterian Church.

73. George Sanchez describes a smiliar phenomenon among Mexican Americans. Sanchez, *Becoming Mexican American,* 149.

74. Ruiz, *From Out of the Shadows,* 50.

75. Susan Kalcik, "Ethnic Foodways in America: Symbol and Performance," in *Ethnic and Regional Foodways in the United States: The Performance of Group Identity,* ed. Linda Brown and Kay Mussel (Knoxville: University of Tennessee Press, 1984), 38.

76. Evans, *Born for Liberty,* 176.

About the Editor

RIZALINE R. RAYMUNDO was born in Modesto, California, on July 14, 1929, just two weeks short of Angeles's seventeenth birthday. As a child of migrant workers, Riz grew up in the Central Valley and Salinas Valley living in one *campo* after another. She worked for the County of Santa Clara as law enforcement clerk for the Sheriff's Department and secretary for the Commission on the Status of Women and the Office of Human Relations. She is an active member of the Santa Clara Valley Chapter of the Filipino American National Historical Society.

About the Contributors

JONATHAN OKAMURA received a Ph.D. from University of London and teaches at the Ethnic Studies Department of University of Hawai'i at Manoa. He is the author of *Imagining Filipino American Diaspora: Transntiional Relations, Identities and Communities* (1998).

DAWN BOHULANO MABALON received a Ph.D. in history from Stanford University and an M.A. in Asian American Studies from UCLA. Dawn was born and raised in Stockton, California, the granddaughter of Filipina/o immigrants who arrived in the 1920s. Her research focuses on Filipina/o American women's and community history, gender, youth and popular culture. She founded the Little Manila Foundation in Stockton, which advocates for historic preservation and revitalization of the Little Manila Historic Site, and she is a member of the Filipino American National Historical Society.